Introduction to
# ORGANIZATION THEORY

# Introduction to ORGANIZATION THEORY

## Structure and Design of Organizations

Sanghamitra Bhattacharyya BE, FPM
Formerly Associate Professor, Department of Management Studies,
Indian Institute of Technology Madras

Universities Press

UNIVERSITIES PRESS (INDIA) PRIVATE LIMITED

Registered Office
3-6-747/1/A & 3-6-754/1, Himayatnagar, Hyderabad 500 029 (A.P.), India
E-mail: info@universitiespress.com

Distributed by
Orient Blackswan Private Limited

Registered Office
3-6-752 Himayatnagar, Hyderabad 500 029 (A.P.) India

Other Offices
Bangalore / Bhopal / Bhubaneshwar / Chandigarh / Chennai / Ernakulam / Guwahati / Hyderabad / Jaipur / Kolkata / Lucknow / Mumbai / New Delhi / Noida / Patna



ISBN: 978 81 7371 737-6



Typeset in IowanOldSt BT 11/13.5 by
OSDATA, Hyderabad 500 029.

Printed in India at

Verdhman Printers Delhi

Published by
Universities Press (India) Private Limited
3-6-747/1/A & 3-6-754/1, Himayatnagar,
Hyderabad 500 029 (A.P.), India.

# Preface

Organizations are an integral part of our lives at every stage, from the time we are born, to the time we die, though for the most part, we might not be consciously aware of them. Organizations represent complex social entities which exist to create some value in society, by interacting with their environment and by utilizing resources – men, machines, materials, knowledge – in a coordinated manner. It is this interaction and coordination among various entities that this book aims to depict.

The management principles that we are familiar with today have evolved over more than a century, and have witnessed wide swings and variations in perspectives. These range from the classical school, through the human relations school to the contemporary school of thought. A study of organization design and theory provides conceptual tools for the practicing manager at all levels of a corporate entity to influence various such organizational situations that she is likely to encounter.

This book is the result of an experiment at IIT Madras to convert recorded classroom lectures into textbooks based on various taught courses at the institute. It is meant to serve as a basic textbook for students of business management, and introduces them to the concept of organization theory, structure and design. A comprehensive understanding of organizations is possible only through a combination of individual, interpersonal and organizational perspectives. Ideally, students should have gone through a previous course on organizational behavior, where they have been given an overview on topics dealing with individual and interpersonal (team) issues and interactions such as personality theories, theories of leadership and motivation, power, politics and conflict management, and group dynamics, among others. This book builds on that understanding; it concentrates on the organization as a whole and tries to understand its behavior and survival mechanisms in relation to its environment.

The focus in this book is on the structure and design of organizations, the theory underlying the design of structures, the effectiveness of organizational design in ensuring its survival and growth, and managing organizational restructuring and change so as to prevent decline and failure. A desirable, though not compulsory, prerequisite for this course would therefore be a basic course in Organizational Behavior from an individual and interpersonal perspective.

The flow of chapters has been designed, keeping in mind the integrated nature of the concepts under discussion. The book begins with an introduction to the concept of organizations (Chapter 1). It discusses various perspectives, describes various types of organizations, and offers a brief introduction to the concept of organization design, structure and theory. After a detailed description of various models and tools for measuring and evaluating the effectiveness of organizations in Chapter 2, the student is provided with a detailed explanation of organization structure (Chapter 3), the various dimensions to define structure, as well as the various types of structural configurations used by organizations.

Over the next four chapters (Chapter 4 to 7), the discussion revolves around understanding how contextual factors such as strategy, size, environment, technology and culture, individually and together, affect the structure of the organization. Chapter 8 adds a note of caution with a discussion of what constitutes failure in organizations, along with issues that managers need to be careful about in order to prevent their organizations from failure and decline. Since an understanding of organizational structure is essential for managers to handle any necessary restructuring required, either for growth or for preventing decline and failure, the concluding chapter (Chapter 9) is devoted to understanding organizational restructuring from a change management perspective with all its implications, including managing resistance to change, conflict management and models of change management, in an organization's endeavor to evolve into a learning organization.

The target audience is primarily students and scholars of business management, aspiring to be practicing managers in the corporate world. While time limitations often constrain theoretical discussions in a classroom setting, I have made use of theoretical concepts and frameworks in this book to lend depth to the discussions, without making it too 'weighty', or compromising on the readability and practical relevance of the topics.

A common query that we often face from students in class is the relevance/applicability of the theories discussed to the Indian context, since most standard textbooks on organizational theory currently in use are by foreign authors, citing predominantly foreign (US/European) examples. To address this lacuna, I have included two Indian case studies in each chapter, in addition to numerous Indian examples of organizations in respect of the theories discussed in the contents, to exemplify the relevance of theory to the Indian context. The suggested pedagogy for this course would be a mix of classroom discussions (PowerPoint slides for each chapter are provided as support material to help the faculty), case discussions and practice project assignments (suggested at the end of each chapter), to reinforce the practical applicability of the concepts discussed in class.

I would like to take this opportunity to thank Professor B. Ramamurthy, former Chairman, CCE, IIT Madras, for facilitating this project, Professor L. S. Ganesh, former Head of the Department of Management Studies, IIT Madras for his very valuable and insightful suggestions to improve the depth and readability of the contents, my students, S. Balaraman and M. Alexander, for painstakingly noting down my class lectures, the staff of CCE for their transcriptions of the recorded material, and my student, V. Vijayalakshmi, for editing the transcribed material. I am also grateful to the authorities of IIT Madras for making available to me the required infrastructural and moral support, which enabled me to complete this project.

*Sanghamitra Bhattacharyya*

# Contents

*To the memory of my father,*
*Professor Samirendranath Ray*

CHAPTER 1

# Understanding Organizations

**CHAPTER OUTLINE**

What is an organization?

❖

Definitions

❖

Organization theory: A historical perspective

❖

Different forms of organizational reality

❖

Why do organizations exist?

❖

Viewing organizations from an open systems perspective

❖

Viewing organizations from a life-cycle perspective

## ORGANIZATIONAL INSIGHT

The game of cricket is India's *de facto* national sport; it has emerged as the country's most popular sport, even though field hockey continues to remain the national sport of India. The development of cricket in India is closely tied to its political and cultural history. In 1911, an all-India cricket team visited England for the first time. Featuring the best cricketers of the time, it was sponsored and captained by the Maharaja of Patiala. In 1926, an English cricket team, led by Arthur Gilligan, visited India, and went back impressed with the Indian team's performance. Gilligan was an active participant in a meeting in Delhi in February 1927. The Maharaja of Patiala, a British businessman named Grant Govan, and Anthony De Mello, an Indian cricket administrator, were the other attendees. At this meeting, Gilligan praised Indian cricket, and promised to press for India's inclusion in the ICC, if all the promoters of cricket in the land came together to establish a single controlling body. Govan, Patiala and De Mello in turn assured Gilligan that they would do their bit. They convened a meeting in Delhi on 21st November 1927, which was attended by around 45 delegates. These comprised cricket representatives from Sind, Punjab, Patiala, Delhi, the United Provinces, Rajputana, Alwar, Bhopal, Gwalior, Baroda, Kathiawar and Central India. A consensus was reached to create a Board of Cricket Control for cricket in India. It was thought to be essential to ensure the following:

- ❖ Advance and control the game of cricket throughout India.
- ❖ Arrange and control inter-territorial, foreign and other cricket matches.
- ❖ Make arrangements incidental to the visits of teams to India, and to manage and control all-India representatives playing within and outside India.
- ❖ If necessary, to control and manage all or any inter-territorial disputes.

Another meeting, on December 10, 1927, resulted in a unanimous decision to form a 'provisional' Board of Control to represent cricket in

India. In December 1928, the BCCI was formed with only six associations affiliated to it as against the eight envisaged earlier. R.E. Grant Govan was made its first president. The Board of Control for Cricket in India, or BCCI, is the only national apex governing body for cricket in India, headquartered at Mumbai. As a member of the International Cricket Council (ICC), it has the authority to select players, umpires and officials to participate in international events and exercises total control over them. The BCCI has 27 state association members across five zones (viz. North Zone, South Zone, East Zone, West Zone and Central Zone) in India, with some states having multiple associations. It is India's richest sporting body; it organizes various domestic cricket competitions in the country, such as the Ranji Trophy, Irani Trophy, Duleep Trophy and Deodhar Trophy and the NKP Salve Challenger Trophy, as well as international tournaments (test matches, one-day matches and the recently introduced twenty-twenty (T20) matches). India's triumph in the World Cup of 1983 emboldened the BCCI to bid for the 1987 World Cup along with its Pakistani counterpart. This successful event, further reinforced by India's recent phenomenal win in World Cup 2011, has enabled the BCCI to showcase its organizational capabilities.

The BCCI is an example of an organization.

## 1.1 What is an organization?

Organizations are complex realities; they are concrete and tangible entities in which resources (men, machines, and materials) are utilized in a coordinated manner.

Consider the following:

- The *Taj* group of hotels
- *Apollo* hospitals
- Indian Institutes of Management
- *State Bank of India*
- *Child Rights and You* (CRY)
- *Infosys Technologies Ltd.*
- A shopping mall
- The Indian army

Despite their obvious differences, each of them represents some form of organization. So, how do we define an organization? While most of us have an intuitive understanding of its meaning, defining an organization poses a much greater challenge. The organizations given as examples above have many underlying dimensions common to each other, in spite of apparent differences between them.

- Each of them functions through a coordinated system of management using well-established routines and procedures (*conscious coordination*), which require groups of people to interact with each other in a coordinated manner, as also in part linking their sense of 'self' to these interactions (*social entity*).

- Each of these entities has *identifiable boundaries* (both physical and virtual), built up through implicit or explicit contracts with their members, which help to differentiate between members and non-members. These organizational members engage in regular interaction for the period of time that they remain with the organization (*continuing bond*).
- All these activities are geared toward achieving a super-arching *common goal*, one which transcends the different, and often conflicting, individual goals of individual members. This goal can be in the form of a product or service or a combination of both, to serve some specific needs of society. Thus, organizations exist to satisfy some collective need of society which cannot be satisfied through individual effort alone.

Chester I Barnard's (1938) classic definition describes an organization as '*a system of consciously coordinated activities of groups of two or more persons.*' Scholars have attempted to define organizations from various approaches, a few of which are given below. Hence, organizations:

- *Signify a method of social control, a means for imparting order, structure and regularity to society (Wolin, 1960)*
- *Are groups of people who work interdependently toward some purpose (Stern and Barley, 1996)*
- *Are consciously coordinated social entities, with an identifiable boundary that function on a relatively continuous basis to achieve a common goal or set of goals (Robbins, 2000)*
- *Are entities that enable societies to pursue accomplishments that cannot be achieved by individuals acting alone (Gibson et al, 2003)*
- *Are social entities that are goal directed, are designed as deliberately structured and coordinated activity systems, and are linked to the external environment (Daft, 2004)*
- *Are formal structures of relationships among people in order to achieve aims and objectives (Mullins, 2005)*

Organizations are complex realities; however, the definitions above refer to a concrete and tangible entity where resources (men, machines, materials) are utilized in a coordinated manner.

### 1.1.1 Types of organization and the concept of intrapreneurship

Depending on the domain of operation, type of holding, etc., organizations may take various forms, some of which are discussed below:

- **Sole proprietorship:** A sole proprietorship is a business owned by one person. The owner may operate on his or her own or may employ others. The owner of the business has personal liability for the debts incurred by the business. Typical examples of sole proprietorships would include mom-and-pop grocery stores, professional service providers, day care operators, the carpenter who is a true independent contractor, those who work part-time in various occupations to supplement the family's main source of earnings, etc.

- **Partnership:** A partnership is a business entity in which partners (owners) share with each other the profits or losses of the business. Partnerships are often favored over corporations for taxation purposes, as the partnership structure does not generally incur a tax on profits before it is distributed to the partners (i.e. there is no dividend tax levied). However, depending on the partnership structure and the jurisdiction in which it operates, owners of a partnership may be exposed to greater personal liability than the shareholders of a corporation. If the number of partners is more than 20, it has to be registered as a company. A **limited liability partnership (LLP)** is a specific type of partnership in which some or all partners (depending on the jurisdiction) have limited liability. It therefore exhibits elements of both partnerships and corporations. In an LLP, one partner is not responsible or liable for another partner's misconduct or negligence.
- **Corporation:** A corporation is either a limited or an unlimited liability entity that has a separate legal personality from its members. A corporation can be organized for-profit or not-for-profit. A corporation is owned by multiple shareholders and is overseen by a board of directors, which hires the business's managerial staff. In addition to privately-owned corporate models, there are state-owned corporate models. A Public or Statutory Corporation is an autonomous corporate body set up under a special Act of Parliament or State Legislature. Examples of statutory corporations in India include *Airports Authority of India, Central Warehousing Corporation, Food Corporation of India*, etc. A public corporation seeks to combine the flexibility of private enterprise with public ownership and accountability. The essential features of a public corporation are:
    - **Corporate body:** It is a body corporate established through a special Act of Parliament or State Legislature. The Act defines its powers and privileges and its relationship with government departments and ministries.
    - **Legal entity:** It enjoys a separate legal entity with perpetual succession and common seal. It can acquire and own property in its own name. It can sue and be sued and can enter into contracts in its own name.
    - **Government ownership:** The public corporation is wholly owned by the Central and/or State Government(s).
    - **Financial independence:** It enjoys financial autonomy. Its initial capital and borrowing are provided by the government, but it is supposed to be self-supporting. It can borrow money from the public and is empowered to plough back its earnings.
    - **Accounting system:** The corporation is not subject to the budgetary, accounting, and audit regulations applicable to government departments. It is generally exempt from the rigid rules applicable to the expenditure of public funds.

- **Management and personnel:** A public corporation is managed by a Board of Directors appointed by the Government. However, its employees need not necessarily be civil servants. They can be employed on terms and conditions laid down by the corporation itself.
- **Service motive:** The primary motive of the corporation is public service rather than private profit. It is, however, expected to operate in a business-like manner.

Intrapreneurship is a management style involving entrepreneurial approaches such as risk-taking and innovation, within a large corporation.

***'Intrapreneurship' in corporations:*** In 1992, The American Heritage Dictionary acknowledged the popular use of a new word, **intrapreneur** to mean 'a person within a large corporation who takes direct responsibility for turning an idea into a profitable finished product through assertive risk-taking and innovation'. **Intrapreneurship** is now known as the practice of a corporate management style that integrates risk-taking and an innovative approach, with rewards and motivational techniques that are more traditionally thought of as being the province of entrepreneurship.

The difference between an entrepreneur and an intrapreneur is that an **entrepreneur** takes substantial risk in being the owner and operator of a business with expectations of financial profit and other rewards that the business may generate. An **intrapreneur**, on the other hand, is an individual employed by an organization for remuneration, which is based on the financial success of the unit he is responsible for. Intrapreneurs share traits such as conviction, zeal and insight with entrepreneurs. As the intrapreneur continues to express his ideas vigorously, the gap between the philosophy of the organization and the employee becomes evident. If the organization supports him in pursuing his ideas, he succeeds. If not, he is likely to leave the organization and set up his own business. An intrapreneur thinks like an entrepreneur, looking out for opportunities that profit the organization. Intrapreneurship is a novel way of making organizations more profitable, where imaginative employees entertain entrepreneurial thoughts. It is in the interest of an organization to encourage intrapreneurs, as intrapreneurship is a significant method for companies to reinvent themselves and improve performance.

John Warnock and Charles Geschke, the founders of *Adobe*, are classic examples of intrapreneurs. They were both employees of *Xerox* and were frustrated because their new product ideas were not encouraged. They quit *Xerox* in the early 1980s to begin their own business. Currently, *Adobe* has an annual turnover of over $3 billion. *HCL Technologies, India* is an organization which actively encourages intrapreneurship. *HCL Comnet*, their subsidiary, was formed as a result of this approach. Currently, the founder of *HCL Comnet*, Vineet Nayar, is the CEO of *HCL Technologies*. The 'Skunk Works' group at *Lockheed Martin* formed in 1943 under the directorship of Kelly

Johnson to build P-80 fighter jets is another example of successful intrapreneurship. Similarly, *3M* has a very strong 'intrapreneurial' culture, where employees can spend 15% of their time working on the projects they like for the betterment of the company. Based on the initial success of the project, *3M* even provides funds for further development. More popularly, Robbie Bach, J. Allard and team's *XBOX* might not have been feasible without *Microsoft*'s money and infrastructure. The project required hundreds of millions of dollars and quality talent to make the product.

- **Cooperative:** Often referred to as a 'co-op', a cooperative is a limited liability entity that can be organized for-profit or not-for-profit. These are organizations which undertake business activities with the prime objective of providing service to their members. Although some amount of profit is essential to survive in the market, their main intention is not to generate profit and grow. They pool available resources from their members, and utilize the same in the best possible manner: the benefits are shared among the members. A cooperative differs from a corporation in that it has members, as opposed to shareholders, who share decision-making authority. Cooperatives are typically classified as either consumer cooperatives or worker cooperatives. Cooperatives are fundamental to the ideology of economic democracy. Examples of successful cooperatives in India include *Amul, Aavin, Indian Coffee House* and the *Shri Mahila Griha Udyog Lijjat Papad*. The main objective of a cooperative is social development, and the emphasis is on rendering service rather than profit, mutual help instead of competition, and self help instead of dependence.
- A **subsidiary**, in business matters, is an entity that is controlled by a separate higher entity. According to the Companies Act, India, a company 'is deemed to be a subsidiary of another if that other controls the composition of its Board of Directors; or where the first-mentioned company is an existing company in respect of which the holders of preference shares issued before the commencement of this Act have the same voting rights in all respects as the holders of equity shares; exercises or controls more than half of the total voting power of such company; or where the first-mentioned company is any other company, holds more than half in nominal value of its equity share capital; or the first-mentioned company is a subsidiary of any company which is that other's subsidiary'. The controlled entity is called a company, corporation, or limited liability company; and in some cases, it can be a government or state-owned enterprise, and the controlling entity is called its parent (or the parent company). The reason for this distinction is that a lone company cannot be a subsidiary of any organization. Contrary to popular belief, a parent company does not have to be the larger or 'more powerful' entity; it is possible for the parent company to be smaller than a subsidiary, or the parent may be larger than some or all of its subsidiaries (if it has more than one).The parent and the subsidiary do not necessarily have

to operate in the same locations, or operate the same businesses, but it is also possible that they could conceivably be competitors in the marketplace. Also, because a parent company and a subsidiary are separate entities, it is entirely possible for one of them to be involved in legal proceedings, bankruptcy, tax delinquency, indictment and/or be under investigation, while the other is not. For example, *Union Carbide India Ltd* (UCIL) was the Indian subsidiary of the US-based, *Union Carbide Corporation,* which is now a subsidiary of *Dow Chemicals. IBP* is the merged subsidiary of *Indian Oil Corporation Ltd,* and *Infosys BPO* is a subsidiary of *Infosys Technologies Ltd.*

- A **parent** company, or **holding** company, is one that owns enough voting stock in another firm to control management and operations by influencing or electing its Board of Directors.

Before proceeding further, a few terms need to be clarified to put our subsequent discussions in perspective.

## 1.2 Definitions

### 1.2.1 Organization design

This is the process whereby managers select and manage various dimensions and components of an organization's structure to enable the organization to achieve its goals. It deals with constructing and changing an organization's structure to achieve these goals. This implies making decisions about integrating various behaviors and activities in a coordinated manner among the various units and departments in the organization. A manager responsible for achieving goals through other people would have to assign resources and decide how organizational members would work together. To be effective, all managers would have to understand the implications of the design choices they make. An effective organization design would be one which not only enables current goals to be achieved, but also fosters adaptation over time to changing circumstances. A combination of contextual and structural dimensions is used to describe an organization's design parameters. **Structural dimensions** (complexity, formalization, centralization) provide labels to describe the internal characteristics of the organization, while **contextual dimensions** (strategy, environment, technology, size, culture) describe the organizational setting that influences and shapes the structural dimensions. Figure 1.1 depicts these dimensions:

> Organizational design is the constructing and changing of an organization's structure to achieve the organization's goals.

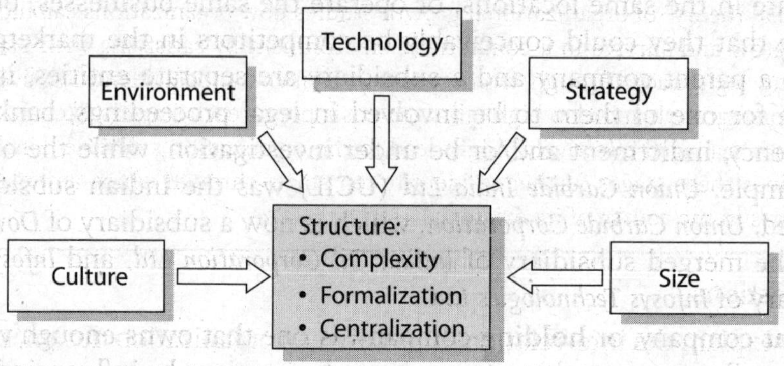


**Figure 1.1** *Dimensions of organization design*

### 1.2.2 Organization structure

> Organization structure establishes a balance between the differentiation and integration requirements of an organization, through the dimensions of complexity, formalization and centralization.

This is the formal system of task and authority relationships that control coordination of resources to achieve the organization's goals. It defines how tasks are allocated, who reports to whom, the coordination mechanisms and interaction patterns that will be followed. Essentially, organization structure helps to establish a balance between the differentiation and integration requirements of organizations. Structure is a multi-dimensional concept, typically described through three components, viz. **complexity, formalization** and **centralization.**

- ***Complexity*** is concerned with the various ways in which the workforce in the organization is differentiated, based on a variety of factors.
  - *Specialization* describes the degree to which organizational jobs are divided into separate jobs, on the basis of professional qualifications and expertise.
  - *Hierarchy* describes differentiation based on formal designation, reporting relationships and span of control. **The organization chart** gives a pictorial depiction of the hierarchy existing in an organization.
- ***Formalization*** describes the extent of an organization's reliance on formal rules and procedures to control and direct employee behavior.
- ***Centralization*** describes the extent to which an organization's decision-making focus is concentrated on an individual unit or dispersed across the ranks.

### 1.2.3 Organization theory (OT)

This is the discipline that studies how organizations function and how they affect and are affected by the environment in which they operate. It seeks to understand how organizations evolve, and how factors such as strategy, size, environment and technology might determine an organization's structure through various design options, to enable it to achieve its final goal. Unlike organizational behavior, as it is commonly understood, its unit of analysis is the organization itself. However, organizational theory is best understood from a combined perspective, rather than from a purely micro (individual and teams/groups) or purely macro (organization as a whole) approach. Internally, structural factors impact the individual behavior of organizational members; externally, structure causes organizational members to perceive and respond to the environment in different ways.

> Organizational theory studies how organizations function and how they affect and are affected by the environment in which they operate.

Organizations are an integral part of our life at every stage, right from the time we are born, to the time we die, though for the most part, we might not be consciously aware of them. When we walk into a restaurant, we are given a menu and we indicate our choices. On the other hand, when we go to a hospital, treatment is prescribed based on the nature of the illness; we are rarely provided with a menu of choices (of medicines or procedures of treatment) to choose from. In primary school, we are taught courses prescribed by the school authorities and/or examination boards, without any choice. In higher educational institutions, a combined approach is followed: students take some fixed courses and choose others based on preference.

So, why do different organizations behave in different ways? Why do two different organizations in the same industry, offering similar products and/or services, have different outcomes? Conversely, why do two organizations in different fields, offering different products or services, have similar outcomes? While we might have some intuitive understanding of these issues based on our experiences and observations, a formal course in organizational theory helps structure our intuitive thought processes and gives greater clarity of understanding of these issues. Since organizations exist to satisfy some needs of society, an understanding of how they operate will help us learn how to control and change organizations so that they can create wealth and resources for society. Moreover, any practicing manager, irrespective of her/his functional area of specialization and designation in the organization, will have to deal with organizational changes and restructuring, to varying degrees, as part of her/his job responsibilities. A study of organization design and theory provides conceptual tools for the practicing manager at all levels to influence various such organizational situations which she/he is likely to encounter. Because of the complexity of organizations, managers who make sense of and use multiple perspectives are better able to bring their knowledge of organization theory to bear on the wide range of analyses, decisions and plans that their organizations make every day.

## 1.3 Organization theory: A historical perspective

The management principles that we are familiar with today have evolved over more than a century, witnessing wide swings and variations in perspectives. With time, the dimensions of each practice have either died out or morphed into newer forms. Typically, parts of each approach have survived and have been incorporated into modern perspectives on management. The historical evolution of organization theory has witnessed a transition from the 'classical' approaches to management, through the 'social' or 'human relations' perspective, and thence to the contemporary approaches of management and organizations. Each of these approaches is very briefly outlined below.

### 1.3.1 The classical school

Characterized by the works of stalwarts such as Adam Smith (division of labor), Frederick Taylor (scientific management), Henri Fayol (administrative management), Max Weber (bureaucracy) and Ralph Davis (rational planning), each of these perspectives viewed organizations as rational, closed systems and provided guidelines and principles for achieving their goals in the most efficient manner possible. Hence, while **Adam Smith**'s division of labor advocated breaking up a job into smaller tasks for greater efficiency and cost saving, **Taylor**'s scientific management highlighted the importance of replacing rules of thumb with scientific determination, and a 'one-best-way' of maximizing productivity to maximize output and returns. **Henri Fayol** enunciated fourteen principles of management for the efficient functioning of organizations, which, with a few exceptions (e.g. unity of command, stability of personnel tenure) are highly relevant even in today's context. **Weber** conceptualized 'bureaucracy' as the most efficient form of organization, having as its basis, principles of authority, rationality, impersonality, rule-directed behavior and merit-based selection, to promote technical efficiency. It is unfortunate and ironic that despite its promise, faulty implementation and abuse of its principles over the past century has made 'bureaucracy' synonymous with inefficiency and its attendant ills. Finally, **Davis**' rational-planning approach proposed that a firm's main objective was economic service, and structure was the logical outcome of this objective.

### 1.3.2 The human-relations school

The proponents of this school included Elton Mayo (Hawthorne Studies), Chester Barnard, Emile Durkheim, Douglas McGregor (Theory X–Theory Y), Mary Parker Follett (workplace democracy) and Warren Bennis (flexible adhocracies). Recognizing the social nature of organizations, where both the social and psychological needs of employees are given importance, these scholars have viewed organizations as being made up of both tasks and people. By recognizing the importance of group work and acceptance, and viewing workers as being separate from machines, the **Hawthorne**

**studies** pioneered the age of 'organizational humanism'. **Chester Barnard** went a step further in redefining authority in terms of subordinates, and propounded that a manager's responsibilities should include subordinate development and communication. **Durkheim** highlighted the difference between formal and informal organizations and stressed the need for paying attention to workers' social needs in addition to the needs of formal work-organizing. **McGregor** postulated that managers viewed their subordinates differently based on negative (Theory X) or positive (Theory Y) assumptions about them, which would in turn affect their behavior toward their subordinates. McGregor proposed that managers should use a Theory Y approach to get the best efforts from their subordinates. However, it is now acknowledged that a mix of both approaches, depending on the demands of the situation, would be more effective.

The workplace democracy advocated by **Mary Parker Follett** is based on the concept of self-government and work delegation in organizations in order to facilitate individual growth and the growth of the groups they belong to. Finally, **Warren Bennis** countered Weber's concept of bureaucracy with that of flexible adhocracy, and proposed that the ideal form of organizing should involve decentralization of decision making, flexible work groups, democratic structures, and influence based on expertise rather than authority.

### 1.3.3 The contemporary school

The contemporary approach to management attempts to take a more balanced perspective, neither too mechanistic nor overly humanistic. The contingency approach advocated by **Herbert Simon** ('principles' and guidelines to be replaced by an understanding of the situation and response based on the context), **Katz** and **Kahn's** environmental approach (the open systems approach to organizations where decisions would be dependent on environmental demands), **March** and **Simon's** redefinition of rationality in decision-making, and **Pfeffer's** conceptualization of organizations as power coalitions, are some seminal perspectives in this school of thought.

## 1.4 Different forms of organizational reality

As was evident from the various definitions given in an earlier section, given their complicated nature, organizations have been conceptualized from multiple perspectives, a representative list of which is provided below. In the remaining chapters of the book, all these perspectives will be discussed in some context or the other. In fact, a comprehensive understanding of organizations would imply looking at all these approaches holistically from a combined perspective, rather than treating each approach as independent and separate. Each of these perspectives represents some reality of organizations, and a combination of all these approaches provides a more complete picture of an organization, while any one or some of these would describe only some aspects of an organization.

- *Organizations as rational goal-seeking entities:* The main objective of any organization is to achieve a set of goals, and members' behaviors are essentially directed toward such goal achievement.
- *Organizations as machines:* Organizations are built around systems which are geared towards efficient and reliable performance.
- *Organizations as power coalitions or political entities:* Organizations are made up of work groups, each of which seeks to satisfy their self-interest, and use their power to influence the distribution of resources in the organization.
- *Organizations as systems:* Organizations take in inputs from the environment, process them in loosely-coupled, relatively independent, though interlinked and coordinated units, to achieve the desired output to be sent back to the environment.
- *Organizations as information processing units*: Organizations are capable of planning for an envisioned future, by interpreting their environment, processing information, and creating meaning out of them to facilitate decision-making regarding present and future strategies of action, and build up a climate of learning.
- *Organizations as psychic prisons*: Organizations segregate or 'imprison' employees in terms of job descriptions, departmentation, hierarchy and reporting relationships, along with prescribed rules and norms of conduct, hence creating psychological 'dominance' over the members in terms of acceptable standards of behavior.
- *Organizations as social contracts*: Organizations function on the basis of mutually accepted written and unwritten contracts where employees perform certain actions or behave in particular ways in return for promised or expected compensations.

## 1.5 Why do organizations exist?

> Organizations exist to create value in society by satisfying certain needs of its stakeholders.

As mentioned above, organizations exist to create value in society by satisfying certain needs of its stakeholders (people who have an interest, claim, or stake in the organization, in what it does, and how well it performs). They provide the setting for people to work together collectively, to produce goods and/or services, and hence, create greater value than people working separately. For example, hospitals satisfy people's health-related needs, educational institutions cater to the needs of learning and knowledge creation in society, banks exist to facilitate transactions in society through monetary instruments of exchange, and so on. An organization helps increase specialization and division of labor, facilitates use of large-scale technology where required, manages the environment and economizes on transaction costs, all of which increases the value that an organization helps create. In fact, the value creation process is best understood by an open-systems approach to understanding organizations.

## 1.6 Viewing organizations from an open systems perspective

A biological metaphor is commonly used to gain insights about how organizations function. As with living organisms, organizations are born, pass through stages of development and maturity, and may even deteriorate and die if the energy they expend is not replenished. A unique characteristic of the systems approach is the interrelationship of parts within the system. As in the human body, for example, where each part (heart, lungs, liver, etc.) performs a different function and yet all parts are held together by the skeleton and central nervous system, so too, organizations are made up of a number of different units, each with its specialized tasks and functions, and all units are held together through integrating mechanisms (supervision, rules, procedures, and policies) to function as a unified whole. Each unit or subsystem in turn is a part of a larger system.

The systems perspective also accepts that any system is a part of the larger environment and, to a lesser or greater extent, needs to depend on the environment for its survival and growth. Based on the degree of interaction, systems are classified as closed or open systems. A **closed system**, has its roots in the physical sciences, it views a system as self-contained and independent. Hence, a perfect closed system would be one that neither receives energy from the outside environment, nor releases any energy into the environment. This, however, is a theoretical concept with little relevance to understanding organizations, since no organization can be a perfectly closed system. At most, their dependence on the environment might be lesser in degree compared to that of an open system. An **open system** recognizes the dynamic interaction of the system, as depicted below (Figure 1.2):

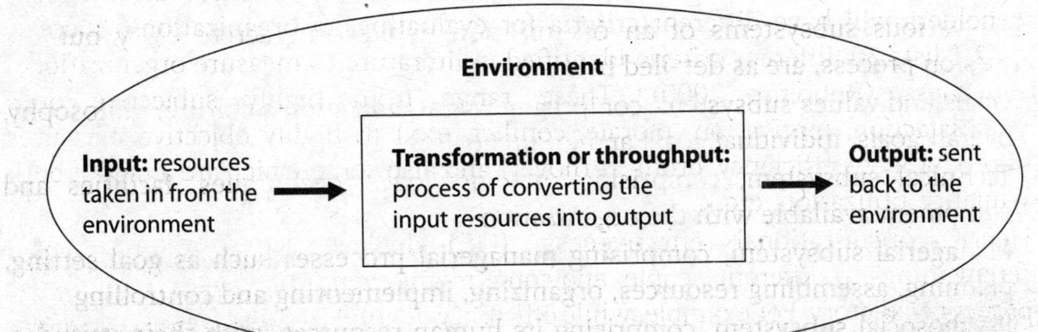


**Figure 1.2** *An open system*

An organization too receives its energy (raw material, manpower, funds, information) from the environment, processes them to produce the final product or service, and releases the finished product back into the environment. The revenues from customers go back into the system again, and are used for the repayment of its loans to financial institutions, payment of wages to its labor force, and payment to its suppliers for goods received from them, all of which ensure continued supply of resources (manpower, money, raw materials) from these input agencies. Feedback from customers also serves as an input in terms of ensuring acceptable product quality.

Hence, organizations create value for society as depicted diagrammatically in Figure 1.3 below:

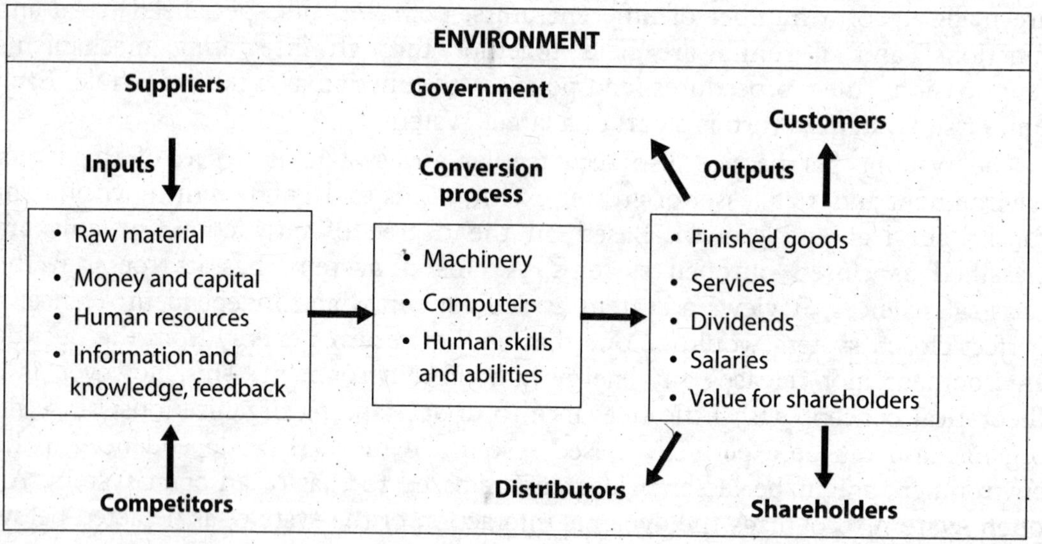


**Figure 1.3** *Organizations create value for society*

The various subsystems of an organization, which interact to carry out the conversion process, are as detailed below:

a) Goals and values subsystem, comprising the organization's culture, philosophy, overall goals, individual goals and group goals
b) Technical subsystem, comprising the knowledge, techniques, facilities and equipment available with the organization
c) Managerial subsystem, comprising managerial processes such as goal setting, planning, assembling resources, organizing, implementing and controlling
d) Psychosocial subsystem, comprising its human resources, with their attitudes, perceptions, motivations, group dynamics, leadership, communication, and interpersonal relations

e) Structural subsystem, comprising the tasks, workflow, authority, information flow, rules, and procedures

### 1.6.1 Characteristics of open systems

Apart from the dimensions discussed above, open systems have some unique characteristics which help us develop our understanding about organizations further (Robins, 2000):

1. *Awareness of the environment*: An open system's interdependence with its environment implies that there is a boundary, either physical or otherwise, that separates it from its environment. In organizations, the inflow and outflow of materials, products, and information occurs across these defined boundaries. Hence, without a boundary there can be no system, and these boundaries determine where systems and subsystems start and stop. Therefore, the concept of boundaries is required to understand organizations from a systems perspective.
2. *Feedback:* An open system continually receives information from the environment which helps it to adjust and allows it to take corrective action to rectify deviations from its prescribed course of activity. From an organizational perspective, this feedback (either favorable or unfavorable) could be from customers (payments, quality complaints, market perceptions) and other stakeholders, which allows a part of the output to be fed back into the system as inputs (money, information, resources, etc.), so as to modify subsequent outputs.
3. *Cyclical character:* In an open system, the outputs provide means for new inputs that allow the cycle to be repeated. In Figure 1.3, revenue from customers provides the means for paying creditors (employees, suppliers, and financial institutions), enabling inflow of further resources (funds, raw materials, man power, etc.) into the organization which perpetuates the cycle.
4. *Negative entropy:* Entropy refers to the dispersal of energy from a system, or the propensity of a system to run down or disintegrate. A closed system, being self-contained and independent, has no interaction with the environment, and therefore does not import energy or new inputs; hence, it is expected that it will eventually run down and disintegrate over time. An open system, on the other hand, is characterized by 'negative entropy': it brings in energy from outside (materials, money, manpower, etc. in the case of organizations), and hence can repair itself, maintain its structure and even grow, when it imports more 'energy' than it gives out.
5. *Steady state:* The outflow of energy from an open system is continually compensated by inflow of energy. In organizations too, outflow of products and services is compensated for by continuous inflow of manpower, funds and materials which help the organization (system) to maintain its basic structure and character and steady state.

6. *Movement toward growth and expansion:* As the concept of negative entropy signifies, open systems import energy from outside to maintain and even grow. That is, it brings in excess energy. Organizations too, utilize a part of their inputs to produce goods and services and build in slack (some margin of safety beyond the immediate level of existence), which can be utilized to grow and expand their operations. Hence, open systems, in addition to maintaining their current state, also strive toward continuous growth and expansion.
7. *Balance of maintenance and adaptive activities:* Any open system is simultaneously involved with two apparently contradicting activities. At one level, maintenance activities have to be carried out to maintain a balance between the various subsystems, and to ensure that the total system is in accord with the environment. At another level, adaptive activities are required to ensure that the system is able to continually adapt itself to changes in internal and external demands over time. From an organizational viewpoint, activities such as recruitment and training of employees, enforcement of rules and procedures, purchase, maintenance, and overhauling of machinery and equipment ensure stability and preservation of status quo, while planning for change, market research, new product development, etc. drive the organization to adapt to changing conditions. Both maintenance and adaptive activities are required for a system to survive. In fact, any organization has to seek to strike a fine balance between the dualities of maintenance and adaptation. Figure 1.4 illustrates some of the dualities continually faced by organizations.
8. *Equifinality:* The principle of 'equifinality' states that in open systems, a given end state can be reached by many means. For organizations, it implies that organizational systems can accomplish their objectives in a variety of ways, using different inputs and transformation processes. This concept highlights the importance for managers in organizations to consider a variety of methods and solutions, rather than searching for the one best way to achieve a goal. For example, the *dabbawalas* in Mumbai use virtually no technology, are heavily reliant on grossly under-educated manual labor and minimum investment, but are as, if not more, effective and successful, than the United States postal service, a multi-billion dollar system involving sophisticated technology for tracking and receiving deliverables, which nonetheless suffers from low delivery reliability and an inability to individualize operations.

For managers in organizations, the systems perspective enables them to perceive the organization as made up of interrelated and interdependent parts. It also helps them appreciate that any decision taken by them in one subsystem of an organization is likely to affect other interrelated subsystems, and their environmental responses, thereby reemphasizing the importance of responsible decision-making.

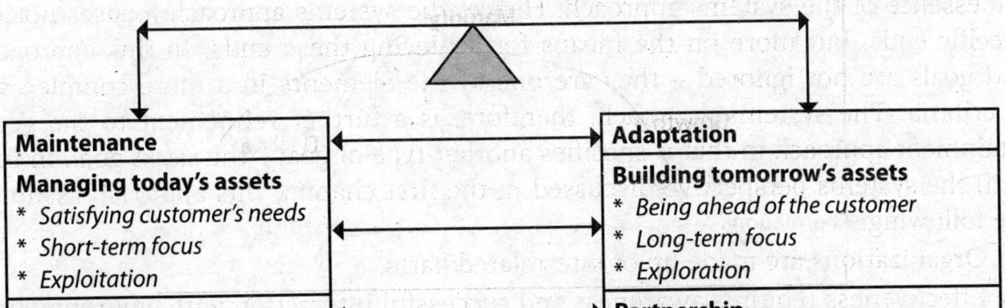


**Figure 1.4** *The duality continuum (Adapted from Evans, Pucik and Barsoux, 2002).*

## 1.7 Viewing organizations from a life-cycle perspective

As mentioned earlier, organizations, like living organisms, are born, pass through stages of development and maturity, and may even deteriorate and die. That is, organizations undergo predictable and repetitive patterns of behavior as they grow and develop. This sequence of stages of growth and development that organizations pass through is termed the **organizational life cycle**. Of course, not all organizations die or go into decline: some may even change their form and be 'reborn'. Organizations typically pass through four stages in their life cycle (Figure 1.5):

1. *Birth (or entrepreneurial) stage:* Organizations are 'born' when individuals/entrepreneurs recognize and take advantage of opportunities to use their skills and competence to create value. This stage is marked by ambiguous goals, high creativity, informal structure and communication patterns. This stage has the greatest chance of failure, since such organizations typically experience what is

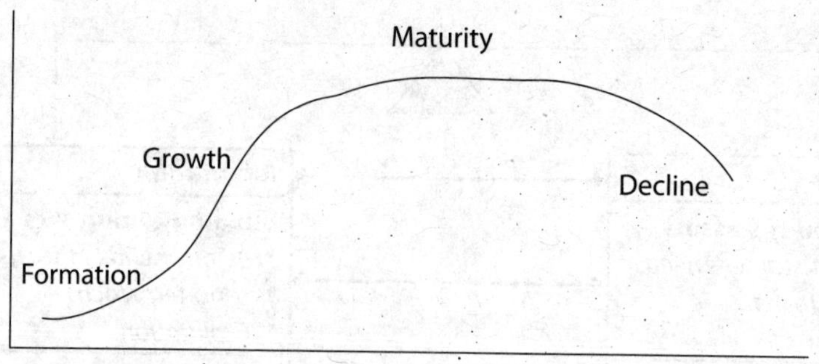


**Figure 1.5** *Organizational life cycle*

known as the '*liability of newness*' – the dangers associated with being the first in a new environment. The **'population ecology theory'** (Hannan and Freeman, 1977) explains the factors that affect the rate at which new organizations are born and die in a population of existing organizations. Using the analogy of Darwinian evolution, this theory seeks to find an explanation for the founding rates and death rates of organizational populations. According to this theory, the availability of resources determines the number of organizations in a population. The amount of resources in an environment limits **population density** (the number of organizations that can compete for the same resources in a particular environment). The rate of birth in a new environment increases rapidly at first and then tapers off as resources become less plentiful and competition increases. Hence, this theory posits that (a) the relationship between density and mortality rates is U-shaped and (b) the relationship between density and founding rates is inverted U-shaped. Over time, organizations develop routinized procedures, which ensure reliability and accountability of their products and services.

> Population ecology theory posits relationships between the availability of resources in the environment and the survival of organizations in a population.

Initially, when the density of organizations within a new niche is low, mortality rates are higher, since routines and procedures which aid in stability, have not yet been established. After a while, as procedures get established and accepted, the attractiveness of the niche increases and mortality rates decrease. However, as the niche becomes more populated, competition escalates, and so does mortality. On the other hand, when the niche is new and lacks legitimacy, founding rates are low. After a while, as the niche stabilizes and becomes popular, the founding rate rises. However, with corresponding increase in competition, the niche gradually becomes overcrowded and loses popularity, leading to a decline in founding rates again.

New organizations are always emerging to take advantage of new opportunities. Ultimately, however, it is the process of natural selection which ensures that only those organizations with skills and resources that best fit the environment survive over time, while others that do not gradually decline and die out.

2. *Growth stage:* Sometimes referred to as the collectivity stage, this is the stage in which organizations develop value creation skills and competences that allow them to acquire additional resources. At this stage, the mission of the organization is clarified, though communication patterns and structure continue to be informal. Members demonstrate high commitment to the organization. The '**institutional theory**' (DiMaggio and Powell, 1983) of organizational growth studies how organizations can increase their ability to grow and survive in a competitive environment by satisfying their stakeholders. **Institutional environment** is defined as the set of values and norms in an environment that govern the behavior of a population of organizations. Organizations which follow the norms of their environment are perceived to be legitimate and trustworthy by stakeholders; this increases their chances of survival and growth. In fact, a new organization can strengthen its perceived legitimacy by imitating the goals, structure and culture of successful organizations in its population. This leads to an increase in 'organizational isomorphism' among organizations in a population: consequently, we find similar organizational configurations in similar environments. The institutional approach highlights three processes to explain why organizations become similar to one another:

> Institutional theory posits that organizations increase their ability to survive in a competitive environment by increasing their perceived legitimacy in the eyes of their stakeholders, by following certain accepted norms of behavior.

   - *Coercive isomorphism*: An organization adopts certain norms because of pressures exerted by other organizations and/or by society in general. The coercion stems from an organization's dependence on other organizations and the cultural expectations in the society in which the organization functions.
   - *Mimetic isomorphism*: Organizations intentionally copy or imitate one another (often their more successful competitors) to increase their legitimacy, and their environmental uncertainties.
   - *Normative isomorphism*: Organizations indirectly adopt norms and values of other organizations, through (a) similar theoretical inputs provided by educational institutions and (b) cross-pollination of norms and values across organizations in a population, owing to movement of their professionals and managers between similar or competing organizations.

3. *Maturity stage:* This stage is characterized by two main phases:
   - *Formalization and control*: The structure of the organization stabilizes, with the imposition of formal rules and procedures to guide members' behaviors.

Focus is more on efficiency and stability, rather than innovation. With formal systems in place, the organization now begins to exist beyond the individual.

- *Elaboration of structure*: Having reached a stable stage, the organization can now look to diversifying its products or service markets, and searches for newer opportunities. The organization becomes more complex and elaborate; decision-making becomes decentralized.

4. *Decline stage:* An organization enters this stage when it fails to anticipate, recognize, avoid, neutralize or adapt to external pressures that threaten its long-term survival. Common symptoms characterizing this stage include shrinking market share, increased employee turnover, increasing conflicts and politicking, and centralized decision making to manage crises. Needless to say, all organizations need not reach this stage, and can continue to flourish in the previous stages, continue to remain in the growth stage or even exist simultaneously in more than one stage. Nor is it necessary to follow this life-cycle pattern in a chronological manner. Organizational decline and death will be addressed in greater detail in Chapter 8.

Using a life-cycle perspective to view organizations helps increase one's appreciation that an organization has not always been the way we perceive it at present, nor will it be the same in future. It also helps the decision-maker appreciate that different stages require different responses to environmental demands; hence, what works in one stage might not work in another, and vice versa.

### 1.7.1 Greiner's life-cycle model of organizational growth

While institutional theory is one way of understanding organizational growth, Greiner (1972) has proposed a five-stage model to explain how organizations evolve and grow. This model (Figure 1.6), taken in conjunction with the life-cycle model discussed earlier, depicts the various stages of organizational evolution. Each stage identified by Greiner is expected to end with a crisis which has to be resolved before the organization can progress to the next stage:

Stage 1: *Growth through creativity*: In this stage, the entrepreneur develops the skills and abilities to create and introduce new products for new market niches. Consequently, a great deal of organizational learning occurs at this stage; integration is through norms and shared values, rather than formalized structures and rules. As the organization is established and secures a niche for itself, some internal forces begin to change the entrepreneurial process. The founders begin to realize that entrepreneurship is very different from management. Often, beyond the initial stages, entrepreneurs or founders find themselves unequal to the task of running and managing the organization they helped set up; in spite of this awareness, however, they are often unwilling to 'let go'. Even if they do continue to be in control, a

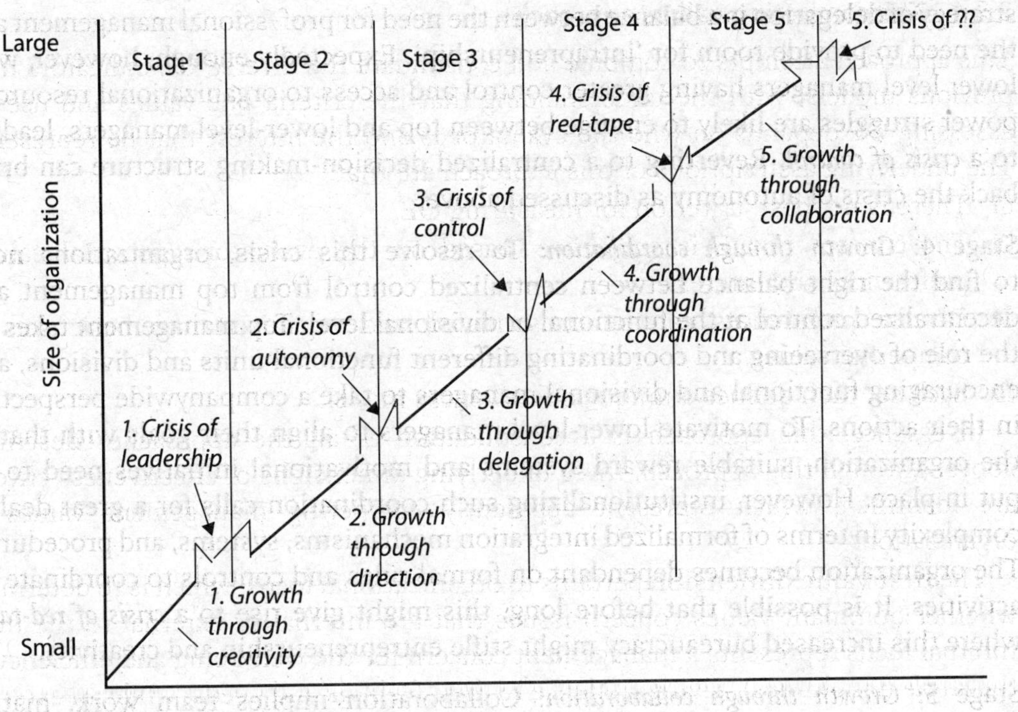


**Figure 1.6** *Greiner's model of organizational growth*

**crisis of leadership** might occur, when shareholders might decide that the founder/entrepreneur is not necessarily the best person to manage the company, and might demand that a professional manager take over from the founder in running the company.

Stage 2: *Growth through direction*: The crisis of leadership ends with the recruitment of a strong top-management team of professional managers to lead the organization and take responsibility for directing the company's future strategy, while lower level managers assume key functional responsibilities. However, as the organization continues to grow with professional managers running the show, creative employees in R&D, product engineering, marketing, etc. start becoming frustrated by their lack of control over innovation and new product development. With innovation being de-emphasized in the interest of stability and efficiency, and bureaucratic controls and approvals required for any new initiatives, motivation for experimentation and risk-taking are lowered. Unless resolved, this *crisis of autonomy* can lead to loss of talented, creative manpower.

Stage 3: *Growth through delegation*: To address this crisis of autonomy, organizations start delegating authority to lower level managers in all functions, reinforced with suitable reward practices to encourage responsibility and accountability. In fact, this strategy of delegation is a balance between the need for professional management and the need to provide room for 'intrapreneurship'. Expectedly enough, however, with lower level managers having greater control and access to organizational resources, power struggles are likely to emerge between top and lower-level managers, leading to a *crisis of control*. Reverting to a centralized decision-making structure can bring back the crisis of autonomy as discussed above.

Stage 4: *Growth through coordination*: To resolve this crisis, organizations need to find the right balance between centralized control from top management and decentralized control at the functional or divisional level. Top management takes on the role of overseeing and coordinating different functional units and divisions, and encouraging functional and divisional managers to take a companywide perspective in their actions. To motivate lower-level managers to align their goals with that of the organization, suitable reward systems and motivational initiatives need to be put in place. However, institutionalizing such coordination calls for a great deal of complexity in terms of formalized integration mechanisms, systems, and procedures. The organization becomes dependant on formal rules and controls to coordinate its activities. It is possible that before long, this might give rise to a *crisis of red-tape*, where this increased bureaucracy might stifle entrepreneurship and creativity.

Stage 5: *Growth through collaboration*: Collaboration implies team work, matrix structure, confronting interpersonal differences, replacing formal controls by social control and self-discipline, and going in for strategic alliances. Collaboration makes organizations more flexible, by making greater use of mutual adjustment and less use of standardization. However, changing from a mechanistic to an organic structure might give rise to varieties of problems, both cultural and otherwise, which need to be managed wisely.

### 1.7.2 Adizes' corporate life-cycle stages

Ichak Adizes (1988) has elaborated these stages further to include ten phases through which organizations typically grow and/or decline:

1. The *courtship* stage: This represents the first stage of an organization's development. At this stage, the organization has not been formally 'born' or incorporated, but exists more as a dream of the founder(s). However, while the initial enthusiasm and excitement of the idea exists, the goals, objectives, and road maps are fuzzy or probably not articulated clearly.
2. The *infancy* stage: At this stage, the organization begins its activities, following its inception. 'Infant' organizations are generally action-oriented and leader-driven, and often suffer from inconsistent performance. Because of lack of stability in systems and operations and lack of managerial depth, minor problems could escalate to crises levels in a very short time. Because of the high risk of 'infant

mortality' among such organizations, this stage is particularly risky in terms of sustainability.

3. The *go-go* stage: At this stage, the organization has a successful product or service, and experiences rapid growth in sales and cash flow. Characterized by rapid and energetic growth, this stage is likely to witness a great deal of chaos and unstructured functioning. Often, organizations in this stage, in the excitement of high growth, might try to diversify into other areas, without consolidating the existing business sufficiently. This stage is also likely to be vulnerable to the risk of 'founders' trap', especially when the founder is unable to let go of control over all operations and hand over the reins of management to more professional experts.
4. At the *adolescence* stage, the organization is still evolving, but is more structured and formal in comparison with the previous stages. This is the stage in which the organization finds a new identity for itself, not necessarily tied to its founder. Organizations might experience substantial turbulence at this stage, brought on by internal conflicts and turf wars.
5. The *prime* stage: At this stage, the organization is at its peak form in terms of health, performance, morale, competitiveness, market share, stability, etc. The organization has achieved the optimum balance between control and flexibility. Processes and systems are stable, there is clarity of vision and the company operates in a focused and predictable manner.
6. The *stability* stage: At this stage, the organization is still effective and continues to enjoy market leadership. However, complacency and a sense of well-being and contentment among managers might result in decreased entrepreneurial spirit, and the organization might begin to lose its leading edge and market share, becoming vulnerable to market challenges in the process.
7. The *aristocracy* stage sees the firm still going strong by virtue of market presence and consolidated accumulated successes, but beginning to be perceived as slow and traditional, focused on past achievements rather than future vision and definitely losing market share to competitors, new technologies, and new trends.
8. The *recrimination* stage: As problems start escalating, threats, internal issues, politicking, blame games, etc. start overshadowing the original purpose of the organization. This results in large scale turnover of talented employees. In this paranoid setup, personal survival becomes the focus, with little concern about customers or outside stakeholders. Organizations at this stage often become prime targets for takeovers.
9. The *bureaucracy* stage witnesses a regression to inward-focused administration, compounded by cumbersome decision-making, exit-seeking, or divestment, and beset with continuous operating and marketing challenges. There is little pressure to perform, as long as rules are followed.

10. *Death*: This stage witnesses closures, sell-offs, bankruptcies, or takeovers, till the organization ceases to exist in its original form.

## CHAPTER SUMMARY

Organizations are groups of people which function through a coordinated system of management using well-established processes and procedures, with identifiable boundaries, where members engage in regular interactions to achieve a common goal, in order to satisfy some collective needs of society. Organizations can take various forms, viz. sole proprietorships, partnerships, cooperatives, corporations, subsidiaries, holding company, etc. Organization design deals with constructing and changing an organization's structure to achieve the organization's goals. A combination of contextual and structural dimensions is used to describe an organization's design parameters. Organization structure helps to establish a balance between the differentiation and integration requirements of organizations by defining how tasks are allocated, who reports to whom, the coordination mechanisms and interaction patterns that will be followed, through the multiple dimensions of complexity, formalization and centralization.

Organization theory (OT) is the discipline that studies how organizations are affected by the environment in which they operate, and how factors such as strategy, size, environment, technology, and culture might determine an organization's structure. OT in its present form has evolved through various stages, beginning with the classical school of thought with their focus on efficiency and the 'one-best-way' of doing business, through the human-relations approach with a predominantly 'humane' orientation and sensitivity to the 'social' aspect of employment,and thence to the contemporary approach with its contingency focus. A study of OT provides conceptual tools for the practicing manager at all levels to influence various organizational situations which she/he is likely to encounter.

Organizations exist to create value in society by satisfying certain needs of its stakeholders. The open systems view of organizations looks at organizations as living organisms, made up of numerous interrelated, interdependent parts and subunits, working in a coordinated manner to take in inputs (raw material, manpower, funds, information, and other resources), processing them within its component units to transform them into tangible/intangible products (or services) and releasing it into the environment outside to satisfy various expectations and needs of its stakeholders. Environmental feedback of its output in turn helps to perpetuate the cyclical nature of this process. For managers in organizations, the systems perspective helps them to appreciate the implications of any decision taken by them in one subsystem of an organization which might affect other interrelated subsystems, and their environmental responses.

The life-cycle perspective looks at the sequence of stages of growth, development, and possible decline that organizations pass through in the course of their existence. Typically, organizations pass through four broad stages in their 'lives': birth, growth, maturity, and decline. All organizations need not reach this last stage, and can continue to flourish in the previous stages, continue to remain in the growth stage, or even exist simultaneously in more than one stage. The 'population ecology theory' helps explain the factors that affect the rate at which new organizations are born and die in a population of existing organizations. The 'institutional theory' of organizational growth studies how organizations can increase their ability to grow and survive in a competitive environment by satisfying their stakeholders, and gaining legitimacy through isomorphism. Greiner's model identifies five stages of organizational growth and also highlights the crisis points each stage is likely to encounter, which, if not managed effectively, might lead to the organization's decline. Finally, Adizes' model refines these stages further to identify ten stages through which an organization is likely to pass in the course of its existence.

## Review Questions

1. Briefly explain the interrelationships between organization design, organization structure, and organization theory.
2. Highlight the similarities and differences between the classical school, the human-relations school, and the contemporary school of organization theory.
3. Explain the terms 'equifinality' and 'negative entropy' with the help of examples.
4. Analyze how population ecology theory and institutional theory help to explain the evolution and growth of organizations.
5. Compare and contrast Greiner's model of organizational growth and Adizes' corporate life-cycle model.

## Project Assignment

Refer to the organizations mentioned at the beginning of this chapter.

1) Analyze each of these organizations from an open systems perspective, identifying their different interrelated, interdependent subunits, as well as their stakeholders, the expectations of each of the stakeholders, the inputs, processes, and outputs.
2) Analyze the 'dualities' faced by each of these organizations with respect to the dimensions mentioned in Figure 1.6 in the chapter.

## CASE ILLUSTRATION: 'HELPING HANDS'

*Udavum Karangal*, whose literal English translation means 'Helping Hands', has been doing just that for the past quarter of a century; it has been reaching out to help and serve orphans and the destitute in distress. Established in 1983 by S. Vidyaakar (affectionately called *Pappa*), a social worker serving in the slums of Chennai, Tamil Nadu, *Udavum Karangal* is a registered non-governmental, non-profit organization. Beginning with caring for an abandoned, sickly infant, the organization, in over 25 years, has grown to its present form, providing care and accommodation to nearly 2000 orphans and elderly destitute, through five centers in Chennai and two centers in Coimbatore. 'Shishu Bhavan' houses little infants, 'Shantivanam' rescues and shelters the mentally ill, while 'Gokulam' houses children between 4 and 14 years of age. Other units include 'Karunalayam' for the terminally ill and dying destitutes, 'Malarvanam' for HIV infected/AIDS patients, and 'Mukthi' for the aged destitute. The organization continues to grow, with an average intake of 24 people per year. In addition to rehabilitation and residential care facilities, *Udavum Karangal* also provides healthcare, educational facilities, ambulance and mortuary services, disaster management to victims of social and natural calamities, and guidance and counseling services. Awards and accolades have become a fact of life at *Udavum Karangal* – the 'International Award for Most Outstanding Voluntary Organization in India' given by *Matsushita*, Japan in 1992, 'Maschio Humanitarian Award' in 1996, 'Award for Best Institution in 2002' from the government of Tamil Nadu, 'Recognition for Outstanding Services' in 2003 from the City of Philadelphia, citation for services provided for tsunami victims in 2005 – are only a representative few in a long list of honors that have been heaped on *Udavum Karangal* over the years. Notwithstanding this, the organization continues to maintain a low profile, preferring to let its actions do the 'talking'. Its India chapter does not have any fund raising events, but the US and UK chapters do try and spread awareness regarding its activities, to overseas Indians. This has resulted in eminent personalities like Manoj N. Shyamalan coming forward to support their cause. The entities which contribute to *Udavum Karangal's* success include their army of around 100 volunteers of all ages, experts from various walks of life who work part time or full time, solving problems at the various 'homes', 130 full-time paid employees to handle the administrative activities, their dedicated board of directors, corporate partners such as *Apollo* hospitals and pharmaceutical companies, donors (purely through word of mouth), and other NGOs with whom they have resource-sharing arrangements. Many inmates spend their entire life at *Udavum Karangal*, entering as infants, completing their education there, and becoming volunteers to other inmates. The only NGO of its kind to be duly certified by ISO, *Udavum Karangal* represents a beacon of light for the homeless and destitute of Tamil Nadu.

### Critical enquiry

*What do you think could have been the possible challenges that Udavum Karangal might have faced in its various stages of growth till date? What are the likely survival and growth challenges you envisage for it in the future?*

***Key words and phrases***: organization, organization design, organization theory, organization structure, organizational reality, dualities, open-systems approach, population ecology theory, institutional theory, organizational life cycle

CHAPTER 2

# Organizational Effectiveness

**CHAPTER OUTLINE**

What is organizational effectiveness?

❖

Approaches for measuring organizational effectiveness

## ORGANIZATIONAL INSIGHT

In an effort at making the voluntary sector in India more democratic, transparent, and accountable in its functioning, a consortium of voluntary organizations – the Credibility Alliance (CA)* – was formed in 2004, as a nodal agency, to ensure good governance practices in the social sector and to increase its credibility. Its vision – *A voluntary sector, which is responsive to the needs of the society, is democratic and transparent in its functioning and accountable to all concerned* – and mission – *To build the credibility of the voluntary sector through creation and promotion of norms of good governance and public disclosure* – are indicative of its objectives, which include:

- ❖ the development of norms of governance for voluntary organizations, based on participation, consultation, and consensus
- ❖ promotion of an accreditation system for the voluntary sector
- ❖ promotion of capacity-building initiatives for voluntary organizations to enable compliance with norms, and
- ❖ policy advocacy for enhanced credibility, acceptability, and recognition of the work done by the voluntary sector in the eyes of the government, the donor community, the corporate sector, the media, and the public.

While the alliance functions on principles of self-regulation on the part of its members by way of compliance – the members participate in the process of evolving suitable guidelines based on voluntary disclosure of information and adhere to them – it enables donors and other stakeholders to gauge the effectiveness of this sector while making a conscious choice to engage with it. The process of setting the norms for enhancing the credibility of the voluntary sector have been initiated and led by the sector itself. The norms are designed in such a way that organizations, small and large, local and international, working in India, are able to comply. While the promotion and modification of the norms evolve in a participatory manner, accreditation/evaluation against these norms is a separate process that is carried out by agencies other than the CA. The norms emphasize disclosure, in keeping with the principles of transparency and accountability, rather than for value judgment. The values espoused by the CA include autonomy and self-governance, integrity, not-for-profit existence, voluntarism, democracy and participation, respect for human rights, respect for diversity, social and gender justice, and are also reflected in the clear definitions of vision, mission, mission statement, objectives, constituency, stakeholders, needs assessment, monitoring, and evaluation, all of which are integral to the concept of effectiveness measurement for organizations.

* **Source:** *http://www.credall.org.in/about_us/aboutus.htm (accessed on 21st May 2010)*

## 2.1 What is organizational effectiveness?

As mentioned in Chapter 1, organizations exist to deliver value to their stakeholders. So, an organization can be thought of as a value-creating tool that can be used simultaneously by different groups of stakeholders to accomplish a variety of goals. Hence, it is natural that different groups of stakeholders would want to evaluate an organization to decide whether the organization is being effective in meeting their expectations. The question of how to decide the best criteria for measuring an organization's effectiveness has held the interest of researchers for years. In fact, the issue of organizational effectiveness has proved to be one of the most critical, yet most elusive, subjects of research in the field of organization theory.

Since organizations must perform diverse activities – from obtaining resource inputs to delivering output – in order to be successful, it is evident that one unequivocal measure of effectiveness would be difficult to arrive at. Different stakeholders will have different criteria for evaluating an organization's success. Table 2.1 lists 30 different criteria identified in literature to measure organizational effectiveness (Robbins, 2000). These range from highly subjective ones (e.g. satisfaction, motivation, morale, conflict, etc.) to highly objective measures (e.g. productivity, efficiency, profit, turnover) and also some which are a mix of both (e.g quality, utilization, etc.).

Different stakeholders will use different criteria to measure an organization's effectiveness.

Hence, organizational effectiveness (OE) means different things to different people, and some might even appear contradictory. For example, while efficiency denotes optimum use of resources, implying strict control of all inputs and *absence of slack*, flexibility is achieved through

**Table 2.1** *Organizational Effectiveness Criteria*

| | |
|---|---|
| 1. Overall effectiveness | 16. Planning and goal setting |
| 2. Productivity | 17. Goal consensus |
| 3. Efficiency | 18. Internalization of organizational goals |
| 4. Profit | 19. Role and norm congruence |
| 5. Quality | 20. Managing interpersonal skills |
| 6. Accidents | 21. Managerial task skills |
| 7. Growth | 22. Information management and communication |
| 8. Absenteeism | 23. Readiness |
| 9. Turnover | 24. Utilization of environment |
| 10. Job satisfaction | 25. Evaluation by external entities |
| 11. Motivation | 26. Stability |
| 12. Morale | 27. Value of human resources |
| 13. Control | 28. Participation and shared influence |
| 14. Conflict/cohesion | 29. Training and development emphasis |
| 15. Flexibility/adaptation | 30. Achievement emphasis |

surplus or buffer, implying *presence of slack* in the system to allow for experimentation. What the above table indicates are the different interests of an organization's evaluators, because of the diverse nature of its activities. Moreover, the above criteria can be used to measure both for-profit and non-profit organizations. Hence, any operational definition of OE must necessarily reflect this complexity of multiple criteria.

Tom Peters and Robert Waterman (1982), in their seminal work, *In Search of Excellence,* have identified eight common characteristics of highly effective or 'excellent' companies. These are:

- *A bias for action and for getting things accomplished*
- *An ability to stay close to customers to fully understand the customers' needs*
- *Willing to allow employees a high degree of autonomy and foster the entrepreneurial spirit*
- *Seeking to increase productivity through employee participation*
- *Their employees know what the company stands for and their managers are actively involved in problems at all levels*
- *They stay close to the businesses they know and understand*
- *Their organizational structures are elegantly simple, with a minimal number of people in staff activities*

- *They blend tight, centralized controls for protecting the company's core values with loose controls in other areas to encourage risk-taking and innovation*

Despite criticism regarding research methodologies and conclusions, these eight criteria were viewed as 'commandments' by organizations in their quest for effectiveness. However, it would be wise to take an objective view of such 'prescriptions', as appreciating the other side of the coin is equally important and valid, though not specifically stated. Hence, for example, long-range, strategic planning (which does not involve any apparent or visible 'action') is as important to an organization's success as a bias for action; staying close to the customer is recommended provided the organization's considerations of cost-effectiveness are not compromised; promoting autonomy and entrepreneurial freedom to employees dovetails with the organization's long-term strategies and visions; and hands-on involvement of managers does not affect their long-term vision or ability to see the big picture. This reinforces the fact that evaluating organizations is a very complex process, and there is a need to take a multiple-perspective approach, rather than a one-size-fits-all approach.

Broadly, researchers have accepted that organizational effectiveness is the degree to which an organization achieves its goal, though this would be a very simplistic approach, since goals themselves can have various definitions. A number of approaches can be used to measure organizational effectiveness. A combination of all these approaches may then yield a comprehensive understanding of OE. These approaches are discussed in subsequent sections.

## 2.2 Approaches for measuring organizational effectiveness

### 2.2.1 The goal-attainment approach

> The goal-attainment approach evaluates an organization's effectiveness by the extent of fulfillment of its output goals (ends goals) only.

This approach consists of identifying an organization's output goals (for example, the number of units sold, revenue generated, percentage of profit, number of complaints settled, etc.) and assessing how well the organization has achieved these goals. Hence, organizational effectiveness should be appraised in terms of accomplishment of ends rather than means, the implication being that irrespective of the means employed, it is the final end or bottom line that counts. It is similar to the Management By Objectives (MBO) approach, in that it assumes that (a) organizations are rational, goal-seeking entities who (b) have ultimate goals that are (c) identified, well-defined, and understood by all, and (d) few enough to be achievable and manageable, and objectively measurable. In the MBO approach (Drucker, 1954), the vision and mission of an organization cascade through successive layers of the hierarchy through a process of participatively set goals and objectives, down to individual goals. The basic characteristics of MBO include participatively set, objective, measurable goals that are understood and accepted by all, and a continuous system of feedback and review. It is based on the assumption that when employees are involved in the process of goal setting in line with the overall mission and goals of the organization, it not only motivates them, but also makes the process of organizing and managing easier through clarity of communication and understanding, and committed and motivated employees.

*Utility of this approach:* This approach may be used in business organizations where output goals such as profitability, growth, market share, return on investment (ROI), etc. can be readily measured. However, some problems in making this approach operational could be issues such as multiple or conflicting goals (whose goals?), short-term or long-term goals, official goals or actual goals, reflecting espoused or enacted values of the organization, and the issue of whether the goals reflect actions to be taken, or are a justification for actions taken in the past. Because of goal multiplicity, there could be some subjective goals which are not objectively measurable, but the achievement of which is, nonetheless, equally crucial to the organization's success. Hence, the validity of the goal-attainment approach can be increased by:

- ensuring that input is received from all those who have a major influence on formulating official goals
- including actual goals by observing the behavior of organization members
- recognizing that organizations pursue both short-term and long-term goals, accepting that both short-term and long-term goals are important for an organization
- insisting on tangible, verifiable, and measurable goals rather than relying on vague statements that merely mirror societal expectations
- viewing goals as dynamic and changing over time, not as rigid or fixed statements or purpose

### 2.2.2 The systems approach

This approach uses a combination of a resource-based approach and an internal process approach to emphasize those criteria which will increase the long-term survival of the organization. The resource-based approach looks at the input side of the transformational process and assumes that an organization must be successful in obtaining and managing scarce, valued resources from the external environment in order to be effective. The internal process approach measures organizational health and efficiency in terms of employee satisfaction, economic efficiency, etc. Hence, a combination of these two approaches implies that organizations need to be judged not only on end goals but also on their ability to acquire inputs, process these inputs, channel these outputs, and maintain stability and balance, which represent the essence of the systems approach. Hence, the systems approach focuses not on specific ends, but more on the means for achieving these ends. In this approach, end goals are not ignored – they are one of the elements in a more complex set of criteria. The systems approach, therefore, is a further refinement to the goal-attainment approach in that it specifies another type of goal – the *means* goal. In line with the systems perspective discussed in the first chapter, this approach assumes the following:

- ❒ Organizations are made up of interrelated parts
- ❒ Effectiveness requires awareness and successful interaction with environmental constituencies
- ❒ Survival requires steady replenishment of those resources consumed

The effectiveness criteria used in this approach are given in Table 2.2:

**Table 2.2** *Effectiveness criteria – Systems approach*

| *Resource-based approach* | *Internal process approach* |
|---|---|
| Relations with the environment to ensure continued input of valued raw resources and favorable acceptance of output | Clarity of internal communications |
| Ability to perceive and correctly interpret environmental signals | Level of conflict among groups, and conflict-resolution mechanisms |
| Flexibility of response to environmental changes | Work culture in organization |
| Efficiency of transforming inputs into outputs | • Rewards for performance, growth, and development of subordinates<br>• Team spirit, group loyalty, and team work<br>• Degree of employee job satisfaction |

Commonly used measures of OE in this approach include:

- Output/input (O/I): e.g. no. of students graduating/total no. of students enrolled
- Transformations/input (T/I): e.g. no. of students graduating with a master's degree/total no. of students enrolled
- Transformations/output (T/O): e.g. total no. of international publications by faculty in top line journals/total no. of publications by faculty
- Changes in input/input ($\delta I/I$): e.g. increase in number of students enrolled, over that of previous year/total no. of students enrolled in current year

While this approach represents a more robust perspective of organizational effectiveness, considering both ends and means, the main challenge lies in measuring and quantifying the criteria, since many of these goals are subjective in nature.

*Utility of this approach:* The main utility of this approach lies in the fact that managers are less likely to look for immediate results; it allows them to concentrate on creating robust and sustainable systems and processes. This might, at times, imply having to sacrifice short-term gains in order to get long-term, sustainable benefits. Otherwise, a greater focus on end goals might often compromise long-term benefits for short-term, short-lived gains. This approach also increases managers' appreciation of the interdependent nature of organizational processes. Finally, this approach is useful in cases where end goals are vague or not amenable to objective measurement.

> The systems approach evaluates an organization's effectiveness by evaluating the extent of fulfillment of ends goals as well as the efficiency of the process (means goals) for achieving these output goals.

### 2.2.3 Strategic constituencies approach (also known as stakeholder approach or multiple-constituencies approach)

The dependence of an organization on its environment has already been discussed in the previous chapter. The assumptions of this approach are essentially an extension of that concept. The strategic constituencies approach maintains that an effective organization is one that satisfies the demands of those constituencies in its environment from whom it requires support for its continued existence. This is similar to the assumptions of the systems approach – both consider the interdependencies of the organization and its environment. However, the strategic constituencies approach is concerned with only those entities in the environment which are crucial to, or can threaten, the organization's survival at that point of time, while the systems approach considers the environment in its entirety. In a way, therefore, this approach represents a more refined version of the systems approach in specifying the exact stakeholders in the larger body of the environment. Hence, the choice of OE criteria in this approach represents an organization's efforts to appease and live up to the expectations of only those significant stakeholders in its environment who can threaten its existence and survival at a particular point in time. Therefore, the satisfaction of those strategic stakeholders or constituencies can be considered to be a measure of the organization's effectiveness at that point of time. And since, at any point of time, there will be multiple stakeholders who are crucial to an organization's survival, the organization would have to fulfill multiple sets of expectations, of these different stakeholders. Table 2.3 provides a representative list of criteria vis-à-vis various strategic constituencies or stakeholders of an organization.

> The strategic constituencies approach evaluates an organization's effectiveness by its ability to satisfy the expectations of its different stakeholders.

**Table 2.3** *OE criteria as per Strategic Constituencies Approach*

| *Constituency* | *Typical Effectiveness Criteria* |
|---|---|
| Owners | ROI; growth in earnings; financial return |
| Employees | Compensation; fringe benefits; satisfactory working conditions, supervision |
| Customers | Price satisfaction; quality; service |
| Suppliers | Payments satisfaction; future sales potential; satisfactory transactions |
| Creditors | Ability to repay debts |
| Unions | Competitive wages and benefits; satisfactory working conditions, fair bargaining process |
| Local community officials | Organizational involvement in local affairs; conserving local environment |
| Government agencies | Compliance with laws; avoidance of penalties; paying taxes and duties |

At any point in time, the organization would be dependent on all or a combination of these stakeholders, whose expectations need to be met, for the organization to survive. Hence, the assumptions underlying this approach are that:

- Organizations are political entities where vested interests compete for control over resources.
- An organization has a number of constituencies, with different degrees of power, each trying to satisfy its demands.
- Each constituency has different sets of values.
- Goals selected by managers represent a response to those interest groups that control the resources necessary for the organization to survive.

The strength of this approach lies in the fact that it takes a broad view of effectiveness and examines factors in the external environment as well as within the organization. By handling several criteria simultaneously – inputs, internal processes, outputs – it acknowledges and reinforces the fact that there is no single measure of effectiveness. This approach implies that if survival is important, managers need to understand who this survival is contingent upon. Moreover, by rendering this approach operational, managers decrease the chance that they might ignore or upset a group whose power could hinder the organization's operations.

However, operationalization of this approach is likely to pose a challenge. The primary issue would be that of separating 'strategic constituents' from the larger environment. Given the dynamic nature of today's environment, the degree of 'strategicness' of each constituent would differ. What is strategic today might not be strategic in future, and vice versa. This is likely to be affected by the life-cycle stage of the organization too. For example, constituencies or stakeholders who are crucial to an organization's survival in the birth stage (e.g. banks and financing institutions, suppliers, etc.) would most likely be different from those in its maturity stage (e.g. customers), when the organization is looking to expand its offerings or area of operations. In this context, we also have to remember that different departments or units of the organization have different sets of strategic constituencies. So, strategic constituencies for the marketing department are likely to be different from those of the finance and accounts department, or the production department. Second, identifying and accurately predicting the expectations of each of these constituencies or stakeholders could prove a daunting task. Hence, the success of this approach depends on ever-vigilant managers to constantly scan the environment and identify suitable signs to periodically 'update' the list of strategic constituencies in order to predict the exact responses called for in respect of each.

In a similar fashion, some other models have also used multi-dimensional approaches which have found favor with organization theorists (Rojas, 2000). **Bhargava and Sinha's** (1992) **model** posits that organizational structure has the potential to improve the overall perceived effectiveness of organizations. Four components – productivity, commitment, leadership, and interpersonal conflict – were assumed to predict OE. An organization with a heterarchical structure is expected to have higher productivity, higher commitment levels, effective leadership, and less interpersonal conflict, and hence is likely to be more effective than a hierarchical structure. However, making these constructs operational among organizations in different domains was thought to be problematic.

The second, the **Ridley and Mendoza model** (1993), evaluates OE based on an organization's need for survival and maximization of return on contributions. The model specifies eleven key processes for organizational effectiveness. While organizational survival and maximization of returns are considered the two super-ordinate processes, the other nine processes are self-regulation, internal-external boundary permeability, sensitivity to status and change, contribution to constituents, transformation, promoting advantageous transactions, flexibility, adaptability, and efficiency.

The third, **the Jackson model** (1999), is based on perceptions of preselected effectiveness indicators and uses six criteria for OE:

- management experience
- organizational structure
- political impact
- board of directors' involvement
- volunteer/stakeholder involvement
- internal communications

The most robust multi-dimensional OE model conceptualized till date is the **competing values framework**, which has found large-scale acceptance among organizational researchers. This is described in greater detail below.

### 2.2.4 The competing values approach

This approach attempts to combine and consolidate the diverse OE indicators from previous models, with the understanding that the criteria one values and uses in assessing OE depends on who the evaluator is and the interest that he represents. The underlying assumptions of this approach are that:

- There is no 'best' criterion for measuring OE.
- The concept of OE is subjective, based on the evaluator's personal values, preferences and interest.
- Diverse preferences can be consolidated and organized into basic sets of competing values.
- Each set then defines a unique effectiveness model.

In essence, this approach is a consolidation of all the approaches described above. Through this approach, three underlying dimensions of effectiveness criteria are identified, which represent apparently competing management values in organizations.

The **first value dimension** pertains to organizational focus, which is to determine whether dominant values concern issues that are internal or external to the firm. Internal focus represents a management concern for the well-being and efficiency of the *people* (employees), giving credence to their feelings and needs, while an external focus represents an emphasis on the well-being of the *organization* itself with respect to the environment, and a concern for productivity and task accomplishment.

The **second value dimension** pertains to organization structure, and whether *control* (stability) or *flexibility* is the dominant structural consideration. Flexibility values innovation, learning, adaptation, and change; while control favors stability, order, predictability, and efficiency. The **third value dimension** pertains to organizational *means* versus *ends*. A means focus stresses internal processes and long-term orientation (also emphasized in the systems approach); an ends focus emphasizes final outcomes and a short-term orientation (also exemplified by the goal-attainment approach).

Each of these three sets of values represents a dichotomy of approaches. And because of the apparent contradictions in each of these values, organizations are likely to experience tension among the various organizational effectiveness attributes. All organizations have a need for some level of stability as well as a need to be flexible and adaptable; a need for control and discipline as well as a need to allow some degree of freedom and autonomy; a need to focus on processes (means) as well as to ensure that these means are contributing to the final outcome (ends). Hence, an organization's effectiveness would depend on its ability to maintain the right balance among these apparently conflicting attributes, as required by the organization's objectives and situation.

A diagrammatic representation of these competing values is given in Figure 2.1 below:

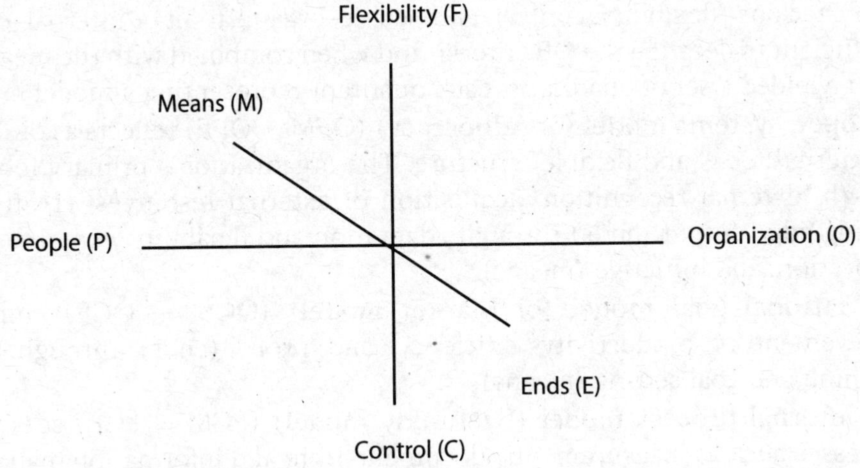


**Figure 2.1** *A three-dimensional model of organizational effectiveness*

These cells can be further combined to form eight cells or sets of OE criteria (viz. OFM, OFE, OCM, OCE, PCM, PCE, PFM, PFE), as shown in Table 2.4 below:

**Table 2.4** *OE criteria cells*

| *Cells* | *Description* | *Definition* |
|---|---|---|
| OFM | Flexibility | Able to adjust well to shifts in external conditions and demands |
| OFE | Acquisition of resources | Able to increase external support and expand size of workforce |
| OCM | Planning | Goals are clear and well understood |
| OCE | Productivity and efficiency | Volume of output is high; ratio of output to input is high |
| PCM | Availability of information | Channels of communication facilitate informing people about things that affect their work |
| PCE | Stability | Sense of order; continuity and smooth functioning of operations |
| PFM | Cohesive workforce | Employees trust, respect, and work well with each other |
| PFE | Skilled workforce | Employees have the training, skills, and capacity to do their work properly |

The above eight cells, taken in particular combinations, yield four different models of organizational effectiveness, reflecting the multiplicity of stakeholder interests and the organization's multiple responses. It has been demonstrated that two of the combinations (flexibility–control, and people–organization or internal–external) were sufficient to describe the OE criteria, and when combined with the means–ends continua, yielded a set of quadrants, each quadrant representing a model by itself.

- The **open systems model** (or **Adhocracy**) (OFM + OFE) reflects a combination of external focus and flexible structure. The organization's primary focus is on growth, external recognition, acquisition of external resources, creativity and cutting-edge output (ends) through adaptation and flexibility, experimentation, innovation, and initiative (means).
- The **rational goal model** (or **Market model**) (OCM + OCE) emphasizes achievement of productivity, efficiency, and profit (ends) through internal planning and goal setting (means).
- The **internal process model (Hierarchy model**) (PCM + PCE) sees internal processes such as measurements, documentation, and information management as methods to achieve stability, timeliness, efficiency, and order (ends) through efficient communication, to facilitate information flow and decision-making (means).
- And finally, the **human-relations model (Clan model**) (PFM + PFE) sees participation, discussion, and openness as ways to improve morale and achieve commitment. Hence, it focuses on the development of team work and a skilled workforce (ends) through cohesion and morale-building, commitment, and training opportunities (means).

Each of these models represents a particular set of values and has a polar opposite with another apparently competing set. The human-relations model for example, with its effectiveness criteria reflecting people and flexibility, appears to be in sharp contrast to the rational goal model's stress on organization and stability. The open systems model, emphasizing organization and flexibility seems to run counter to the internal process model focusing on people and stable structures. Hence, operationalizing this model would involve identifying the strategic constituencies and calculating the importance that each constituency places on each of the above eight value sets. A diagrammatic representation of these four competing models of effectiveness is reproduced in Figure 2.2.

To reiterate, the competing values approach therefore is a consolidation of the previous three approaches into a coherent whole, it factors in an organization's end goals (goal-attainment approach), means goals (systems approach), and multiple effectiveness criteria for multiple stakeholders (strategic constituencies approach), to come up with an integrated model.

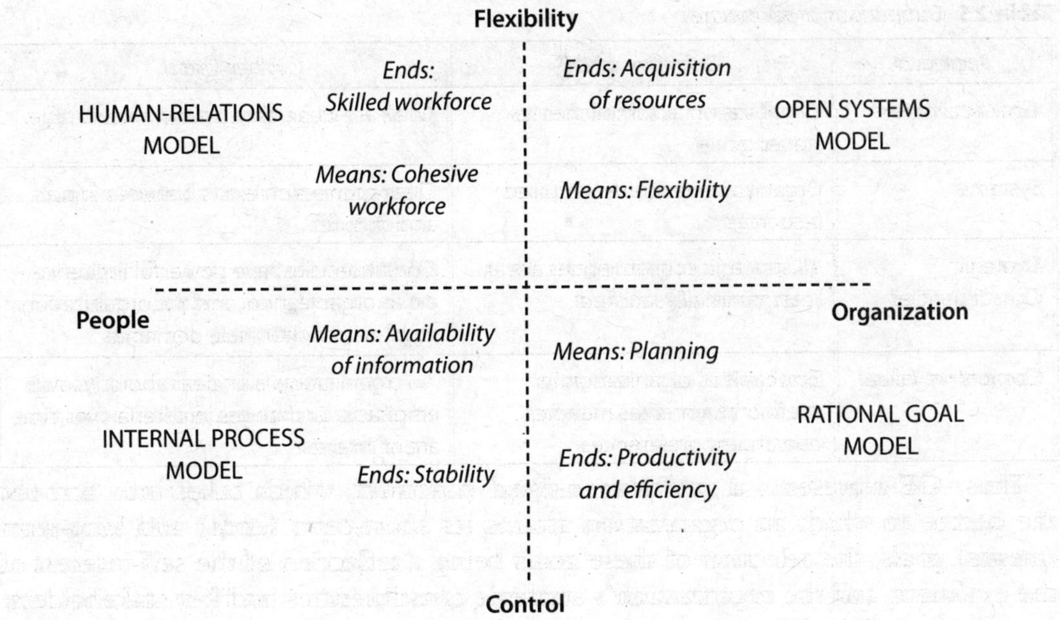


**Figure 2.2** *Four competing models of organizational effectiveness*

> The competing values approach assumes that there is no 'one' best criterion for measuring effectiveness, and multiple criteria and conflicting interests coexist at the same time.

*Utility of this approach:* The strength of this approach lies essentially in the acknowledgement that multiple criteria and conflicting interests coexist at the same time, and underlie efforts at defining and assessing OE. Dominant values in an organization change over time, and are expected to differ across life-cycle stages. Hence, by reducing large numbers of OE criteria into four broad conceptually elegant categories, it enables the practicing manager to identify the relevance and appropriateness of different criteria to different constituencies and different life-cycle stages. Managers therefore have to decide which values they wish to pursue and which values will receive less emphasis, at a given point in time. Table 2.5 tabulates a comparison of the four approaches and represents a handy tool for managers to make informed judgments about OE criteria.

**Table 2.5** *Comparison of approaches*

| *Approach* | *Definition of OE* | *When Useful* |
|---|---|---|
| Goal Attainment | Organization accomplishes its stated goals | Goals are clear, time bound, measurable. |
| Systems | Organization acquires required resources | Clear connection exists between inputs and outputs |
| Strategic Constituencies | All strategic constituencies are at least minimally satisfied | Constituencies have powerful influence on an organization, and the organization must respond to these demands |
| Competing Values | Emphasis of organization in the four major areas matches constituent preferences | An organization is unclear about its own emphasis, or changes in criteria over time are of interest |

Thus, OE represents a multidimensional construct, which takes into account the degree to which an organization attains its short-term (ends) and long-term (means) goals, the selection of these goals being a reflection of the self-interest of the evaluator, and the organization's strategic constituencies and key stakeholders, at every stage of its life cycle.

## CHAPTER SUMMARY

The question of correctly evaluating an organization's effectiveness has been a challenge to organizational researchers for decades. Organizations create value for different groups of stakeholders, by accomplishing a variety of goals. Hence, different groups of stakeholders evaluate an organization to decide whether the organization is being effective in meeting their expectations. Since organizations must perform diverse activities, one unequivocal measure of effectiveness would be difficult to arrive at. Different stakeholders will have different criteria for evaluating an organization's success.

Various approaches have been conceptualized to explain the construct of OE, each of which has its usefulness as well as limitations. The goal-attainment approach consists of identifying an organization's output goals and assessing how well the organization has achieved these goals. However, selection of inappropriate goals and ambiguity in goal selection could be major limitations of this viewpoint. The systems approach is a refinement on the goal-attainment approach, using a combination of resource-based and internal process-based perspectives. It implies that an organization should be judged not only on end goals but also on the means, i.e. its ability to maintain its relationship with the external environment in acquiring inputs, processing these inputs, channeling the outputs, and maintaining stability and balance. However, difficulty in operationalizing means goals is a possible limitation of this approach.

The strategic constituencies approach further refines the systems approach by specifying those stakeholders in the environment who are strategically important for the organization's survival at that point of time and whose expectations have to be satisfied. Hence, OE criteria in this approach would be a reflection of the strategic importance of the stakeholders concerned.

However, differentiating between the strategic importance of different stakeholders could be a constraint in correctly deciding on evaluation criteria for OE. Finally, the competing values approach consolidates these models into a comprehensive whole by identifying three sets of apparently contradictory value systems which any organization will have to satisfy: flexibility vs control, people vs organization, and means vs ends. These three dichotomous pairs of value systems represent four models of effectiveness, each with a different focus, and an organization's overall effectiveness will depend on its ability to maintain the right balance among these apparently conflicting attributes.

## Review Questions

1. Why is it not possible to have a unique measure of organizational effectiveness?
2. What are the limitations of the goal-attainment approach? Under what conditions would you want to use this approach for evaluating OE?
3. How is the strategic constituencies approach different from the systems approach to OE evaluation?
4. Which of the four models: open systems, human-relations, rational goal and internal process, do you think is the most appropriate for evaluating OE? Qualify your response with suitable justifications.

## Project Assignment

Look up a detailed version of your institute's vision and mission statements. Using any of the approaches described in the chapter, analyze each statement to draw up a list of OE criteria that emerge, which an outsider can use to evaluate your institute.

## CASE ILLUSTRATION: A STUDY IN EFFECTIVENESS: IIT MADRAS*

*'The primary objective of the Indian Institutes of Technology is to provide scientists and technologists of the highest calibre who would engage in research, design and development to help building the nation towards self-reliance in her technological needs'*

—Pandit Jawaharlal Nehru.

The Indian Institute of Technology, Madras (IITM) at Chennai, set up by the Government of India, with German collaboration, was a realization of Nehru's dream. Inaugurated on July 30, 1959, it was declared an Institution of National Importance by Parliament in 1961. Located in South Chennai in a beautiful campus spanning 633 acres, the institute is self-contained and houses around 5000 students as well as the families of members of faculty and staff. It owes its reputation for excellence in technical education, research, and industrial and educational consultancy to motivated and talented students, highly qualified and dedicated faculty, comprehensive experimental and computing facilities, and well-trained technical and administrative supporting staff.

IIT Madras has passed through various stages of development and growth. During the first decade, the Institute concentrated on faculty/staff recruitment, developing curricula, examination systems, placement of students, and setting up infrastructural facilities. A strong emphasis was given to academic excellence and on laying a good research foundation. During the next two decades, postgraduate and doctoral programmes as well as research, technology development, and consultancy projects were actively promoted. During the fourth decade, the Institute experienced substantial growth on all fronts. Currently, the Institute offers undergraduate and postgraduate programmes leading to the B.Tech, Dual degree, M.Sc, M.B.A., M.Tech, Integrated M.A, M.S, and Ph.D., degrees in a variety of specialisations. Over the years, the Institute has responded to environmental changes and user needs by reshaping curricula, offering new programmes and organizing continuing education programmes. In addition to close collaboration with German universities, IITM has active linkages with academic/research organisations in Austria, Belgium, Canada, France, Japan, Malaysia, Nepal, the Netherlands, Russia, Singapore, Switzerland, Thailand and the USA.

The vision and mission statements of IIT Madras reflect its awareness regarding its multiple stakeholders, and its sensitivity in terms of addressing the stakeholders' diverse expectations. The vision statement of IIT Madras is 'to be an academic institution in dynamic equilibrium with its social, ecological, and economic environment, striving continuously for excellence in education, research and technological service to the nation.' IIT Madras' mission statement elaborates this dream further. Its mission is:

- to create and sustain a community of learning in which students acquire knowledge and learn to apply it professionally, with due consideration for ethical, ecological, and economic issues
- to pursue research and disseminate research findings
- to provide knowledge-based technological services to satisfy the needs of society and the industry
- to help in building national capabilities in science, technology, humanities, management, education, and research

In the recent past, however, a plethora of changes, both globally and nationally, have thrown up challenges as well as opportunities for IIT Madras. The sources of these environmental changes are wide ranging and include diverse factors, viz. the knowledge revolution, the need for sustainable development, government policy initiatives, including new paradigms of funding, growing competition in higher technological education, rapid and complex changes in markets and technology, unprecedented growth in the service sector, and multiple dimensions of institutional accountability. These unprecedented changes, both at the global and local levels, require IITM to build enduring relationships with different entities in order to achieve its vision and mission.

* *(http://www.iitm.ac.in/TheInstitute/)*

## Critical enquiry

Analyze the effectiveness of IIT Madras using (a) the strategic constituencies approach, and (b) the competing values framework. How should the Organizational Effectiveness (OE) criteria for IITM be altered in order to overcome possible challenges in future and to capitalize on future opportunities?

***Key words and phrases:*** organizational effectiveness, strategic constituents, competing values

CHAPTER 3

# Organization Structure

**CHAPTER OUTLINE**

What is organization structure?

❖

Dimensions of organization structure

❖

Organizational configurations: Types of organizational structure

❖

Global organization design

## ORGANIZATIONAL INSIGHT

In 2004, three associates set up a creative startup, with the aim of creating high-quality games for mobile phones.* Two of the associates were from the video game industry – PC games, while the third had been involved in website creation. Their first game was an original in-house production, commercialized at the end of 2004. Although the game was quite good for the standards of the time, the firm encountered difficulties in marketing it. Luckily, however, it came to the notice of a major game publisher, who hired the firm to produce a mobile phone game for a franchise he possessed and had already exploited for PC and console productions. This was a new opportunity for the firm, which then decided to produce games for the major publishers that were relatively standard in their concepts, and to produce in parallel its own original games.

The evolution of the firm though various stages was also accompanied by various structural changes. In the beginning, all the founders were actively involved in the production of games, doing programming, level design, and testing. The firm has grown in size since then, and in 2008, it had 25 employees, and had succeeded in producing 15 games in less than four years of inception. In addition to the increase in the number of employees, the skill mix and competences had also undergone significant changes, along with their qualifications and missions. For example, in 2005, the firm hired an individual who had several tasks to fulfil: to organize the beta test with users, to market the original games they produced, and to handle relations with the game publishers. Earlier, these responsibilities had been borne by the founders themselves.

In the first months, the firm operated reasonably well without any formal governance mechanisms. The founders knew each other very well; each had a specific task to do. The governance was *de facto*. As the organization grew, the increase in the number of employees was accompanied by an increase in specialisation in the tasks performed;

hence, some organization schemes had also to be defined. With increasing number of product offerings, the complexity increased. From a governance perspective, rules had to be enforced and an integration mechanism had to be in place for the different information flows. The need to coordinate interdependent member activities and integrate member contributions in a production context was likely to exacerbate the need for a shared basis of authority.

The firm tried to enhance the existing rules, or to adapt them. It soon became clear that the firm could not impose its rules, only give a broad direction. This was accompanied by the use of more contributors outside the firm; information and work done by different communities created the need for clearer governance rules. For efficient governance, the firm decided to set up efficient knowledge management portals. Hence, with increasing complexity, the firm responded by restructuring in a manner to suit the specifics of the situation.

* **Source:** Adapted from Burger-Helmchen, T and Llerna, P (2008). "A case study of a creative start-up: governance, communities and knowledge management". *Journal of Innovation Economics*. 2(2). 125–146.

## 3.1 What is organization structure?

In recent times, a glance at the headlines of any newspaper, business supplement, or magazine very often throws up some mention of restructuring activities being undertaken by some organization. Restructuring is a corporate management term implying dismantling or reorganizing an existing structure. So, what is this entity called 'structure' which is being dismantled or reorganized? An intuitive response to this question is likely to be **'the organization chart'**, which is the visual representation of a whole set of underlying activities and processes in an organization, depicting different groups or parts of the organization, their interrelationships, and how each position and department fits into the whole. However, the concept of **structure** goes far beyond a merely pictorial depiction of reporting relationships.

Organization structure is the formal decision-making framework whereby job tasks are divided, grouped, and coordinated. An earlier definition by **Child** (1972) described structure as 'the formal allocation of work roles and the administrative mechanisms to control and integrate work activities, including those which cross formal organizational boundaries.' Researchers have come up with various definitions of structure, which involve both division of work as well as the means of integrating this differentiation. Hence, any structural configuration would include criteria by which various roles, activities, and coordination mechanisms can be differentiated as well as grouped together in the organization. Table 3.1 depicts the various dimensions or criteria which have been used to describe structure.

**Table 3.1** *Dimensions of organizational structure*

| |
|---|
| **Administrative component**: Number of line supervisors, managers, and staff personnel relative to total number of employees |
| **Autonomy**: Extent of freedom given to employees to carry out their designated tasks and responsibilities |
| **Centralization**: Concentration of power arrangements, locus of decision-making |
| **Complexity**: Number of occupational specialties, professional activity, professional training of employees |
| **Delegation of authority**: Empowering lower level managers with decision-making powers |
| **Differentiation**: Number of specialty functions |
| **Formalization**: Defining employees' roles through formal documentation |
| **Integration**: Extent of collaboration among departments, feedback and coordination mechanisms |
| **Span of control** : Number of subordinates that an individual manager can and should supervise |
| **Standardization**: Range of variation tolerated within rules defining the jobs |
| **Vertical span**: Number of levels in the authority hierarchy from the top to the bottom |

However, a closer look reveals that the decision-making process for ensuring this balance between differentiation and integration of organizational activities can be categorized under three broad criteria or dimensions as depicted by the terms **complexity, formalization,** and **centralization**. Hence, structural configurations among organizations would differ mainly based on differences in the degree of these three dimensions. That is, one organization would be more or less complex, more or less formalized, and more or less centralized relative to another: there is no absolute extent of complexity, formalization, or centralization.

In fact, an organization's structure can be thought of as a combination of a 'superstructure' depicted by the organization chart showing departments and important reporting relationships in the organization, and an 'infrastructure' comprising the roles performed by various organizational members, based on the extent of their formal authority, degrees of centralization, formalization, and their specialization.

## 3.2 Dimensions of organization structure

### 3.2.1 Complexity

Defined as 'the degree of differentiation that exists within an organization', complexity determines the number of ways in which the same workforce can be divided based on different responsibilities or functions. Some of the commonly practiced divisions include:

Complexity determines the different ways in which the same workforce can be divided along different dimensions

- *Horizontal differentiation*, referring to the degree of differentiation between units based on orientation of members, nature of tasks, education and training. Organizations have various alternatives for differentiating horizontally.

**Specialization** refers to particular grouping of activities performed by an individual. Specialization is normally of two types:

- *Functional specialization*, with jobs broken down into simple and repetitive tasks, more commonly referred to as division of labor. This form of specialization creates high substitutability among employees, and facilitates their easy replacement by management.
- *Social specialization*, where individuals, rather than their work, are specialized, and possess professional skills that cannot be routinized. Replacebility or substitutability is naturally lower in comparison.

While organizations are increasingly relying on social specialization in today's 'knowledge economy', division of labor continues to work, primarily because of the many advantages it accords, namely, (a) time-saving, (b) standardization and quality control through efficiency resulting from repetitive work (up to an optimum point; beyond this, boredom sets in, thereby decreasing output and efficiency), and (c) cost-effectiveness and better utilization of resources (paying for skills used, rather than skills possessed), among others.

While greater functional specialization implies greater need for coordinating between different tasks, higher social specialization implies greater challenge in motivating and handling a highly skilled set of employees with unique needs and expectations. Hence, higher specialization which implies differently skilled employees with different levels of expectations, who have to be managed together, and whose tasks have to be integrated for the overall organizational outcomes, gives rise to a higher degree of complexity.

**Departmentation** refers to the grouping of specialists; it may be based on simple numbers, function, product or service, client, geography, or process. Here too, the need for integrating the activities of different departments increases the level of complexity.

- *Vertical differentiation* refers to the number of hierarchical levels; it also denotes depth in structure. Normally, it is a logical response to horizontal differentiation. Increasing specialization makes it difficult to coordinate tasks. Since high horizontal specialization implies employees with diverse skills and training, working in different departments or groups, someone has to supervise the

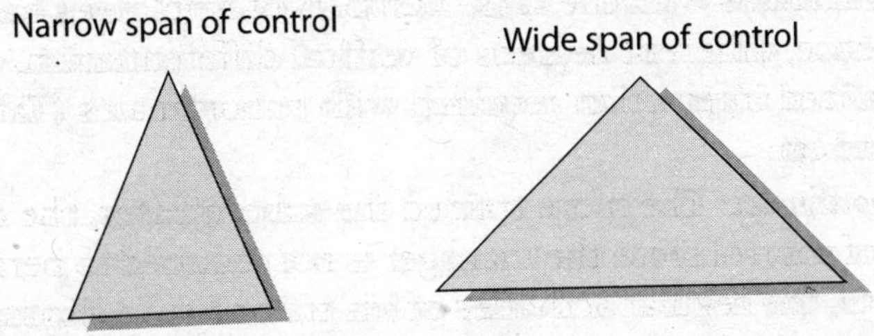


**Figure 3.1** *Contrasting spans of control*

activities of each of these diverse occupational groups; this need for increased coordination shows itself in the development of vertical differentiation. However, different organizations with the same number of employees would have different numbers of vertical levels, depending on the **span of control**, i.e. the number of subordinates that a manager can effectively direct (Figure 3.1):

A narrower span of control would necessitate more hierarchical layers in the organization, while a wider span would reduce the number of layers. As with any other organizational variable, there is no 'ideal' span or number of levels. Both narrow and wide spans have their advantages and disadvantages, as shown in Table 3.2:

**Table 3.2** *Comparison between narrow and wide spans of control*

| ***Tall organization structures (organizations with narrow spans)*** | |
|---|---|
| *Advantages* | *Disadvantages* |
| Close supervision | Superiors tend to get too involved in subordinates' work |
| Close control | Many levels of management |
| Fast communication between subordinates and superiors | High costs due to many levels |
| | Excessive distance between lowest level and top level |
| ***Flat organization structures (organizations with wide spans)*** | |
| *Advantages* | *Disadvantages* |
| Superiors are forced to delegate | Tendency of overloaded superiors to become decision bottlenecks |
| Clear policies must be made | Danger of superior's loss of control |
| Subordinates must be carefully selected | Requires exceptional quality of managers |
| Superiors are forced to delegate | Tendency of overloaded superiors to become decision bottlenecks |

Different organizations with the same numbers of employees have different spans of control, and hence, different degrees of vertical differentiation, depending on the extent of personalized interaction required with subordinates (Table 3.3), which in turn would depend on:

- *Training of subordinates:* The more trained the subordinates, the easier it is to have a wider span of control since the manager is not required to personally supervise, at a micro level, the regular activities of his trained subordinates.
- *Clarity of delegation of authority:* When instructions with respect to lines of responsibility, scope, and authority are clear and unambiguous, there is not much scope for misunderstanding instructions, necessitating less amount of personal contact needed with the manager.
- *Clarity of plans:* Similarly, when work plans are laid out in a clear and transparent manner, subordinates will not need to depend on their managers to clarify doubts and ambiguity.

**Table 3.3** *Factors influencing span of control*

| *Narrow spans (great deal of time spent with subordinates)* | *Wide spans (less time spent with subordinates)* |
|---|---|
| Little or no training | Thorough training of subordinates |
| Inadequate or unclear authority delegation | Clear delegation to undertake well-defined tasks |
| Unclear plans for non-repetitive operations | Well-defined plans for repetitive operations |
| Non-verifiable objectives and standards | Verifiable objectives used as standards |
| Fast changes in internal and external environments | Slow changes in external and internal environments |
| Use of poor or inappropriate communication techniques, including vague instructions | Use of appropriate techniques, such as proper organization structure, written and oral communication |
| Ineffective interaction of superior and subordinate | Effective interaction between superior and subordinate |
| Ineffective meetings | Effective meetings |
| Greater number of specialties at lower and middle levels | Number of specialties at upper levels (TM concerned with external environment) |
| Incompetent and untrained manager | Competent and trained manager |
| Complex task | Simple task |
| Subordinates' unwillingness to assume responsibility and reasonable risks | Subordinates' willingness to assume responsibility and reasonable risks |
| Immature subordinates | Mature subordinates |

- *Use of objective standards:* Objective evaluation and appraisal criteria add to the transparency and clarity of organizational processes, reducing the possibility of ambiguity based on personal interpretations of the criteria.
- *Rate of change:* The higher the rate of change and dynamism in the external environment, the greater is the need for faster responses and customized solutions, requiring discussions and collaborations. This is possible with low span of control.
- *Communication techniques:* Organizations which practice clear and unambiguous communication techniques are more likely to go in for a wider span of control since it lessens the need for personalized interventions by managers to clarify doubts and misconceptions.
- *Variation by organization level:* By and large, the lower levels of the hierarchy are likely to have a wider span of control, since the nature of the tasks are more routinized and repetitive. At higher levels of the hierarchy, tasks and responsibilities are more likely to require customized solutions, necessitating higher degrees of discussion, collaboration, and personalized interaction, and consequently, lower span of control.

An organization's structure has to be designed to provide both the vertical and horizontal information flow necessary to accomplish the organization's overall goals. However, there would always be an inherent tension (Figure 3.2) between vertical and horizontal mechanisms in an organization: while vertical linkages are designed primarily for control and efficiency considerations, horizontal linkages are designed for coordination and collaboration to promote learning outcomes, which usually means reducing control.

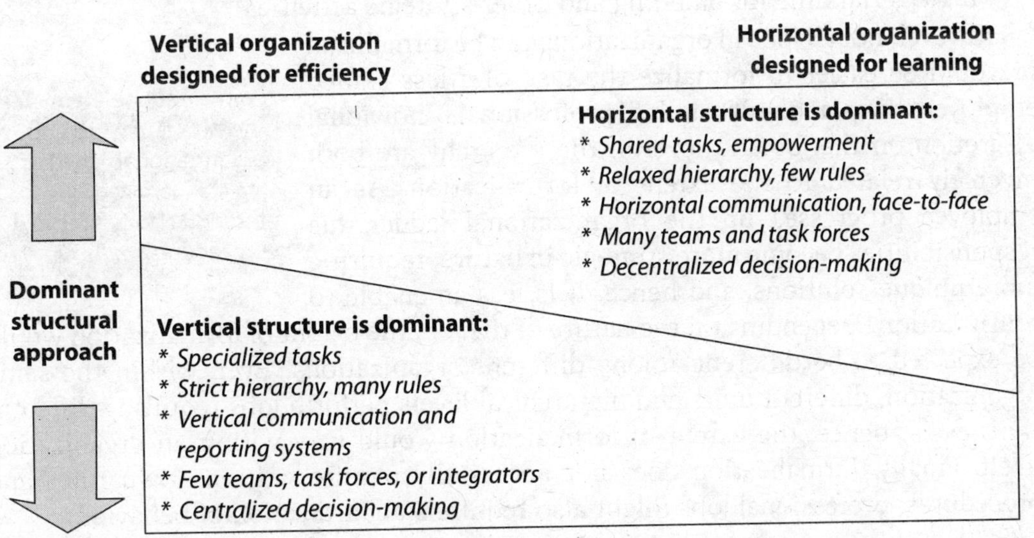


**Figure 3.2** *Relationship of organization structure to efficiency vs learning outcomes*

- *Spatial differentiation*: This refers to the degree to which the subunits and personnel of an organization are geographically separated.

While most modern organizations today typically operate on all or a mix of the above levels of differentiation, it has to be kept in mind that greater differentiation of any kind adds to the complexity within the organization, since it increases the need and difficulty of coordinating and controlling the activities of diverse groups of employees. In fact, this represents a paradox of sorts: the economies created by complexity are counterbalanced by the increased costs of integration and coordination in holding the differentiated organization together. A systems perspective to the issue of complexity is that organizations grow to survive. And organizations that survive will, over time, become more complex as their environment becomes more complex.

### 3.2.2 Formalization

This is defined as 'the degree to which jobs within an organization are standardized'. By introducing detailed rules, meticulous work-procedures, and clear job descriptions, organizations ensure that any input is handled in a standard manner to produce a uniform output. Conversely, less formalization implies that jobs are less 'programmed' and hence provide sufficient discretion to employees to deal with their work. There could be various reasons for an organization to introduce formalization. Formalization helps:

1) To reduce variability, and hence ensure standardization and quality assurance
2) In the coordination of interdependent and complex tasks
3) To reduce the need for direct supervision and control, and free up crucial managerial time for planning and other strategic activities

However, not all jobs in organizations can be formalized. It would be easier to formalize the task of a less skilled employee than a highly skilled professional. Individual discretion on the job and level in the hierarchy are both inversely related to the extent of formalization. As an employee progresses up the organizational ladder, his responsibilities become more strategic in nature, requiring more unique solutions, and hence, it is less amenable to routinization. Depending on the nature of the job, the extent of formalization would be expected to be different among different organizations. Even within the same organization, different units and hierarchical levels perform jobs requiring different skill levels; hence, the extent of formalization would vary within an organization itself. Finally, formalization does not necessarily require written down rules and procedures; professional jobs might also require standardization of behavior.

> Formalization determines the extent to which organizational activities are standardized through clearly specified procedures.

'**Organizational formalization**' refers to explicit rules and procedures laid down by organizations to control its employees' behavior and actions, and is most often used for routine, unskilled work. '**Professional formalization**' is implicit, based on internal values and socialization, and is used for skilled, non-routine work. However, for all practical purposes, the term formalization normally refers to the explicit, written regulations of an organization. To differentiate, high formalization would imply externalized behavior (behavior driven by external rules and procedures), while professionalization implies internalized behavior (behavior driven by socialization, by internalizing the values, norms, and expected behaviors). Hence, a '*make*' or '*buy*' decision would depend on the extent of formalization required in a job. Highly standardized jobs could be 'made' in-house through employee development, while for less standardized, professional jobs depending on individual expertise, a 'buy' decision is preferable.

The degree of socialization refers to the adaptation process by which individuals learn the values, norms, and expected behaviors of an organization. For 'make' decisions, the socialization process would 'teach' the employees to behave in a particular fashion; for a 'buy' decision, the socialization is expected to have occurred outside the organization.

Organizations employ a variety of formalization techniques, viz.

1) Selection and recruitment, to ensure a proper person–organization 'fit' with respect to commonly held values, norms, and ideas.
2) Specific role/job descriptions to spell out the dos and don'ts for an employee, which helps to regulate and control his/her behavior.
3) Rules and procedures to provide detailed guidelines for acceptable behavior.
4) Training and rituals, to reinforce desired behavioral patterns and expectations among employees.

*Formalization and complexity*: There appears to be a strong association between specialization and formalization, depending on the nature of horizontal differentiation. Hence, a high degree of functional specialization is associated with a high degree of explicit formalization, while a high degree of social specialization is associated with low degree of explicit formalization, or high degree of professional formalization.

### 3.2.3 Centralization

This third dimension of organization structure is defined as the degree to which the formal authority to make discretionary choices is concentrated in an individual, unit, or level (usually high up in the organizational hierarchy). That is, centralization is concerned with the dispersion of authority within the organization to make decisions. Thus, a high degree of centralization would imply minimum amount of decision-making input by lower-level employees in their work. However, certain issues have to be kept in mind, to understand the true implication of centralization.

a) *Formal authority*: Centralization/decentralization refers to the distribution of *formal* authority. While informal leaders and interest groups might influence such decisions, it cannot be interpreted to affect the degree of centralization in any way.

b) *Policies and decentralization*: Centralization is concerned with decision-discretion. Some organizations claim to decentralize by delegating decision-making to the lower-level members, but constrain the discretion of decision-makers through elaborate formal policies and procedures. In such cases, policies can override decentralization. Such organizations can be said to be more centralized than decentralized.

c) *Concentration at a single point*: Centralization of decision-making may be with a single person, unit, or level. This point should, however, be placed at a higher level in the organization's hierarchy. If this concentration is at a lower level, it can be interpreted to be more decentralized.

d) *IT and centralization*: Advanced information technology and communication can facilitate decentralization to the lower levels, but at the same time, enable senior managers to closely monitor the decision-making process. This control however, does not decrease the extent of decentralization or make the process more centralized as the discretion in decision-making still rests with the lower-level manager.

e) *Control of information by lower-level members*: In a centralized decision-making scenario, the top managers often depend on information from the lower-level managers, who might filter out some information, or control the extent of information input to the top: this effectively reduces the discretion of the top managers to make an objective decision. Hence, while management decisions are centralized, if concentrated at the top, the more the information input into those decisions is filtered through others, the less centralized is the decision.

Figure 3.3 depicts the organizational decision-making process, especially in terms of the points of discretion available to the decision-maker.

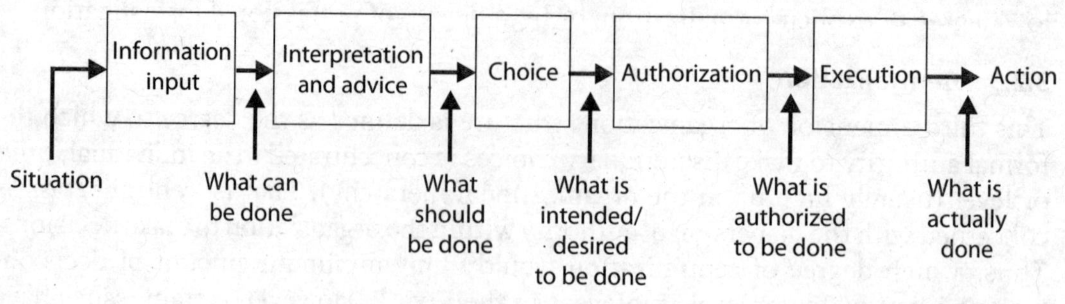


**Figure 3.3** *Organization decision-making process*

Decision-making would be absolutely centralized if the decision-maker controls all the steps. In large, professionally-run organizations, this is not normally the case. The decision-maker might control the process of making choices, while all other steps are controlled by others. Hence, in large organizations, decision-making is likely to be relatively decentralized. Until recently, nearly all organizations followed Weber's concept of bureaucratic structures (see Chapter 1) with centralized decision making. The increased complexity of multinational organizations created the necessity of a new structure that Drucker (1974) called 'federal decentralization'. In **federal decentralization**, a company is organized so that there are a number of independent units operating simultaneously. Each unit has its own management which, in effect, runs its own autonomous business. This structure has resulted in large conglomerates which have diversified into many different fields in order to minimize risk.

As already mentioned, no organizations can have absolute levels of centralization or decentralization. There would be variation in degrees of centralization, both among organizations and between different departments of the same organization. Since both centralization and decentralization have inbuilt advantages and disadvantages (Table 3.4), managers have to strive for a balanced approach between both, depending on situational factors.

**Table 3.4** *Centralization and decentralization: A comparison*

| *Centralization* | *Decentralization* |
|---|---|
| **ADVANTAGES** | |
| • Uniformity of policies, standards, and actions<br>• Enables closer control and coordination<br>• Maximizes economies of scale; eliminates duplication<br>• Reduces risk-factor in decision-making by less informed or less skilled subordinates<br>• Benefits whole organization, not any special interest group | • Greater flexibility and appropriateness in responding to local situations<br>• Helps counter information overload of top managers<br>• Hence, allows top management to focus on policy issues<br>• Facilitates intra-unit communication<br>• Increases opportunity for on-the-job training for subordinates<br>• Increases morale and commitment |
| **DISADVANTAGES** | |
| • Too much decision load on top management<br>• Causes alienation and lack of initiative among junior employees<br>• Inappropriate response to tactical requirements | • Causes problems of control and coordination<br>• Causes conflicts of goals and interests among units<br>• Loss of economies of scale; duplication of efforts |

*Centralization, Formalization and Complexity:* As complexity increases, information processing becomes more complex. In parallel, increasing complexity might also imply higher levels of expertise, where employees can contribute knowledgeably to the decision-making process in the organization. Hence, increase in complexity has an inverse relationship with centralization: higher complexity facilitates higher decentralization. However, the centralization–formalization relationship is more ambiguous. While increase in functional complexity might serve to increase centralization, increase in social specialization will more likely facilitate decentralization. Conversely, one might argue that higher formalization facilitates decentralization, at least at the tactical level, even with functional specialization, since rules and procedures are explicitly laid down, without any need for interpretation and understanding, rendering decision-making by the lower levels an easier proposition. Again, highly professional employees might expect high decentralization in decisions that directly affect their work, but would prefer centralized decision-making for personnel issues, which ensures predictability and standardization of their expectations from the organization. Thus, the relationship between centralization and formalization seems unclear at best.

Centralization determines the extent to which organizational decision-making authority is concentrated in a single individual or group.

## 3.3 Organizational configurations: Types of organizational structures

Mintzberg (1980, 1981, 1983) provided a comprehensive model for classifying organizational structures. An organization can be seen as composed of five basic parts:

1. *The operating core*: Employees who perform the basic work related to the production of products and services.
2. *The strategic apex*: Top-level managers, who are charged with the overall responsibility for the organization.
3. *The middle line*: Managers, who connect the operating core to the strategic apex.
4. *The techno-structure*: Analysts, who have the responsibility for ensuring certain forms of standardization in the organization.
5. *The support staff*: People who fill the staff units; who provide indirect support services for the organization.

Any one of these five parts can dominate an organization. Moreover, depending on which part is in control, a given structural configuration is likely to be used. Figure 3.4 depicts how organizational configurations have undergone transformations with time, as a response to increasing demands for flexibility, stability, and ease of information processing.

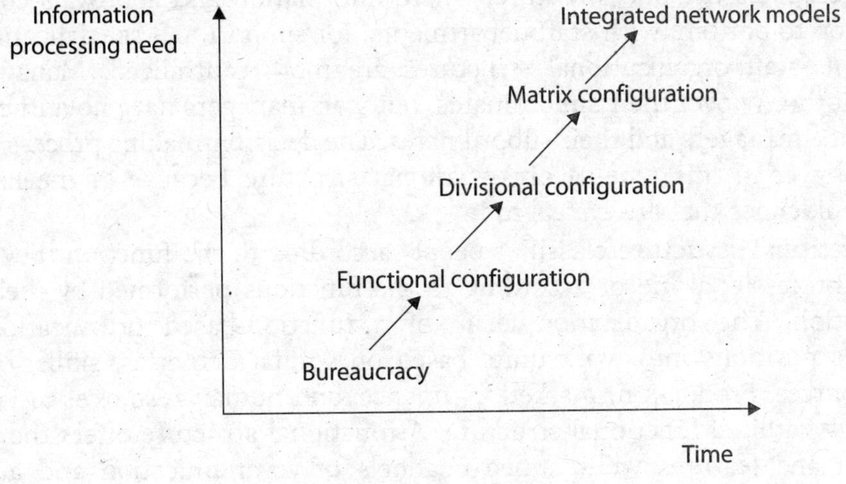


**Figure 3.4** *Structural configurations from a time perspective*

Some commonly used structural configurations among organizations include simple structures, professional bureaucracies, divisional structures, matrix organizations, and adhocracy. A company should choose the one that best suits their needs. A small business will require a simple organizational structure, while large multinational companies or universities with several colleges under their control would need a large or complex organizational structure.

**Traditional structures** are based on functional division and departments. These are the kind of structures that follow the organization's rules and procedures meticulously. They are characterized by having precise authority lines for all levels in the management. Traditional structures could be of various forms:

- *Simple structure*: A primary school or a start-up private limited company is a good example of a simple organizational structure. Apart from the management, these organizations have fewer employees compared to big organizations. The main advantage of a simple organizational structure is the simplicity in carving out day-to-day activities.
- *Line structure*: This structure has a very specific line of command. The approvals and orders come from top to bottom in a line. Hence the name, line structure. It is suitable for smaller organizations like small accounting firms and law offices. This sort of structure allows for easy decision making and is also very informal in nature. There are fewer departments, which makes the entire organization more decentralized.
- *Line-and-Staff structure*: Although line structure is suitable for most organizations, especially small ones, it is not effective for larger companies. This is where the line-and-staff organizational structure comes into play. It

combines the line structure, where information and approvals come from top to bottom, with staff departments, for support and specialization. Line-and-staff organizational structures are more centralized. Managers have authority over their subordinates, but staff managers have no authority over line managers and their subordinates. The decision-making process becomes slower in this type of organizational structure because of the layers and guidelines that are typical to it.

A **functional structure** classifies people according to the function they perform in their professional life or according to the functions performed by them in the organization. The organization chart of a function-based organization group organizes positions into work units based on similar activities, skills, expertise, and resources. Production, marketing, finance, and human resources are common groupings within a functional structure. A functional structure offers the simplest approach and features well-defined channels of communication and authority/responsibility relationships. Not only does this structure improve productivity by minimizing duplication of personnel and equipment, but it also makes employees comfortable and simplifies training. However, the functional structure has many downsides that may make it inappropriate for some organizations:

- The functional structure can result in narrowed perspectives because of the separateness of different departmental work groups. Production managers may have a hard time relating to marketing, for example, which is often in an entirely different grouping. As a result, anticipating or reacting to changing consumer needs may be difficult. In addition, reduced cooperation and communication may occur.
- Decisions and communication are slow to take place because of the many layers of hierarchy. Authority is more centralized.
- The functional structure gives managers experience in only one field – their own. Managers do not have the opportunity to see how all the firm's departments work together and understand their interrelationships and interdependence. In the long run, this specialization results in executives with narrow backgrounds and little training in handling top management duties.

**Divisional structures** are based on the different divisions in the organization. Because managers in large companies may have difficulty keeping track of all their company's products and activities, specialized departments may develop. These departments are divided according to their organizational outputs. Examples include departments created to distinguish among production, customer service, and geographical categories. These departments allow managers to focus their resources and results better. Divisional structure also makes performance easier to monitor. As a result, this structure is flexible and responsive to change.

These structures can be further divided into:

- *Product structure*: This is based on organizing employees and work on the basis of different types of products. If the company produces three different types of products, they will have three different divisions for these products.
- *Market structure*: This structure is used to group employees on the basis of the specific market the company sells in. A company could operate in three different markets, each would be a separate division in the structure.
- *Geographic structure*: Large organizations have offices at different places; for example, there could be a north zone, south zone, west, and east zone. The organizational structure would then follow a 'zonal region' structure.

However, divisional structure does have its drawbacks. Because managers are so specialized, they may waste time duplicating each other's activities and resources. In addition, competition among divisions may develop due to limited resources.

**Bureaucracy** was an organizational configuration conceptualized by Weber as the most efficient form of organization. The key characteristics of a bureaucracy as conceptualized by Weber were:

> Bureaucracy was conceptualized as the most efficient form of organizing, characterized by job specification, responsibility and authority, documentation, hierarchy, and merit-based progress

1. Specification of jobs with detailed rights, obligations, responsibilities, scope of authority
2. System of supervision and subordination
3. Unity of command
4. Extensive use of written documents
5. Training in job requirements and skills
6. Application of consistent and complete rules (company manual)
7. Assigning work and hiring personnel based on competence and experience

Despite its robust conceptualization designed to remove human errors to the maximum extent possible, improper implementation on account of informal hierarchies, goal-displacement and goal non-achievement, and misuse of authority has unfortunately led to bureaucracy in its current form being predominantly viewed as inefficient, slow, and corrupt. Nonetheless, bureaucracies, if implemented correctly, would be very effective for businesses involving routine tasks that can be well-specified in writing and do not change quickly, but probably not as effective in industries in which technology changes rapidly or is not yet well-understood.

**Matrix structure** is a combination of function and product structures. This structure combines functional specialization with the focus of the divisional structure. It uses permanent cross-functional teams to integrate functional expertise with a divisional focus. Employees in a matrix structure belong to at least two formal groups at the same time – a functional group and a product, program or project team. They also report to two bosses – one within the functional group and the other within the team. This structure not only increases employee motivation, but it also allows technical and general management training across functional areas as well. Potential advantages include:

- Better cooperation and problem solving
- Increased flexibility
- Better customer service
- Better performance accountability
- Improved strategic management

Predictably, the matrix structure also has potential disadvantages:

- The multiple-boss system is susceptible to power struggles, as functional supervisors and team leaders vie with one another to exercise authority.
- Members of the matrix may suffer task confusion when taking orders from more than one boss.
- Teams may develop strong team loyalties that cause a loss of focus on larger organization goals.
- Adding the team leaders, a crucial component, to a matrix structure can result in increased costs.

The **network structure** relies on other organizations to perform critical functions on a contractual basis. In other words, managers can contract out specific work to specialists. This approach provides flexibility and reduces overheads because the size of staff and operations can be reduced. On the other hand, the network structure may result in unpredictability of supply and lack of control because managers are relying on contractual workers to perform important work.

Therefore, it is clear that the manager has before him a choice of alternative structural configurations to choose from, the ultimate choice would depend on his understanding of the context in which the organization operates, and its life-cycle stage. For example, where machine bureaucracies and functional configurations were suitable and efficient in terms of utilizing formalization and specialization with clear hierarchical relationships, the lack of flexibility and lack of responsibility and accountability for the end product necessitated the creation of more flexible configurations. However, as customers became more demanding and the need for innovative products and solutions increased, the requirement of focusing on the end product and creating profit centers through decentralization necessitated the creation of divisional configurations.

While divisional structures were effective at some levels, splitting the organization into divisions brought with it attendant inefficiencies, ranging from possibilities of duplication of products, to integrative problems between divisions. To counter these inefficiencies, the matrix configuration, whose dual hierarchy brought in both specialization and flexibility, was conceptualized. The salient features of some of these configurations are summarised in Table 3.5 overleaf.

### 3.3.1 Global organization design

The last three decades have seen dramatic changes in the approach of organizations to business. With the globalization of world markets gaining momentum, more and more firms are moving outside their domestic borders into the dynamic world of international business. Internally too, what were once considered safe markets are now becoming fierce battlegrounds for firms fighting for market share against both foreign and domestic competitors. The motivating reasons for these could be many, predominant among them being factors related to economies of scale, economies of scope, and low production costs.

**Economies of scale** are the cost advantages that a business obtains due to expansion. These are factors that cause a producer's average cost per unit to fall as output rises. For many companies, domestic markets no longer provide the necessary volume of sales required to sustain and achieve economies of scale. For example, *Wipro* spent more than US $250 million on acquisitions at home and in foreign markets such as Sweden and Finland, and plans bigger deals in the years ahead to boost economies of scale and to lower costs. Economies of scale also enable companies to obtain volume discounts from suppliers, lowering the firm's cost of production.

**Economies of scope** are conceptually similar to economies of scale. Whereas economies of scale primarily refer to efficiencies associated with supply-side changes, such as increasing or decreasing the scale of production of a single product type, economies of scope refer to efficiencies primarily associated with demand-side changes, such as increasing or decreasing the scope of marketing and distribution of different types of products. Having a presence in multiple countries provides higher marketing power and synergy compared to the same-sized firm that has a presence in fewer countries. For example, *Infosys Technologies* has added to its product scope by offering BPO services ('*Progeon*') in addition to its existing suite of products; this has enhanced its economies of scope in international markets, given the significant opportunities to leverage resources and people across both the IT and BPO services segment.

In an effort to reduce their **cost of production**, many firms turn to other countries as a source of cheap labor. For example, India as a developing market offers a host of low cost advantages, including highly skilled manpower and low labor costs. Hence, India has already become a hub of activity for Information Technology and Business Process Outsourcing, mainly in the services sector and ITES. Some global car manufacturers such as *Suzuki* and *Hyundai* are also using India as an outsourcing hub for automotive components, services, and even complete vehicles.

Firms pass through several stages of organizational evolution in their journey to internationalization. In the domestic stage, while the firm's operations are limited due to domestic barriers, managers are well aware of the global environment and

**Table 3.5** *Types of organizational structures*

| *Types of structure* | *Salient features* | *Strengths* | *Weaknesses* | *When to use* |
|---|---|---|---|---|
| Simple structure | • Low complexity<br>• Low formalization<br>• High centralization<br>• A flat structure<br>• Organic operating core<br>• One-person strategic apex | • Flexible<br>• Cost-effective<br>• Clear accountability<br>• Minimum goal ambiguity | • Inappropriate with large size<br>• Concentration of power on one person | • Small size<br>• Formative stages; entrepreneurial firm<br>• Simple and dynamic environment<br>• Owner is top manager<br>• Crisis situations and hostile environment |
| Bureaucracy | • Highly routine tasks<br>• High formalization<br>• High vertical differentiation<br>• Tasks grouped into functional departments<br>• Decision-making follows chain of command | • Efficient<br>• Ensures standardization and economies of scale of complex operations<br>• Democratic structure; selection based on expertise and merit | • Creativity and innovation stifled<br>• Subunit conflicts<br>• Obsession with rules; rules can become an end by themselves, rather than a means to an end | • Large size<br>• Maturity stage<br>• Simple and stable environment<br>• Technology can be standardized<br>• Requirement for consistency and stability |

| | | | | |
|---|---|---|---|---|
| Divisional structure | • Power lies with middle management<br>• A group of autonomous units, each a bureaucracy by itself<br>• High formalization within divisions<br>• Limited decentralization | • More accountability and focus on outcomes<br>• Top management can concentrate on strategic matters since tactical decision-making is decentralized<br>• Non-performing units can be disengaged because of autonomous nature | • Duplication of activities and resources<br>• Increased propensity to conflict among divisions<br>• Coordination problems | • Choosing a diversification strategy<br>• Large size<br>• Complicated, multiple technology<br>• Stable, simple environment |
| Adhocracy | • High horizontal differentiation<br>• Low vertical differentiation<br>• Low formalization<br>• Decentralization | • Speed and flexibility of responses<br>• Complicated tasks can be handled | • Conflict<br>• Social stress and psychological strain<br>• Inefficient<br>• Costly | • When individual specialists from diverse backgrounds are required to collaborate<br>• Complex, dynamic environment |
| Matrix structure | • Functional departmentation<br>• Dual reporting<br>• High functional and social complexity<br>• Decentralization | • Facilitates coordination between complicated tasks<br>• Faster information flow<br>• Flexibility of response | • Conflict of interests<br>• Ambiguity and confusion<br>• Power struggles | • Interdependent departments<br>• Economies of scale in using internal resources |

the imperatives for going international. The structure is predominantly functional or divisional. Exporting is typically the initial stage for firms entering international operations. An export department might be set up to handle these operations, or it may be handled through an intermediary or joint venture.

As the firm develops expertise in foreign markets, the company begins to think along **multidomestic** lines, which means competitive issues in each country are independent of other countries; the company deals with each country individually. At this point, an international division, functionally structured, replaces the export department, with specialists hired to handle sales, service, warehousing, etc. abroad. As sales volumes abroad continue to increase, the firm reaches the multinational stage, where the firm has established manufacturing, R&D, after-sales, and marketing facilities in several foreign countries. The structure is geographically dispersed and is product or services centered. The last stage is **the global stage**, where the firm transcends any single country. The business operations are now no longer multi-domestic, that is, a collection of domestic industries; rather, subsidiaries are interlinked so that competitive position in one country significantly influences operations in other countries. The structure is matrix or transnational, with the entire world as its potential market. In fact, truly global companies do not think of themselves with respect to a single home country, but rather as stateless corporations.

Given the speed at which the dynamics of world business is changing, most countries use international strategic alliances as a vehicle for internationalizing. These could be in the form of joint ventures, consortia, virtual networks, acquisitions, etc. For example, *Alcon Inc*, the world's leading eye-care company, is planning to enter into strategic manufacturing alliances and joint ventures with leading Indian drug manufacturers such as *Cipla*, in its bid to enter the Indian market. Again, in a bid to ease overseas investment rules, the *Reserve Bank of India* has liberalized the investment norms for Indian telecom companies by allowing them to invest in international submarine cable consortia through the automatic route. In March 2010, *Bharti Airtel* acquired the African operations of the Kuwait-based, *Zain Telecom*, for US$ 10.7 billion, driving the Indian player into the league of the top ten telecom players globally.

While forces for globalization will continue to rule future businesses, managers have to be clear about whether globalization is really a sound business proposition for them, that it is not merely a mimetic response to other competitors in the industry. Particularly for emerging market economies such as India and China, Dawar and Frost (1999) have identified four distinct strategies – 'defender', 'extender', 'dodger', and 'contender' – based on two parameters: the strength of globalization pressures in an industry and the degree to which a company's assets are transferable internationally. Figure 3.5 depicts the various categories.

Moreover, while internationalizing, managers will have to choose a structure that will help them balance the often contradicting pulls of global standardization against

**Competitive Assets**

| Pressures to globalize in the industry | Customised to home market | Transferable abroad |
|---|---|---|
| High | **Dodger**<br>*Focuses on a locally oriented link in the value chain, enters a joint venture, or sells out to a multinational* | **Contender**<br>*Focuses on upgrading capabilities and resources to match multinationals globally, often by keeping to niche markets* |
| Low | **Defender**<br>*Focuses on leveraging local assets in market segments where multinationals are weak* | **Extender**<br>*Focuses on expanding into markets similar to those of the home base, using competencies developed at home* |

**Figure 3.5** *Strategies for globalization*

local/national responsiveness. When, for example, the requirement for national responsiveness is low, coupled with low forces for global integration, having an international division in an otherwise domestic structure would be sufficient to handle export activities.

However, when national responsiveness has to be high, with low forces for global integration, the firm might need to adopt a multi-domestic strategy, using a global geographic division structure, which would enable it to customize its solutions to the specific location. Companies using this type of structure are typically those with mature product lines and stable technologies. On the other hand, low requirement for national responsiveness combined with high forces for global integration would require adoption of a globalization strategy with a global product division structure. Here, a division handles products that are technologically similar and can be standardized for marketing worldwide. Finally, high requirements for both national responsiveness and global integration would call for a combination of both multi-domestic and global strategy, using a global matrix structure for maximum flexibility, and optimum balance between the interests of both product standardization and geographical localization.

> A multi-domestic strategy helps an organization tailor-make solutions to specific locations. A global strategy helps an organization to offer standardized solutions worldwide.

## CHAPTER SUMMARY

Organization structure is the formal decision-making framework by which job tasks are divided, grouped, and coordinated. Any structural configuration includes criteria by which various roles, activities, and coordination mechanisms can be differentiated as well as grouped together in the organization. An organization's structure can be described through the three broad dimensions of complexity, formalization, and centralization. That is, one organization would be more or less complex, more or less formalized, and more or less centralized relative to another: there is no absolute extent of complexity, formalization, or centralization.

Complexity is defined as the degree of differentiation that exists within an organization and determines the number of ways in which the same workforce can be divided based on different responsibilities or functions (namely, specialization, departmentation, hierarchy). Formalization is defined as the degree to which jobs within an organization are standardized. A high degree of functional specialization is associated with a high degree of explicit formalization, while a high degree of social specialization is associated with low degree of explicit formalization, or high degree of professional formalization. Centralization is concerned with the dispersion of authority within the organization to make decisions and is defined as the degree to which the formal authority to make discretionary choices is concentrated in an individual, unit, or, level (usually high up in the organizational hierarchy). Increase in complexity has an inverse relationship with centralization: higher complexity facilitates higher decentralization. However, the centralization–formalization relationship is ambiguous.

Throughout its life cycle, an organization's structure keeps evolving, starting with a simple structure in the early stages, and passing through functional structure, divisional structure, bureaucratic structure, matrix structure, to the more evolved integrated network models, depending on the scale and complexity of its operations. In recent decades, organizations have been increasingly expanding their sphere of operations into international markets, and globalization has become the watchword of modern businesses. Firms today have a variety of options for internationalizing, depending on various factors such as forces for national responsiveness, vis-à-vis global integration, and transferability of assets vs pressures to globalize in the industry. Each strategic option can be operationalized though a variety of structural configurations designed to suit the internationalization strategy and its expected outcomes.

### Review Questions

1. Define the term 'organization structure'. Explain the various dimensions through which structure can be understood.
2. How are complexity, formalization, and centralization related?
3. Why was bureaucracy considered to be the most efficient form of organizing?
4. Compare and contrast 'functional structure', 'divisional structure', and 'matrix structure' with respect to their advantages and disadvantages.

5. As part of their internationalization strategies, what type of structural configurations do you think each of these categories are likely to have: 'defender', 'extender', 'dodger', and 'contender'?

## Project Assignment

Take one organization each in the following sectors: (a) hospitality, (b) telecom, (c) manufacturing, and (d) higher education. Make a comparative study of the structural dimensions of each of these organizations. What can you infer about the effect of the sector/industry on the structure of an organization?

## CASE ILLUSTRATION: *SYNERGY I-DESIGN*

*Synergy i-Design*, the Indian partner of *CADopia Inc*, USA, was set up in 1998 to concentrate on several IT/ITES/CAD/CAM/CAE/AEC/GIS/BPO projects, engineering applications, software development, 2D and 3D animation, CAD customization, and data processing/warehousing. Though it began as a partnership firm, it was registered as a private limited company under the Companies Act in 2005. *Synergy i-Design* has enabled organizations worldwide to reduce their business processing costs considerably by outsourcing their back office functions such as call centers, document processing, CAD conversion, data entry and validations. In India, *Northern Railways*, *NTPC*, *ONGC*, and *HAL* are its major customers in the field of CAD/CAM/CAE. Apart from these, *Synergy* also provides training on CAD/CAM /CAE/AEC/GIS at the corporate and institutional level.

Being essentially an entrepreneurial set up, Synergy has low levels of formalization in its dealings. While there is a specified reporting time for level three employees, the same has never been documented or enforced strictly, depending more on mutual understanding between the management and employees. There is no specific time for leaving, and employees can leave whenever the work for the day is done. There is a basic appraisal system in place, which is dependent on performance statistics rather than feedback. In terms of specialization, while Synergy began with overall low levels of specialization, with its few initial employees handling a variety of work between them, the organization, with a current manpower of 35 employees, has now reached a stage where engineers and designers are recruited to dedicatedly work on the designing part. However, level three employees are required to undergo job rotation on a need-basis. Hence, while recruiting, the firm makes sure to look for a skill mix combining both software and hardware competencies. With greater need for specialization, *Synergy* is finding it increasingly difficult to get qualified and skilled professionals for the type of specialized jobs that they are into. Over the years, *Synergy* has added to its hierarchical layers by having two top level managers as well as a layer of four middle level administrative personnel. Most of the decisions are taken by the two partners at the top and the four middle level supervisors. Till now, employees have been apparently satisfied with this centralized structure, with nobody demanding more decision-making powers.

At present, *Synergy's* offerings are limited to data entry and word processing services, but it does have ambitious plans of growth, through a diversified offering of services, including data mining and data warehousing, advisory and consultancy services, seismic analysis, as well as through greater geographical spread. Given that *Synergy* is at a relatively young stage of growth, its stakeholder interactions are not very intricate or complex as one would expect from a well-established firm.

However, given that *Synergy* is slowly moving from its entrepreneurial phase to a more mature phase in its journey, there are likely to be radical changes in the firm's mode of doing business.

## Critical enquiry

*Given the ambitious plans that Synergy has for itself, what type of structural adjustments would be required for Synergy to effectively realize its dream?*

***Key words and phrases***: structure, complexity, formalization, centralization, specialization, differentiation, integration, span of control, hierarchy, matrix, bureaucracy, networks, global organizations

CHAPTER 4

# Organizational Strategy

**CHAPTER OUTLINE**

The 'strategy imperative'

❖

What is strategy?

❖

Levels of strategy

❖

Strategic dimensions

❖

The strategy–structure relationship

❖

The size imperative

❖

The industry–strategy–structure relationship

## ORGANIZATIONAL INSIGHT

In recent years, a buoyant Indian economy, aided by supportive government policies, has seen a slew of acquisitions of North American and European companies by Indian organizations, in their bid to become global players. The acquisition of Anglo-Dutch steel producer *Corus Group Plc* by *Tata Steel Limited*, India's leading steel producer, marked the biggest overseas acquisition by an Indian company. Some financial experts claimed that the price paid by *Tata Steel* (608 pence per share of *Corus*) for the acquisition was too high. Nonetheless, this acquisition helped *Tata Steel* emerge as the fifth largest steel producer in the world, with access to *Corus*' strong distribution network in Europe.*

There were many likely synergies between *Tata Steel*, the lowest-cost producer of steel in the world, and *Corus*, a large player with a significant presence in the value-added steel segment and a strong distribution network in Europe. Among the benefits to *Tata Steel* was that it would be able to supply semi-finished steel to *Corus* for finishing at its plants, which were located closer to the high-value markets. *Corus*' expertise in making the grades of steel used in automobiles and in aerospace could be used to boost *Tata Steel*'s supplies to the Indian automobile market. *Corus* in turn was expected to benefit from *Tata Steel*'s expertise in the low cost manufacturing of steel. Other benefits expected from this acquisition included cross-fertilization of research and development capabilities in the automotive, packaging, and construction sectors and a transfer, from Europe to India, of technology, best practices, and expertise of senior *Corus* management. In addition, *Tata Steel* retained access to low cost raw materials and slab for the enlarged group, and exposure to high growth in emerging markets, whilst gaining price stability in developed markets.

This acquisition was stated to be in line with *Tata Steel*'s strategy of growth and globalization.

* **Source:** *http://www.icmrindia.org/casestudies/catalogue/Finance/FINC049.htm*

## 4.1 The 'strategy imperative'

> An organization's structure should support the implementation of strategic objectives, rather than being based on pre-determined templates.

As early as 1974, Peter Drucker noted that: '*...structure is a means for attaining the objectives and goals of an institution. Any work on structure must therefore start with objectives and strategy*'. This is similar to what is commonly known as 'the strategy imperative', signified by the clichéd phrase 'structure follows strategy'. That is, strategy was considered to be the only variable determining an organization's structural configuration. This was based on the assumption that (a) every organization has a goal toward which it moves in a 'rational' manner and (b) the environment within which the organization operates is a given and is stable. However, as depicted in Figure 1.1 of Chapter 1, strategy today is just one of the many, albeit critical, contextual variables which influence an organization's structure; the others include technology, environment, size, and culture. Therefore, the current thinking can be depicted as shown below:

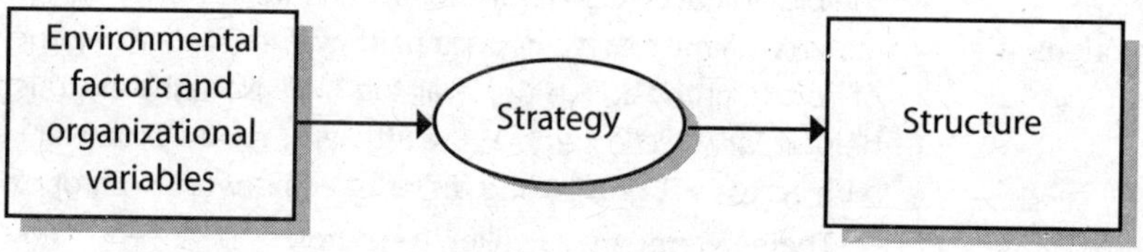


Hence, it is important that an organization's structure should support the implementation of strategic objectives, rather than being based on pre-determined templates.

## 4.2 What is strategy?

> Strategy is the determination of the basic long-term goals and objectives of an enterprise, and the adoption of courses of action and the allocation of resources necessary for carrying out these goals.

With its roots in military terminology, strategy implies long-term goals. However, as seen in our discussions on organizational effectiveness, while goals *per se* signify ends or objectives, strategy also includes the road-map to reach the designated end, including the resources that need to be allocated and committed to achieve those ends. Hence strategy, a combination of 'end goals' and 'means goals', represents a comprehensive plan of action that sets a critical direction and guides the allocation of resources to achieve long-term organizational objectives. Thus, strategy can be defined as *the determination of the basic long-term goals and objectives of an enterprise, and the adoption of courses of action and the allocation of resources necessary for carrying out these goals.* Strategy refers to the specific pattern of decisions and actions that managers take to use the organization's core competences (arising from the possession of specialized resources and the ability to coordinate these resources to add value to its stakeholders), to achieve a competitive advantage and outperform competitors. Any strategy is a choice that specifies how managers plan to move the organization in a competitive environment.

Strategy can be determined in two ways. In the earlier **planning mode**, a definite or explicit set of guidelines is developed in advance. The objectives are decided, followed by a systematic and structured plan of how to get there. However, with the increasing turbulence in the business environment, planning ahead might not always be a viable option for today's organizations. Hence, a more contemporary approach is the **evolutionary mode**, where strategy evolves over time as a response to external and internal changes.

## 4.3 Levels of strategy

An organization's strategy is formulated at three levels: at the corporate, business, and functional levels.

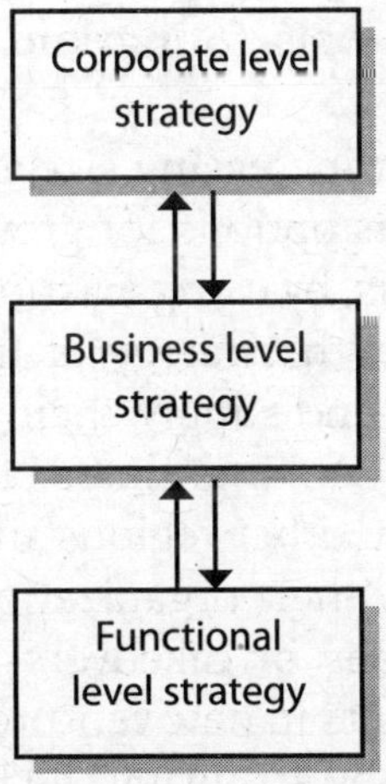


**Corporate level strategy** seeks to answer the question: '*In what set of businesses should the organization be*?' More relevant for a multi-business organizational form, it represents a plan to use and develop core competences, so that the organization can not only protect and enlarge its existing domain but also diversify and expand into newer domains. For example, when *ITC Ltd*. decides to expand its operations in areas as diverse as cigarettes, software, lifestyle, hospitality, food products, etc., to name a few, it is an example of its corporate level strategy. The purpose of corporate strategy is to set direction and guide resource allocations for the total enterprise. Typically, strategic decisions at this level relate to the use of resources for acquisitions, new business development, divestitures, etc.

Once the above decision has been taken, the **business level strategy** then seeks to answer the question: *'How should the organization compete in each of its businesses?'* Hence, business level strategy would refer to a plan to combine functional core competences in order to position the organization so that it has a competitive advantage in its domain. Typical business strategy decisions include choices about product/service mix, facilities/locations, new technologies, etc. For example, when *ITC Foods* decided on biscuits, staples, ready-to-eats, snacks, and confectionaries as part of its basket of offerings, it segmented consumer needs to understand gaps in the market, and accordingly launched different brands of the same product in different regions, or used celebrity advertising to market its products, these are examples of the business level strategies of *ITC Ltd*'s food business. For a smaller organization in a single line of business, the business and corporate level strategy would be the same, but in multiple businesses, each business division would have its own unique business strategy. In fact, the term **strategic business unit** (SBU) is used to describe such divisions, when they operate with separate missions within a larger enterprise. For example, *ITC* is a multi-business corporation, its SBUs are categorized on the basis of the various businesses it competes in, namely, cigarettes, FMCG, hotels, paperboards, packaging, agri business, IT, etc.

At the corporate and business levels, **four grand** or **master strategies** are typically used (Glueck, 1976).

1. *Growth strategies* are aimed at increasing size and expanding current operations. Organizations pursue various options for growth. Some try to grow organically through concentration, that is, by using existing strengths in new and productive ways. For example, the growth strategy of Indian IT major, *Infosys*, is geared toward becoming an end-to-end supply chain solutions provider, expanding its offerings beyond the BFSI (banking, financial services, and insurance) sector, and increasing its presence in other regions and markets, including the growing domestic Indian market. Other organizations grow through *diversification*, through mergers, acquisitions or takeovers of new businesses in related or unrelated areas, or investments in new ventures. For example, *Oracle Corporation* follows a strategy of growth by acquiring the best-of-breed products (e.g. *Siebel* in CRM, *PeopleSoft* in HR, *Hyperion* in Enterprise Performance Management, *Retek* and *ProfitLogic* in Retail, *SPL* in utilities, *G-Log* in logistics, and *MetaSolv* in telecom), and integrating them with its own products to capture market share across all possible industry sectors. The acquisition of Anglo-Dutch steel major *Corus* by *Tata Steel* of India is another such example of growth strategy. On the other hand, the *Reliance ADAG* group in India has grown through unrelated diversification into areas as varied as infrastructure, health, finance, power, communications, entertainment, and media. Although diversifications allow a company to grow, it also brings with it the added challenges of managing in new and unfamiliar domains. Common **diversification strategies** include

horizontal and vertical integration, conglomerate diversification, and joint ventures. However, managers often mistake growth as effectiveness, which need not always be the case. An organization whose long-term objective is to be the number one player in the market might never achieve its goal, despite a slew of diversification and other growth initiatives. Hence, managers would continuously have to be alert for danger signals from the environment, which might threaten their competitiveness and market position, rather than allowing such growth initiatives to lull them into a sense of complacency.

2. A *stability strategy* maintains the current course of action without commitment to any major operating changes. This strategy could be beneficial when an organization is doing well in a receptive environment, or needs time to consolidate its operations. Rather than being a 'do-nothing' strategy, this strategy seeks to continue an existing pattern of operations. The modernization initiatives by the steel plants under the umbrella of *Steel Authority of India* to improve their efficiency and productivity are an example of stability strategy.
3. *Retrenchment strategies* are defensive strategies undertaken to reduce the scale of operations in order to cut losses and improve operating efficiencies. For example, because of huge operating losses, the *Tata* group of companies was forced to liquidate its textile business. Typical retrenchment strategies include downsizing, restructuring, and liquidation. For example, in order to revive its loss-making PSUs, the Government of India decided to disinvest its stake in them and offer these PSUs to joint venture partners or strategic buyers. More recently, after Vikram Pandit took charge, the US-based *Citi* group sold off its *Diners Club International* business to *Discover Financial Services* and exited the payment network business.[1]
4. A *combination strategy* simultaneously employs more than one of the above strategies. A conglomerate, in its quest for overall growth, might pursue growth in some divisions, hive off some non-profitable divisions, and consolidate its operations in other divisions. For example, as part of its overall growth plans, *Pidilite Industries* in India went in for related diversification through expansion of its product portfolio across three business segments: adhesives and sealants, construction paints and chemicals, and art materials. Simultaneously, it divested its specialty chemicals business, and acquired M-Seal from the *Mahindra* group.

Finally, **functional level strategy** refers to a plan of action to strengthen an organization's functional and organizational resources, as well as its coordination abilities, in order to create core competences. Functional strategy guides activities within a specific functional area of operations. Within a typical business, the functions of marketing, manufacturing, finance, human resources, and research

[1] *Business India, June 29, 2008*

and development illustrate this level of strategy. The key question to be answered at this level therefore becomes *'How can we best use functional expertise to support business level strategy?'* For example, *Hindustan Unilever*'s distribution network of 7000 redistribution stockists, designed to cover the entire urban population and about 250 million rural consumers, is an example of its functional level strategy for its distribution function.

Table 4.1 summarises the questions that each level attempts to answer:

**Table 4.1** *Strategic decisions at different levels*

| *Level of strategy* | *Examples of types of decisions* |
|---|---|
| Corporate | • What domain should one operate in?<br>• How should one grow? (vertical integration, unrelated diversification, niche market, strategic alliances?)<br>• What should be the product mix?<br>• What should be the customer mix? |
| Business | • How should resources be allocated?<br>• What should be the pricing policy?<br>• What should be the advertising strategies?<br>• How should activities and functions be structured? |
| Functional | • What should be the plant capacity and production schedules? Service qualities?<br>• How should distribution networks be designed?<br>• What is the manpower requirement in each department? |

However, successful implementation and execution of strategies are not easy. Managers would need to keep some issues in mind for effectively implementing envisioned strategies (Hrebiniak, 2008):

- Since planning and execution are interdependent, involving those responsible for execution at the planning process itself would improve knowledge transfer, commitment to sought-after outcomes and the implementation process in general.
- Successful execution takes time, and can sometimes detract the managers' attention from details. The process of execution has to be adaptive and dynamic, to respond to unanticipated events.
- Execution involves people across levels and hierarchies, and is a collective responsibility.
- Choice of structure is vital to the implementation of strategy.
- Integration mechanisms and coordination across units, clarifying roles, responsibilities and accountabilities, and developing effective incentives and controls is essential for the execution of strategy

## 4.4 Strategic dimensions

Broadly, corporate strategy decisions follow the four dimensions proposed by **Miller**:

- **Innovation:** This is the degree to which an organization introduces new products or services, through meaningful and new innovations.
- **Marketing differentiation:** This is a strategy for creating customer loyalty by uniquely meeting a particular need, through advertising, market segmentation, prestige pricing, etc.
- **Breadth:** This refers to the scope of the market served by the organization's business, in terms of the variety of customers, their geographic spread, numbers of products, etc.
- **Cost control:** This strategy focuses on the extent to which the organization controls its costs, refrains from unnecessary innovation, and cuts prices in selling a basic product.

## 4.5 The strategy–structure relationship

### 4.5.1 Chandler's thesis

In his classic study of nearly 100 American firms, Chandler found that to remain effective and realize economies of growth, a firm's structure has to develop and change in accordance with the changes in the firm's activities, in new areas, functions, or products. In its early stages, a firm typically concentrates on one line of business – either a single product or service. Correspondingly, the structure is simple, with centralized decision-making, low complexity and formalization. However, with time, as the organization expands its scope of activities, there is need for greater interdependencies among units, and greater coordination. The structure likewise changes to a more complex configuration. Figure 4.1 below depicts this relationship:

| Time | t | t + 1 | t + 2 |
|---|---|---|---|
| Product diversification strategy | Low → | | High |
| Structure | Simple | Functional | Divisional |

**Figure 4.1** *Chandler's strategy–structure relationships*

Despite several criticisms regarding his methodology and the generalizability of findings, Chandler's propositions have more or less stood the test of time.

### 4.5.2 Miles and Snow's typologies

Miles and Snow described a framework for categorizing organizations based on their strategic choices. Table 4.2 below describes each of these typologies in relation to their structural characteristics:

**Table 4.2** *Miles and Snow's strategic typologies*

| *Strategy type* | *Goals* | *Environment* | *General description* | *Structural characteristics* |
|---|---|---|---|---|
| Defender | Stability and efficiency | Stable | • Limited product range<br>• Narrow market segment<br>• 'Turf' protection, 'niche' maintenance<br>• Focus on cost and efficiency<br>• Limited environmental scanning | • Horizontal differentiation<br>• Centralized control<br>• Elaborate, formal hierarchy for communication |
| Prospector | Flexibility | Changing | • Finds and exploits new product and market opportunities<br>• Focus on innovation rather than profitability<br>• First mover advantage | • Flexible structure<br>• Low routinization and mechanization<br>• Decentralization<br>• Low in formalization |
| Analyzer | Stability and Flexibility | Dynamic | • Capitalize on best of previous two strategies<br>• Minimum risk, maximum profit opportunity<br>• Imitation | • Mix of standardization and adaptiveness<br>• Moderate centralization |
| Reactor | | | • Responds inappropriately, performs poorly | • Poor fit between strategy and structure |

Defenders adopt a strategic posture which aims at stability, niche maintenance and turf protection in their own domain. Prospectors are the antithesis of defenders in that they operate in dynamic and uncertain environments, calling for constant innovation and change. While these two types represent two ends of a continuum, analyzers fall somewhere in between, representing a judicious blend of the two. Hence, analyzers would try to minimize their risks (defender strategy) and maximize their profits (prospector strategy). The last category, reactor, is likely to lead to organizational failure, subscribing to an unstable and inconsistent pattern of adjustment to the environment. Such strategic failures normally occur because of (a) lack of clear articulation of the organization's strategy by top management, (b) improper fit of an organization's structure and processes to fit the strategy, and (c) reluctance on the part of top management to change the organization's current strategy–structure relationship despite drastic changes in its environment demanding such changes.

According to Miles and Snow, organizations must identify, confront, and solve three problems: entrepreneurial problems, engineering problems, and administrative problems, in order to successfully adapt to the environment. Table 4.2A summarises the differences in adaptation strategies of these three types. Table 4.2B discusses the HR implications of these strategic types, while Table 4.2C clarifies the organizational processes of each of these three categories.

**Table 4.2A** *Differences in adaptation problems of the three strategic types**

| *Adaptation problems* | *Strategic types* | | |
|---|---|---|---|
| | *Defender* | *Analyzer* | *Prospector* |
| Entrepreneurial | How to seal off a portion of the total market to create a stable domain | How to locate and exploit new product/market, while simultaneously maintaining a firm base of traditional products and customers | How to locate and exploit new product/market opportunities |
| Engineering | How to produce and distribute goods/services as efficiently as possible | How to be efficient in the stable portion of the domain and flexible in the changing domain | How to avoid long-term commitments to a single technological process |
| Administrative | How to achieve strict control of the organization in order to ensure efficiency | How to differentiate the organization's structure and processes to accommodate both stable and dynamic areas of operation | How to facilitate rather than control organizational operation |

* **Source:** *Shukla, 1999*

**Table 4.2B** *Differences in HR system profiles of the three strategic types**

| *Dimensions* | *Strategic types* | | |
|---|---|---|---|
| | *Defender* | *Analyzer* | *Prospector* |
| Recruitment and selection | Standardized skills, fewer professionals; recruitment does not need to be selective | Professionals for managerial positions; moderate selectiveness | Highly skilled professionals; highly selective recruitment and selection function |
| Training | Relies on standardized skills and narrow/ specialized job descriptions. Low levels of training | Experts in managerial and professional jobs. Moderate training | Continuous upgrade of skills and high levels of expertise. High levels of training |
| Degree of formalization | Standardized skills and work processes. HR systems emphasize formalization | Experts in managerial and professional jobs. Low formalization for managers and professionals. High for other employees | Many professionals, high personnel turnover likely. Low formalization |
| Compensation | Jobs are well described, easy to monitor, and outcomes are predictable. Low emphasis on incentive compensations | Most jobs are well described and easy to monitor. Managers and professional jobs are exceptions. Moderate emphasis on incentive compensation | Job are loosely described, difficult to monitor, and outcomes are unpredictable. High emphasis on incentive compensation |

* **Source**: *Burton, Erikson, Hakonsson and Snow, 2006*

**Table 4.2C** *Differences in organizational processes of the three strategic types**

| *Dimensions* | *Strategic types* | | |
|---|---|---|---|
| | *Defender* | *Analyzer* | *Prospector* |
| Communication | Jobs and procedures are well described. Few exceptions to daily operations and strategic changes. Low emphasis on communication | Moderate change to jobs and procedures. Moderate changes in daily operations and strategy. Moderate emphasis on communication | Jobs and procedures change frequently. Changes need to be communicated effectively to ensure effective implementation |

*(Contd ...*

*... Contd)*

| | | | |
|---|---|---|---|
| Executive leadership style | Internal process culture. Emphasis on formalization and structure | Rational-goal culture. Results-oriented with hard drivers, producers and competitors as leaders | Developmental culture. Focus on dynamics, entrepreneurship and creativity |

* **Source:** *Burton, Erikson, Hakonsson and Snow, 2006*

This concept of 'fit' between strategy and context and its positive impact on firm performance has been taken further by Venkatraman and Prescott (1990) through their concept of **coalignment**. The concept of 'fit' has been discussed in greater detail in Chapter 5.

### 4.5.3 Porter's competitive strategies

Michael Porter's competitive model identifies forces that govern the state of industry and competition, which must be properly addressed if organizational decision-makers are to formulate effective strategies. These forces are:

- threat of new entrants
- bargaining power of suppliers
- bargaining power of buyers
- threat of substitute products or services
- rivalry among industry firms

> Porter has identified five market forces that should determine an organization's strategies for competitive advantage: threat of new entrants, bargaining power of suppliers, bargaining power of buyers, threat of substitute products and services, and rivalry among firms.

Based on an analysis of these forces, an organization must select a strategy that gives it a competitive advantage. Porter observes that organizations can pursue three generic strategies to gain this competitive advantage. They are:

(a) **Cost-leadership strategy:** Here an organization is the cost leader by virtue of being a low-cost producer in the market, for alternative products or services of comparable quality and specifications being offered by other companies competing in the same field. The required structural configuration for this would be high complexity (high functional differentiation), high formalization, and high centralization. The introduction of *Air Deccan* as India's first low-cost airline in the highly regulated Indian skies is a notable example of cost–leadership strategy in recent times.

(b) **Differentiation strategy:** In this strategy, the organization attempts to be the market leader by virtue of being perceived to be offering some unique value to the customer (high quality, extraordinary service, innovative design, cutting-edge technology, etc.). Whatever the attribute, it should be perceived to be different from those offered by other competitors, and significant enough to merit premium pricing. The flexibility demanded in this type of strategy calls for low formalization, high decentralization, high social specialization. For example, *Domino's* has differentiated itself from its competitors by positioning itself as a home delivery specialist, capable of delivering its pizzas within 30 minutes or else supplying it free to its consumers.

(c) **Focus strategy** aims at a cost advantage or differentiation advantage in a narrow segment. That is, the management will select a segment or group of segments in an industry (such as product variety, type of end buyer, distribution channel, and geographic location of customers) and tailor a strategy to suit that segment, to the exclusion of others, and thereby exploit a narrow segment of market. For example, *Nokia* in India has straddled all customer segments, customizing their product features to suit the particular segment. Hence, for example, handsets targeted at the low-end and rural population have inbuilt torches in them to help people in areas which do not have electricity.

Organizations that are unable to gain a competitive advantage by any of the above strategies are referred to as 'stuck-in-the-middle', who would find it difficult to achieve long-term success. Overreaching beyond one's competitive advantage can sometimes lead to a 'stuck-in-the-middle' situation for unrealistically ambitious companies.

### 4.5.4 Miller's framework

Chandler, Miles and Snow, and Porter all appear to broadly follow Miller's four strategic dimensions of innovation, marketing differentiation, breadth, and cost-control.

Miller has drawn up an integrative framework combining these strategic dimensions with their structural characteristics, as depicted in Table 4.3 below:

**Table 4.3** *Miller's framework*

| *Strategic dimension* | *Challenge* | *Predicted structural characteristics* |
|---|---|---|
| Innovation | To understand and manage more products, customer types, technologies and markets | Scanning of markets to discern customer requirements; low formalization; decentralization; extensive use of coordinative committees and task forces |
| Market differentiation | To understand and cater to customer preferences | Moderate to high complexity; extensive scanning and analysis of customers' reactions and competitor strategies; moderate to high formalization; moderate decentralization |

(Contd ...

... Contd)

| | | |
|---|---|---|
| Breadth:<br>• Breadth innovation<br><br><br>• Breadth stability | To select the right range of products, services, customers and territory | High complexity; low formalization; decentralization;<br><br>High complexity; high formalization; high centralization |
| Cost control | To produce standardized products efficiently | High formalization; high centralization |

The above typologies are similar to those of Miles and Snow's: for example, the prospector category of Miles and Snow requires a similar structural configuration as that of the innovation and breadth types of Miller; Miles and Snow's defender types requires a structural configuration similar to Miller's cost-control strategy. And Miles and Snows analyzers require structural characteristics similar to marketing differentiation, needing flexible marketing and stable production.

While the type of strategy does drive structural configurations, there is often a time lag between implementing a new strategy and restructuring the organization accordingly. The higher the competitive pressures faced by the organization, the faster it would be to adapt structurally with changes in strategy. Conversely, low competitive pressures are likely to result in a greater time lag between changes in strategy and modifications in structure.

Another dimension that needs to be kept in mind is that while strategy determines structure, structural configurations in turn are likely to have an effect on the type of strategic actions taken. One of the key challenges facing an organization is to ensure that its structure supports current and future strategic needs. In fact, an inappropriate organizational structure can actually undermine an organization's strategic performance. For example, a strategic imperative might lead to an increase in complexity. However, since members are more dispersed and differentiated, it is possible that members, bound by parochial and group level biases, might not recognize the decision as strategic and comprehensive, and hence ignore it initially. Therefore, integrating the decision across all the differentiated units would be difficult.

Higher departmentation could also imply that strategic decisions and actions would be the result of an internal process of political bargaining. Moreover, any strategic decision would have to satisfy a large constraint set. However, with increased complexity, it would be difficult to ensure that the decision in fact benefits the organization as a whole and not a select few. Integration of decisions will be low. Likewise, increase in formalization could imply that strategic actions will be initiated only in response to problems or crises that appear in variables monitored by the formal system. Because of the high focus on procedures and processes, means might attain higher importance than the final ends. This could also imply that the level of detail achieved in the standardized organizational processes will be the primary constraint in integrating the strategic action comprehensively. Similarly, increasing centralization in response to some strategic imperative might imply that strategic actions will only be initiated by a dominant few, which also increases possibilities of opportunity-seeking behavior. Moreover, the top management's knowledge limitations might be a constraint in terms of the decision-quality and effectiveness. On the other hand, however, high centralization would ensure a high level of integration of the decisions taken.

Increase in size increases structural differentiation but at a decreasing rate.

## 4.6 The 'size imperative'

The grand strategies or master strategies discussed in section 4.3 are aimed at bringing about a change in the size of the organization's operations, normally manifested by a change in manpower size. Researchers have largely agreed that an organization's size can be defined as the total number of its employees. While the actual number would vary from one organization to the other, depending on the industry and other contextual factors, a broad generalization adopted is that more than 2000 employees constitute a 'large' size for an organization.

Intuitive reasoning seems to imply that as an organization grows, it takes on more employees, and hence would try to take advantage of the economic benefits of specialization. Hence, horizontal differentiation is likely to increase. This would in turn give rise to greater vertical differentiation, in response to greater needs for control and coordination. Spatial differentiation might also increase to take care of this expansion in size. With increasing complexity, top management's ability to control through direct supervision will be severely challenged, necessitating the implementation of formal rules and procedures in place of direct control. With an increase in the number of vertical levels, the ability of top management to make rapid and informed decisions reduces drastically. Hence, increase in size is likely to lead to greater decentralization. Therefore, increase in an organization's size is likely to lead to major structural changes. However, the exact influence of size on each dimension of structure needs to be examined in greater detail. One of the strongest proponents of the size imperative has been **Peter Blau**. He maintains that increasing size promotes structural differentiation but at a decreasing rate. Figure 4.2 depicts this relationship vividly.

An organization's increase in size is initially accompanied by rapid increase in the number of spatial dispersions, the number of hierarchical levels and official designations, the number of functional divisions at the headquarters, and the number

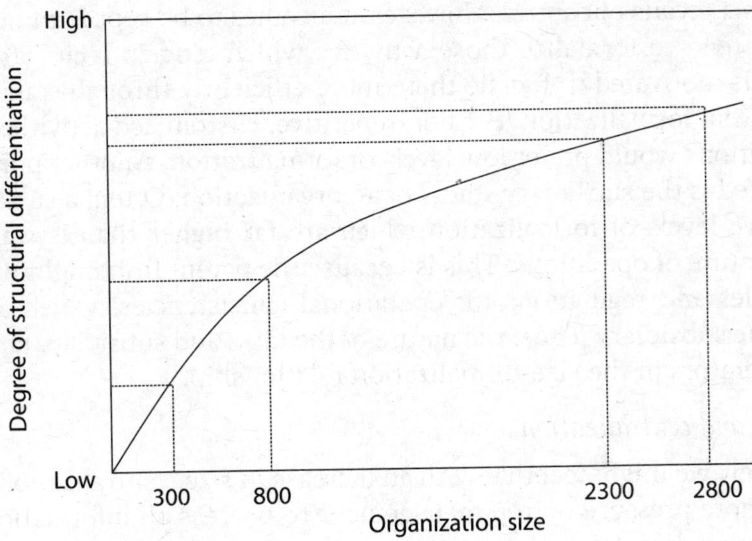


**Figure 4.2** *Organization size and structural differentiation*

of sections per division. Beyond a particular size, however, the structure tends to stabilize, and is less prone to changes, even with incremental changes in size.

### 4.6.1 The size–structure relationship

While a direct relationship between size and structure is not very apparent (some critiques are of the opinion that size is a consequence rather than a cause of structure), some broad relationships between size and various structural dimensions can be predicted, as shown in the subsequent sections:

#### *4.6.1.1 Size and complexity*

Size has been found to be the strongest predictor of vertical differentiation. Increasing size puts a constraint on managers in terms of span of control, necessitating more number of hierarchical levels. A similar relationship holds true for horizontal differentiation as well. The larger the organization, the more pronounced (at declining rates) is the division of labor within it. Intuitively, it also appears that increasing size would lead to an increase in spatial differentiation; this relationship, however, has not been supported too strongly through studies.

#### *4.6.1.2 Size and formalization*

It appears logical to state that with an increase in size, the extent of formalization increases. A small size is amenable to direct supervision by management. However, as size increases and there are more subordinates to supervise, direct supervision becomes a non-viable option; standardized rules and procedures replace direct supervision as a means of control. However, it also has to be kept in mind that large organizations tend to formalize those activities which tend to recur often. Hence, management is motivated to handle them more efficiently through standardization which arises from formalization. For non-repetitive, customized activities, however, large organizations would prefer low levels of formalization. Another point that has to be considered is the subsidiary status of an organization. Often, a subsidiary firm is seen to have levels of formalization which are far higher than is warranted by their size or nature of operations. This is because the parent firm might have certain formalized rules and regulations for operational consistencies, which are in turn imposed on the subsidiary. Thus, the nature of the task, and subsidiary status would be likely moderators in the size-formalization relationship.

#### *4.6.1.3 Size and centralization*

While intuitively we might feel that with an increase in size, centralization decreases since it puts more pressure on top management to process all information on their own, necessitating delegation of decision-making, at least for tactical issues, research has not really been able to support this hypothesis conclusively.

### 4.6.2 What is the optimum size for an organization?

While most organizations would want to grow and expand their scope of activities, there are advantages and disadvantages associated with small and large sizes that organizations need to be aware of before deciding on their growth strategies. The main differences between large and small organizations are tabulated below:

**Table 4.4** *Characteristics of large and small organizations*

| *Large* | *Small* |
|---|---|
| • Economies of scale<br>• Global reach<br>• Vertical hierarchy<br>• Mechanistic structure<br>• Complex<br>• Stable market<br>• Managers or 'organization men' | • Responsive, flexible<br>• Regional reach<br>• Flat structure, organic<br>• Simple<br>• Niche finding<br>• Entrepreneurs |

Large organizations are characterized by economies of scale and huge resources are needed to compete globally. The high level of complexity allows numerous functional specialties within the organization to perform complex tasks. Moreover, large established organizations can help stabilize the market and provide long-term career paths for its employees, which can facilitate organizational loyalty and commitment. Small organizations, on the other hand, provide the responsiveness and flexibility required to compete in the fast-changing global markets. In fact, while large organizations were the norm earlier, technological advancement, development of the Internet and rapid growth of the service sector have all facilitated the growth of numerous small firms in diverse niche segments.

The paradox is that the advantages of small firms enable them to succeed and, hence, grow. However, the flexibility and adaptability of small firms is replaced by more rigid, mechanistic structures as they become victims of their own success and grow in size. Jack Welch, former CEO of *General Electric* proposed the concept of a 'big company/small company' hybrid that combines a large corporation's resources and reaches with a small company's simplicity and flexibility. The divisional structure and matrix structures described in Chapter 3 are a way of achieving this hybrid.

## 4.7 The industry–strategy– structure relationship

Every industry has some unique characteristics (growth possibilities, regulatory constraints, entry barriers, and mobility) that determine the strategies they would choose. This would, in turn, affect the structural characteristics they are likely to have. Geiger, Ritchie, and Marlin (2006) have found that a fit between a firm's strategy and structure is more important for firms that operate in higher concentration industries such as manufacturing (steel, cement, etc.). Figure 4.3 below shows a two-by-two matrix, depicting different industries and their likely structural configurations, where industries are classified along two dimensions: capital requirements and product

| Product innovation rates | Capital requirement: High | Capital requirement: Low |
|---|---|---|
| High | Highly structured and standardized; large size; limited competition<br><br>*e.g. aerospace, large computer manufacturers* | Small firms; less formalization and more decentralization<br><br>*e.g. computer software, publishing* |
| Low | Highly structured and standardized; decentralized; large size; limited competition<br><br>*e.g. metals and mining, appliance manufacturers* | Small firms; more division of labor and formalization<br><br>*e.g. retail, construction material, bicycle manufacture* |

**Figure 4.3** *Industry–strategy–structure relationship*

innovation rates. Firms belonging to the same industry are likely to have a similar structural configuration.

## CHAPTER SUMMARY

An organization's strategy can be defined as the determination of the basic long-term goals and objectives of an enterprise, and the adoption of courses of action and the allocation of resources necessary for carrying out these goals. Strategy is one of the most critical determinants of an organization's structure. Hence, it is important that an organization's structure should support the implementation of strategic objectives, rather than being based on pre-determined templates. Given the increasing turbulence in today's business environment, strategy evolves over time as a response to external and internal changes.

An organization's strategy is formulated at three levels: corporate level, business level, and functional level. While corporate level strategy chalks out the set of businesses in which the organization should be, business level strategy highlights how the organization should compete in each of its businesses. Finally, functional level strategy helps strengthen an organization's functional and organizational resources, as well as its coordination abilities, in order to create core competences.

Various scholars have attempted to chart out the relationship between strategy and structure in organizations. Chandler found that to remain effective and realize economies of growth, a firm's structure needed to develop and change in accordance with changes in the firm's activities. Beginning with a single product or service, and a corresponding simple structure, the organization gradually expands its scope of activities over time, with its structure changing to a more complex configuration. Miles and Snow described a framework for categorizing organizations based on their strategic choices. The strategy typologies identified by them were analyzers, defenders, prospectors, and reactors. Porter's competitive strategies include cost-focus strategies, differentiation strategies, and focus strategies. Miller has consolidated these typologies to identify four dimensions viz. innovation, marketing differentiation, breadth control, and cost control, which corporate strategy decisions follow.

An organization's size can be defined as the total number of its employees. Generally, more than 2000 employees constitute a 'large' size for an organization. With increase in size, there is likely to be an increase in horizontal differentiation, vertical differentiation, spatial differentiation, and decentralization. Therefore, an increase in an organization's size is likely to lead to major structural changes. The concept of a 'big company/small company' hybrid that combines a large corporation's resources and reach with a small company's simplicity and flexibility is now gaining popularity. Every industry has some unique characteristics that determine the strategies they would choose. This would, in turn, affect the structural characteristics they are likely to have. Firms belonging to the same industry are likely to have similar structural configurations.

## Review Questions

1. What is meant by the term 'strategy'? How is strategy formulated?

2. Illustrate with examples the relationship between an organization's corporate level, business level, and functional level strategies.
3. What would be the structural implications for an organization as its strategy cascades down from corporate level to functional level?
4. How can organizations achieve an 'optimum size' for their operations?

## Project Assignment

Examine the evolution of industry structure for the BPO sector in India, using Porter's five forces analysis. Try and predict what type of growth strategies should be undertaken by different categories of BPOs to survive and compete, giving suitable justifications for your suggestions.

## CASE ILLUSTRATION: *CMC LIMITED*

*CMC Limited* is an IT solutions company in India and a subsidiary of *Tata Consultancy Services Ltd*, a *Tata* group company and one of the world's leading IT consulting, services and business process outsourcing organizations. With 18 offices, 150 service locations, 520 non-resident locations and over 3500 employees worldwide, CMC provides a wide spectrum of unique IT solutions and services to a clientele of premier organizations in the government and private sectors. *CMC* started in 1975 with people from *IBM* who had remained in India when *IBM* shut shop. At the time of its inception, it was named *Computer Maintenance Corporation Private Limited*. The Government of India held 100% of its equity share capital. In 1977, it was converted into a public limited company. To reflect its diversified business activities, it was renamed *CMC Limited*, and obtained a fresh certificate of incorporation in 1984.

Following a spurt in the global demand for IT services in the early 1990s, particularly in the United States, *CMC* decided to expand its operations and market its product and service offerings in foreign markets. In 1991, it acquired Baton Rouge International Inc, USA, which was subsequently renamed *CMC Americas Inc.* in 2003; this was one of the first cross-border acquisitions by an Indian IT firm. In 1992, the Indian government divested 16.69% of *CMC's* equity to the *General Insurance Corporation of India*. This was followed in 1993 by *CMC's* shares being listed on the Hyderabad and Bombay Stock Exchanges. To service and develop their clientele in the UK and Europe, *CMC* opened a branch office in London in 2000. A year later, the Indian government divested 51% of *CMC's* equity to *Tata Sons Ltd*, through a strategic sale, and *CMC* became a part of the *Tata* group.

The multi-level strategies followed by *CMC* are reflected in their vision and mission. Hence, *CMC* aims to 'operate globally and bring the benefits of information technology to improve the productivity of our customers, and the quality of their products and services' as its vision. This dream is further elaborated through its mission, which includes the following statements:

- *CMC Limited* will provide comprehensive and cost-effective IT solutions and services to organizations and institutions in India and the rest of the world to improve their competitiveness, building on its strengths in maintenance, systems integration, networking, and software development.
- Exports are a critical area for the healthy growth of the organization, and will receive priority in resource allocation and competence building

- Maintenance will continue to be a key business area and will be strengthened to improve price performance and market share.
- Appropriate business alliances will be entered into, to complement internal efforts toward expansion and growth.
- *CMC*, on an ongoing basis, will review market opportunities and technology trends to focus on niche areas and direct its R&D efforts toward cost-effective, timely products, and package solutions to meet customer requirements.

Spread across five strategic business units (SBUs) – (1) customer services, (2) systems integration, (3) IT-enabled services, (4) embedded systems, and (5) education and training, *CMC*'s products and solutions span a gamut of domains: banking and finance, e-governance, mining, insurance, shipping, power, and transportation. While *CMC*'s strengths lies in government-based projects (e.g. implementing the Computerized Reservation System for *Indian Railways*, a project now replicated in other countries), its acquisition by *TCS* has enabled it to diversify into hitherto untapped domains. Hence, from its previous 'analyzer' status with its focus on status-quo and stability, *CMC* has now transformed into a prospector, on a rapid growth trajectory. Having serviced government clients, *CMC* is one of the lowest-cost players in the market. Alongside this, it offers a unique value proposition by providing clients with innovative designs at low cost, cutting edge technology and high levels of services and client involvement.

*CMC* aims at a cost advantage and differentiation strategy for a narrow segment, i.e. its government clients. A culture of innovation has enabled *CMC* to enhance their client base from PSUs such as *Indian Railways* and *ONGC* to developing complete model software for banking, environment engineering and network management. In terms of breadth, the company operates in diverse areas such as systems and hardware consultancy, software and hardware maintenance, environmental engineering, equipment integration and supply, network management, facilities management, embedded systems, turnkey project management and integration, web hosting/web applications, data centre services and software design and development, among others.

## Critical enquiry

*How do you think the structure of CMC might have altered to accommodate the strategic changes in its operations from a government-owned enterprise to a private sector subsidiary?*

***Key words and phrases***: strategy imperative, corporate level strategy, business level strategies, functional level strategies, strategic dimensions, strategic choices, competitive strategies

## CHAPTER 5

# Organizational Environment

**CHAPTER OUTLINE**

What is environment?

❖

Sources of environmental uncertainty

❖

Structural responses to environmental uncertainty

❖

Environment–structure relationship

❖

Organizational strategies for managing environmental uncertainties

## ORGANIZATIONAL INSIGHT

In recent years, a number of Indian organizations have woken up to the fact that corporations have obligations to society that extend beyond mere profit-making activities. Accordingly, many Indian business houses have launched Corporate Social Responsibility (CSR) initiatives to discharge their obligations to society for their existence, as well as add value to their stakeholders, and thus ensure their sustained competitive survival. Some key sectors in India which have benefited through such CSR initiatives include education, community development, environment, disaster management, health, and safety.

*Bharti Foundation*, the philanthropic arm of *Bharti Enterprises* aims to provide education to the weaker sections of society, to make them employable. The *Azim Premji Foundation*, set up with financial resources contributed by Azim Premji, the founder of *Wipro*, dedicates itself to the cause of universalization of elementary education in India. Other organizations who pledge their resources to provide quality education to underprivileged students include *Infosys Corporation, Oracle India, IBM, Hewlett-Packard, Reliance India, Coca Cola India* and *INTEL*.

In the area of community and livelihood development, *Intel* provides access to affordable computers for underprivileged youth in India. *Technology Informatics Design Endeavour (TIDE)* provides efficient technology products such as stoves, boilers, dryers, kilns, etc. to different informal industry sectors. *Punjab National Bank* reaches out to its rural customers through technology and infrastructure development. *Feedback Foundation*, the not-for-profit entity of *Feedback Ventures*, undertakes community engagement mandates with the aim of fostering inclusive growth for all infrastructural advancements, the *shakti-amma* project of *Hindustan Levers Ltd (HLL)* engages underprivileged women in Indian villages as their roving retailing agents, *ITC Ltd's e-choupal* leverages the Internet to empower small and marginal farmers by providing them with farming know-how and services, timely and relevant weather information, transparent price discovery, and access to wider markets, and the *Coca Cola India Foundation* funds a range of community development activities including water, environment, healthy living, and social advancement.

The CSR activities of *GE India* include blood donation drives, education with mobile crèche projects, AIDS awareness programs, medicine collection drives, finding help for natural disasters, etc. *Sundesh*, the CSR arm of *Dabur India*, is involved in healthcare, education, veterinary services, and income generation activities in rural areas.

Through these and other comparable initiatives, Indian organizations are increasingly reaching out to their stakeholders in the business environment and attempting to meet their expectations of being socially and environmentally responsible in their business dealings.

## 5.1 What is environment?

The open systems approach to viewing organizations focuses on an organization's reliance on its environment in order to survive and grow. A further refinement of this concept occurs while evaluating an organization's effectiveness from a strategic constituency's perspective, by identifying the various environmental dimensions which directly affect an organization's functioning. Hence, the broad question to be answered is: 'what constitutes environment?' While Miller's generic approach (*'....take the universe, subtract from it the organization, and the remainder is environment'*) appears simple enough, it might have sufficed in earlier times, when business conditions were more stable and predictable. In today's unstable and rapidly changing scenario, it is more difficult to identify environmental dimensions, since each organization, as well as different units of the same organization, faces different levels of environmental uncertainties. Hence, organizational strategies would reflect managers' responses for dealing with these uncertainties.

Restructuring represents one way of dealing with environmental uncertainties, in order to match environmental demands. In fact, the population ecology theory discussed in Chapter 1 has its roots in this environmental imperative. That is, the environment 'selects' certain types of organizations to survive and others to perish, based on the fit between certain types of structural characteristics and the characteristics of their environment. While anything outside an organization's boundaries represents the environment, not all environmental constituencies would have a direct or significant impact on an organization's activities. Hence, the **general environment** represents all those constituents which might have an impact on the organization's activities, though their relevance might not always be clear. These would include economic forces such as interest rates, state of the economy and unemployment rates, international forces such as exchange rates, technological forces such as new product development, new information-processing equipment, political forces, environmental forces, etc. The **specific environment**, on the other hand, represents those strategic constituents who are directly relevant to the organization and have an impact on the organization's survival and growth. Unique to each organization, the specific environment would comprise customers, suppliers, public pressure groups, competitors, the government, labor unions, and trade associations.

> The specific environment of an organization represents those strategic constituents who are directly relevant to the organization and have an impact on the organization's survival and growth.

**Domain** refers to the range of products or services that an organization offers and the markets it serves. Depending on the domain chosen by the organization to operate in, the specific environment would be different for each organization. However, definition of the specific environment and their relative uncertainties is a function of perception. The same environment that one organization perceives as static and stable might be perceived as unstable and unpredictable by another organization. For example, a government-aided business school of long-standing repute and credentials is likely to find its environment relatively stable in terms of continued patronage from top recruiters, availability of best quality students and faculty, etc.; on the other hand, a newly set up private business school, despite being in the same domain of higher education, is likely to find the environment very unstable in terms of its ability to attract quality recruiters, students, faculty, funding, etc. Again, managers in different units of the same organization may have different perceptions of the specific or strategic components of the environment. Hence, to a large extent, organizations 'construct' or 'perceive' their environments and the related levels of uncertainties. Therefore, organizational strategies are essentially a response to their 'enacted' environment.

## 5.2 Sources of environmental uncertainty

An organization would like to have a steady and abundant supply of resources so that it can manage its domain and satisfy its stakeholders. All organizations, however, face uncertainties, which make it impossible for managers to control and predict the flow of resources. Three factors give rise to environmental uncertainty: its complexity, dynamism, and richness (capacity). As the environment becomes more complex, less stable, and poorer, the uncertainty in the environment increases. Figure 5.1 provides a three-dimensional depiction of environmental uncertainty.

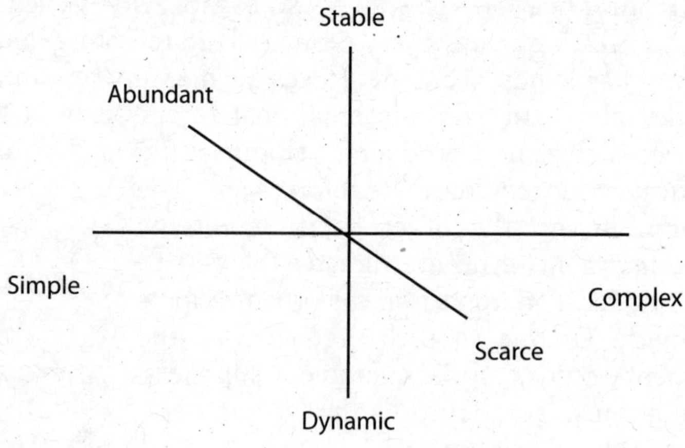


**Figure 5.1** *Dimensions of environmental uncertainty*

Each of the above dimensions is now discussed briefly:

5.2.1 *Environmental complexity* refers to the degree of heterogeneity and concentration among environmental elements. It is a function of the strength, number, and interconnectedness of the environmental constituents that an organization has to manage. The greater the number and dissimilarity of external elements relevant to an organization's operations, the more complex is the environment, and the more difficult it is to predict and control, thereby increasing the uncertainty.

5.2.2 *Environmental dynamism* is a function of how much and how quickly the environmental constituents change over time. The static dimension implies that few forces in the specific environment (e.g. number and nature of competitors, technological breakthroughs, etc.) change, thereby creating significantly less uncertainty for managers. The dynamic dimension, on the other hand, could include rapidly changing government regulations, new competition, rapid obsolescence of technology, or continually changing product preference by consumers, all of which increases the uncertainty faced by the organization, thereby adversely affecting the organization's effectiveness.

5.2.3 *Environmental capacity or richness* is a function of the amount of resources available to support an organization's domain. In rich environments, abundance of resources (skills and knowledge, technology, finance, raw materials, etc.) implies that organizations do not have to compete for resources; hence, uncertainties with relation to the availability of resources are low. Conversely, in poor environments, resources are scarce, and uncertainty is high since organizations have to compete among themselves for limited resources.

## 5.3 Structural responses to environmental uncertainty

It must be remembered that the above dimensions are not static; they might vary in degree over time. Hence, an environment which is simple, static, or rich today might become complex, dynamic, or poor in future. Therefore, managers have to scan their environments periodically to identify sources of uncertainty, and to deal with contingencies. The contingency theory represents a first step in this direction.

> The contingency theory holds that an organization should design its structure to fit the environment in which it operates.

*5.3.1 Contingency theory (Pennings, 1992):* This theory states that in order to manage its environment effectively, an organization should design its structure to fit the environment in which it operates. An organization's environment, in spite of complications in defining the exact dimensions, is likely to vary along a continuum ranging from extremely stable, rich, simple to extremely dynamic, poor, complex, with variations in the degree of stability, complexity, or dynamism. Additionally, different units or departments of the same organization are likely to face differing degrees of environmental stability or dynamism, and hence, different levels of uncertainty.

For example, the administration or accounts departments are likely to face relatively stable and simple environments, dealing as they do with a predictable set of entities. The marketing department of the same organization, on the other hand, is likely to face higher environmental uncertainty, dealing with rapidly changing customer preferences, speed of competitor offerings, etc. An organization operating in a relatively predictable and stable environment (assured supply of resources, less competition, steady demand of products/services, stable technology, etc.) is less likely to need swift and innovative responses to environmental demands. Hence, its activities can be more stable and amenable to routine. On the other hand, an organization operating in a relatively dynamic environment is likely to need faster response times, and hence, more flexibility and adaptability to rapidly changing environmental demands. This would call for greater flexibility and less routinization in its tasks.

Among the scholars who have studied the structural responses of organizations to environmental uncertainties, Burns and Stalker, Emery and Trist, and Lawrence and Lorsch deserve particular mention.

*5.3.1.1 Burns and Stalker:* Based on their study of 20 English and Scottish industrial firms, they concluded that the type of structure that exists in rapidly changing and dynamic environments is significantly different from that in organizations with stable environments. The effectiveness of a firm would be dependent on its structural fit with its environment. They categorized structures along two ends of a continuum, viz. **mechanistic structures** and **organic structures**. A comparison of the characteristic features of mechanistic and organic structures is given in Table 5.1. The more scarce, dynamic, and complex the environment, the more organic will be the structure. The more abundant, stable, and simple the environment, the more mechanistic, the preferred structure.

**Table 5.1** *Mechanistic vs organic structures*

| *Characteristic feature* | *Mechanistic* | *Organic* |
|---|---|---|
| Nature of environment | Relatively stable, simple, and predictable | Relatively dynamic, complex, and uncertain |
| Task definition | Tasks segmented from each other and isolated from the overall organizational goal; rigidly defined into specialties | Task loosely defined in the context of overall organizational goal; flexible; needs constant redefinition through continuous interaction among members |
| Communication | Vertical, primarily to communicate decisions and give instructions | Lateral; primarily to share information and solve problems |
| Authority | Position-based | Expertise-based |
| Control mechanisms | Hierarchical and impersonal (through rules, procedures, etc.) | Reciprocal; through interpersonal negotiations and contracts |
| Decision-making | Autocratic; programmed, computational | Participative, non-programmed, judgmental |
| Influence | Authority | Expertise |
| Formalization | High | Low |
| Centralization | High | Low |
| Integration | Low | High |

Hence, organizations operating in a relatively stable environment are likely to have a mechanistic structure, while those operating in relatively dynamic environments are likely to be more effective by employing an organic structural form, which enables them to respond speedily and flexibly to changing environmental demands. However, it should be kept in mind that no organization is purely mechanistic or organic; it moves toward one or the other based on the changing environment. When the environment is changing rapidly and immediate decisions are required to be taken, lower-level employees would have to be empowered to take decisions, as well as to facilitate rapid communication and information sharing to respond quickly to stakeholders' needs. Figure 5.2 provides a two-by-two framework for assessing changes in environmental uncertainty, along the complexity and stability dimensions

| ENVIRONMENTAL CHANGE | Simple | Complex |
|---|---|---|
| Stable | **Simple + Stable = Low uncertainty**<br>1. Small no. of external elements; elements are similar<br>2. Elements remain same or change slowly<br>*e.g. soft-drink bottlers, breweries, food processors* | **Complex + Stable = Low to medium uncertainty**<br>1. Large no. of external elements; elements are dissimilar<br>2. Elements remain same or change slowly<br>*e.g. educational institutions, appliance manufacturers, insurance companies* |
| Unstable | **Simple + Unstable = High to moderate uncertainty**<br>1. Small no. of external elements; elements are similar<br>2. Elements change frequently and unpredictably<br>*e.g. entertainment industry, fashion clothing, toy manufacturers* | **Complex + Stable = High uncertainty**<br>1. Large no. of external elements; elements are dissimilar<br>2. Elements change frequently and unpredictably<br>*e.g. Software firms, telecom, airlines* |

Simple ENVIRONMENTAL COMPLEXITY Complex

**Figure 5.2** *Framework for assessing environmental uncertainty (Source: R L Daft, 2004)*

of the environment, while Figure 5.3 depicts organizations' structural responses to changing levels of environmental uncertainties.

5.3.1.2 *Emery and Trist* have proposed a more sophisticated categorization of environments, whereby organizations might confront four kinds of environments, with varying levels of uncertainty:

(1) *placid–randomized*
(2) *placid–-clustered*
(3) *disturbed–reactive*
(4) *turbulent field*

ENVIRONMENTAL CHANGE (Stable → Unstable)

| | Simple | Complex |
|---|---|---|
| **Stable** | **Low uncertainty**<br>1. *Mechanistic structure: formal, centralized*<br>2. *Few departments*<br>3. *No integrating roles*<br>4. *Current operations orientation* | **Low to moderate uncertainty**<br>1. *Mechanistic structure: formal, centralized*<br>2. *Many departments, some boundary spanning*<br>3. *Few integrating roles*<br>4. *Some planning* |
| **Unstable** | **High to moderate uncertainty**<br>1. *Organic structure, teamwork: participative, decentralized*<br>2. *Few departments, much boundary spanning*<br>3. *Few integrating roles*<br>4. *Planning orientation* | **High uncertainty**<br>1. *Organic structure, teamwork: participative, decentralized*<br>2. *Many departments differentiated, extensive boundary spanning*<br>3. *Many integrating roles*<br>4. *Extensive planning, forecasting* |

Simple ENVIRONMENTAL COMPLEXITY Complex

**Figure 5.3** *Structural responses to uncertainty (Source: R L Daft, 2004)*

The level of complexity increases with every category, from (1) to (4).

- The relatively stable and unchanging **placid–randomized** environment poses the least level of threat or uncertainty to an organization. Demands for products or services are distributed randomly, and no single stakeholder can have significant impact on the organization's operations. The classical economist's state of pure competition, with enough demand, and low uncertainty, is analogous to this state. Any change takes place slowly over time and is random. The *Indian Railways* or the *Indian Postal Service* are good examples of organizations facing a placid–randomized environment.
- The rate of change is slow in the **placid–clustered** environment too, but the threats are more clustered, rather than random due to greater interlinkages of

environmental constituents. The steel majors (*Tata Steel, SAIL, RINL*) typically face this type of environment.

For both these categories, the level of uncertainty is relatively low; hence, their structures will tend to be more mechanistic in nature, with higher centralization.

- In a **disturbed–reactive** environment, there are many competitors, with two or three large players dominating. White goods manufacturers, automobile manufacturers and other assembly line producers fall in this category. The environment is more complex, and survival calls for flexibility in responses and a decentralized structure.
- Finally, the **turbulent–field** environment is the most dynamic, with the highest level of uncertainty, characterized as it is by unpredictable, ever-changing trends, high interrelatedness between constituents, and many competitors. Software companies and low-cost airlines are some examples of organizations operating in this environment.

For the last two categories, the level of uncertainty is high, and hence, would require more organic structures, to provide the required flexibility and adaptability to rapid changes. The current thinking is that the last two categories would become the dominant environmental form for most organizations.

*5.3.1.3 Lawrence and Lorsch's study:* Their study attempted to identify the influence of uncertainty in an organisation's external environment on its internal environment. It was found that successful firms have a better match between their internal and external environments compared to less successful firms. While the **external environment** might comprise dimensions such as rate of change, clarity of information that management has about the environment, and the amount of time it takes the management to get feedback about its actions from the environment, the **internal environment** is a function of a combination of differentiation and integration dimensions in the organization. **Differentiation** refers to the task segmentation, difference in attitudes, viewpoints, and behaviors, arising out of horizontal differentiation. **Integration** on the other hand refers to the quality of collaboration that exists among interdependent units or departments that are required to achieve unity of effort. Integration devices include rules and procedures, formal plans, hierarchy, and decision-making committees.

> Lawrence and Lorsch have differentiated between the internal and external environments of an organization and advocated a match between them for effectiveness.

According to Lawrence and Lorsch, the organization's interactions with its environment are through its subparts: different parts of organizations deal with different parts of the environment (termed sub-environment). Since different units of the organization have different strategic constituents, an organization's internal structure can be expected to differ from department to department, reflecting the characteristics of the sub-environment with which it interacts. Departmental differentiation is created to meet the needs of sub-environments. Since different departments are likely to face different levels of environmental uncertainties (the marketing department in an organization can be expected to face a more volatile environment compared to the accounts department), the structural characteristics of each internal subunit will be different, and a reflection of the sub-environment it faces. In successful organizations, there is a fit between the internal subunits and external sub-environments.

The main implications of Lawrence and Lorsch's findings are manifold:

1. The higher the turbulence, complexity, and diversity of the external environment, the higher is the degree of differentiation among an organization's subparts. This creates a greater need for formalization and integration, since different departmental managers are likely to have different goals.
2. Subunits of successful organizations meet the demands of their sub-environments. Hence, subunits facing more complex and turbulent environments are likely to have more organic structures, with multiple integration mechanisms, while subunits facing relatively stable environments may be expected to have more mechanistic structures.
3. The key lies in matching differentiation and integration activities, that is, creating differentiation between departments to deal with specific problems, and tasks facing the organization, and getting people to integrate and work as a cohesive unit toward the organization's goals.

While the concept of 'fit' is central to strategy and environment research, this concept has been refined even further by Venkataraman (1989) through his conceptualization of six different perspectives of 'fit':

1) 'fit' as moderation
2) 'fit' as mediation
3) 'fit' as matching
4) 'fit' as gestalts
5) 'fit' as profile-deviations, and
6) 'fit' as covariation

'Fit' as moderation implies that a particular type of strategy is likely to lead to the desired level of performance, depending on the extent to which the strategy 'fits' the environment in which the firm is operating. Hence, the extent of 'fit' acts as a moderator, variable between strategy and the firm's performance. In 'fit' as mediation, structure, an outcome of the 'fit' is assumed to be a mediating variable existing between strategy and the firm's performance. The 'fit' as matching perspective follows Chandler's classical hypotheses that the type of strategy should match the type of structure (e.g a diversification strategy will require a multi-divisional structure). The 'fit' as gestalt is best explained by Van de Ven (1979) as 'that characteristic of environmental niches and organizational forms (that) must be joined together in a particular configuration to achieve completeness in a description of a social system – like pieces of a puzzle must be put together in certain ways to obtain a complete image.' In 'fit' as profile deviation, the degree of adherence to the ideal strategy profile for a particular environment is deemed to be the extent of fit. Finally, in 'fit' as covariation, the concept of fit is operationalised through the notion of internal consistency in strategic resource deployments for major and minor strategic decisions, or the common thread of logic running through the firm's megastrategy.

According to the resource dependence theory, an organization should minimize its dependence on other organizations for supply of scarce resources by designing suitable influence strategies.

## 5.4 Environment–structure relationship

The above findings can therefore be broadly summarised as follows:

1. A dynamic environment has more influence on structure than a static environment; that is, there are likely to be more structural changes in a dynamic environment.
2. The higher the environmental turbulence and complexity, the higher is the complexity in organizations.
3. For boundary spanning units which need to be in constant touch with the environment, the extent of formalization is likely to be low, since these units have to be adaptive and responsive.
4. The higher the environmental complexity and turbulence, the higher is the expected level of decentralization. However, an extremely hostile environment drives organizations to temporarily centralize their structures (e.g. wildcat strike by employees, unions).

## 5.5 Organizational strategies for managing environmental uncertainties: Resource dependence theory

An organization's availability of resources from some of its stakeholders in the environment is dependent on the complexity, dynamism, and richness of the environment. As the environment becomes 'poorer' with increasing competition, there is greater uncertainty due to increased competition for these limited resources. In order to ensure access to resources, organizations need to devise various strategies.

The **resource dependence theory** (Pfeffer and Salancik, 1978) states that the goal of an organization is to minimize its dependence on other organizations for the supply of scarce resources in its environment, and to find ways of influencing them to make resources available. Some strategies that organizations commonly use to manage environmental uncertainties are discussed.

1. **Domain choice**: By changing their domain, the operating environment changes. Hence, an organization might change its domain of operation to one where competition is less, and greater resource availability is ensured.
2. **Recruitment** of people with the right type of professional competence and experience in operating in similar environments gives organizations an advantage in managing their environments.
3. **Vertical integration**: Assuming that the organization is financially sound, this strategy enables the organization to extend its control over the input and output ends of the environment and reduce supply and distribution uncertainties.
4. **Buffering** is a cost-effective alternative to vertical integration, and involves maintaining high inventories of input (e.g. raw materials and spare parts) and output (finished goods), to offset sudden changes in the demand or supply situation.
5. **Smoothening** refers to the strategy of offering attractive incentives to customers to 'smoothen' demand fluctuations to manageable limits, especially in sectors where such fluctuations, though predictable, are steep, and the organization has to repeatedly face problems of overload and under-utilization, alternately, across different seasons.
6. **Advertising** helps to create brand loyalty, lure away customers, and reduce competitive pressures, thus helping to stabilize demand and reduce associated uncertainties.
7. **Contracting**: By entering into long-term contracts with key suppliers and end-users, organizations can reduce demand- and supply-related uncertainties and ensure greater predictability in their resource availability.
8. **Mergers/acquisitions/strategic alliances**: Horizontal integrations such as these (also termed 'coalescing') provide strategic advantages to organizations, by supplementing resources, competencies, and technologies that they might individually lack, as well to increase their market share and thereby reduce demand uncertainties.
9. **Lobbying**: This is a type of political behavior by organizations to try and get favorable treatment from government and regulatory bodies through the formation of consortiums, business forums, etc. in various sectors, thereby trying to reduce the environmental uncertainties due to the regulatory environment, and to help stabilize business in a particular sector, by establishing norms and codes of conduct for businesses in that sector to follow, which would help to increase the predictability further.

Figure 5.4 provides a summarised depiction of the influence of environmental uncertainties on organizational actions.

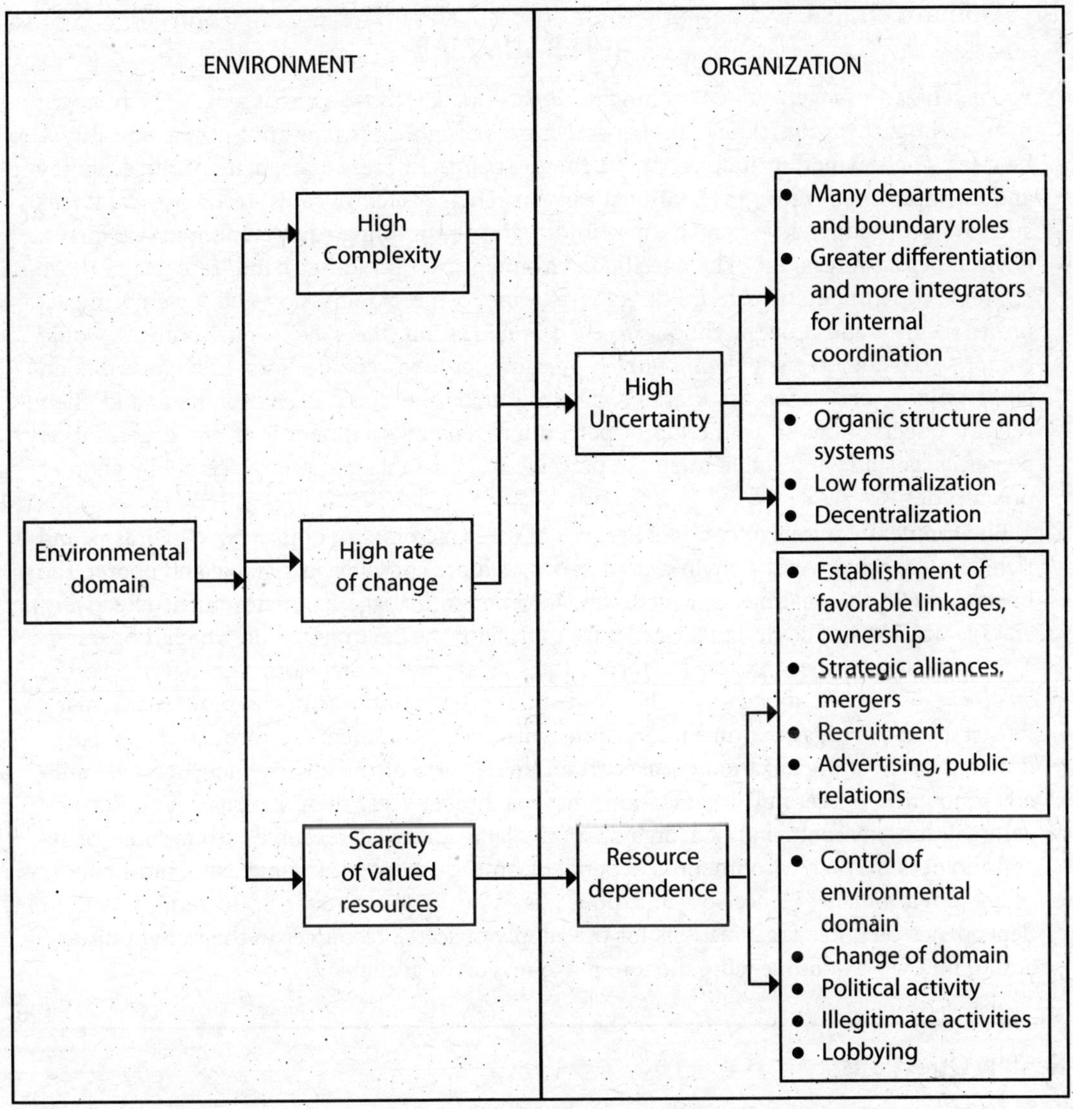


**Figure 5.4** *Environmental uncertainties and organizational actions*

## CHAPTER SUMMARY

An organization's general environment represents all those constituents which might have an impact on the organization's activities, though their relevance might not always be clear. These would include economic forces such as interest rates, state of the economy and unemployment rates, international forces such as exchange rates, technological forces such as new product development, new information-processing equipment, political forces, environmental forces, etc. The specific environment, on the other hand, represents those strategic constituents which are directly relevant to the organization and have an impact on its survival and growth. Unique to each organization, the specific environment would comprise customers, suppliers, public pressure groups, competitors, the government, labor unions, and trade associations. Definition of the specific environment and their relative uncertainties is a function of perception. The environment that one organization perceives as static and stable might be perceived as unstable and unpredictable by another organization.

Environmental uncertainty arises because of three factors: its complexity, dynamism, and richness (capacity). As the environment becomes more complex, less stable and poorer, the uncertainty in the environment increases. In order to manage its environment effectively, an organization should design its structure to fit with the environment in which it operates. The more scarce, dynamic, and complex the environment, the more organic will be the structure. The more abundant, stable, and simple the environment, the more mechanistic its structure. An organization's interactions with its environment are through its subparts: different parts of organizations deal with different parts of the environment (termed sub-environment). Successful organizations have a fit between their internal subunits and external sub-environments. An organization's availability of resources from some of its stakeholders in the environment is dependent on the complexity, dynamism, and richness of the environment. Hence, organizations resort to various strategies to minimize their dependence on other organizations for the supply of scarce resources in their environment, and to find ways of influencing them to make resources available.

### Review Questions

1. Based on your understanding of the systems theory of organizations, explain what is meant by the term 'environment' for organizations.
2. Explain the phrase: '*organizations "construct" or "perceive" their environments and the related levels of uncertainties*'.
3. Describe how the following structural forms: (a) functional, (b) divisional, and (c) matrix are designed to reduce environmental uncertainties.
4. With respect to the resource dependence theory, briefly explain any four strategic responses by organizations to counter environmental uncertainties.

## Project Assignment

Trawl though popular business articles and reports in the press for the past two years and identify at least one organization/real-life example for each of the resource dependence strategies described in the text above.

## CASE ILLUSTRATION: ENVIRONMENTAL CHALLENGES FOR *HRSL*

*Hi-Tech Robotic Systemz Limited (HRSL)*, the brain child of Anuj Kapuria, a technopreneur, is one of India's first robotics and artificial intelligence ventures, engaged in developing and deploying leading-edge robotics, computer/machine vision and artificial intelligence solutions. *HRSL* is a part of the *Hi-Tech Group* – a US $125 million multi-dimensional group of companies. Its solution spectrum integrates products and services to create a continuum of highly customizable as well as standardized applications for every sphere of life, and includes cutting edge products such as machine vision systems (to check critical dimensions and surface defects), automation (process/workstation, online/offline), robotics/ artificial intelligence, computer vision (access control solutions), material handling (bulk and unit), and embedded systems.

The vision of *HRSL* is to 'Change the world with *Made in HRS* Smart Robots serving every sphere of human life.' It aims to fulfill this dream through its mission of customer orientation with quality consciousness, successfully transforming path-breaking ideas into products, creating custom-made solutions, minimizing time to market, and nurturing innovative, motivated and committed people. The industries that *HRSL* serves are automotive, engineering, defense, and education. With 14 patents in state-of-the-art technology at present and a very special award – the Product Innovation Award from *Frost and Sullivan* – the pioneering spirit and synergy of convergence continues to foster technical excellence at *HRSL*.

Nonetheless, the escalating security problems besetting India of late, coupled with various other external changes have been creating substantial environmental turbulence for *HRSL* in recent times. There has been a surge in requirements from the defense sector for AI/hi-tech supported defense solutions such as UAV, moles, etc. At the same time, competition is increasing, with the entry of established players like *Kuka Engineering Solutions, Eicher Engineering*, etc., in designing reengineered business solutions. The automobile industries are becoming more quality conscious with stringent quality requirements, accompanied by a shift from manual to automation/robot-based applications. The same trend is being observed in conventional industries too, with increased acceptance of robotics-based solutions.

Given the very niche area of its operation, *HRSL* requires very high professional skills and competencies from its workforce. However, availability of such special talent and retention of talent in the face of increasing competition and rapid technological obsolescence is proving to be a herculean task for *HRSL*. Finally, government-mandated issues such as international sanctions on the use of sensitive technology, mandatory product disclosure and audit norms, lack of tax concessions and foreign currency fluctuations affecting imports of expensive equipment and technology are adding to the already considerable external pressures on *HRSL*.

Accordingly, the *HRSL* structure has been designed to address these uncertainties. The entire organization is divided into two clear verticals: Business Vertical 1 deals with automation projects, and is headed by a Vice-President and a DGM, the remaining layers in the relatively lean hierarchy comprises project managers, project leaders, their core teams, and staff. Business Vertical 2 focuses on R&D-based new product development, and has designated Centers of Excellence, peopled with competency leaders, designers, and developers. Given the high skill levels involved and the unique competencies, power and influence in the system is based on expertise rather than designation. Communication across the two business verticals is continuous and parallel. Tasks are defined in relation to overall organization goals, with very high levels of integration among the differentiated units. It now remains to be seen whether this structure is an effective fit with the environmental demands being faced by HRSL.

## Critical enquiry

*Analyze the environmental complexity, dynamism, and capacity faced by HRSL. How appropriate do you think is the structure at HRSL to counter these uncertainties? Give justifications for your answer.*

***Key words and phrases***: general environment, specific environment, domain, uncertainty, dynamism, capacity, richness, resource dependence, contingency approach, mechanistic and organic, sub-environment

CHAPTER 6

# Technology in Organizations

**CHAPTER OUTLINE**



## ORGANIZATIONAL INSIGHT

As early as 2002, *SAP*, the world's third largest software company, decided to radically transform itself from being merely a developer to a 'platform' company on its own Web-based platform solution: *NetWeaver*. This meant it had to open its platform to developers outside its own walls, who would drive innovative ways for businesses to use this platform to solve their business problems. It meant it had to 'talk' to a huge, new audience that had not been part of its prior focus: developers across the globe, who may or may not be *SAP* employees. *NetWeaver* would achieve ubiquity by breaking down its walls and embracing a larger, interactive community: the technologists inside and outside the company who recognized that a business solution is the ever-changing product of global collaboration. Additional objectives included a desire to increase adoption of *SAP* products and to provide a platform of innovation for *SAP* and its partners. Further, the *SAP Developer Network* (*SDN*) was seen as a way of providing a learning platform for new customers that would be facilitated by existing customers, and to accelerate the learning curve and adoption of new *SAP* products.

*SAP* is not alone in utilizing the power of social network technologies as a powerful business tool. *Dell Computer* has a strong blogging presence with its *Direct2Dell* forum. Not only is this a chance for bloggers to learn about new products, but it has also helped improve the organization's reputation. The amount of negative blogs dropped from 49% to 22% since the start of the site. *Dell* was able to connect with the customers and immediately address their concerns, comments, and questions through the blog.

*Starbucks* can be found on *Facebook, YouTube, Flickr, Twitter,* and on their own blogging site: 'My Starbucks Idea'. *Starbucks* is considered to have one of the best social media strategies. The focus is geared toward the needs, wants, and likes of existing companies and building that relationship to help gain new customers. *Target* has been successful on

*Facebook* by 'getting real' with customers and displaying products which resonate with the customers. *Target* took time to understand the medium and how to use it to benefit by connecting with the customer. They embraced the learning curve and did especially well by allowing customers to help shape the group.

*3M*'s reputation for innovation is well established, but the company wanted to include more staff in the ideation process. Traditionally, access to the company's annual 'Markets of the Future' brainstorming sessions was limited. By employing a new internal social networking platform, *3M* was able to foster creativity and collaboration among all its employees around the world. In the two weeks the tool was open to employees, it attracted more than 1200 people, who generated over 700 new ideas, which resulted in nine new markets for the company to explore.

Global names such as *Ernst and Young, Deloitte, Hallmark*, and *Apple* are all beneficiaries of *Facebook*'s recruitment strategies. The medium had been successful in creating a strategy to connect with passive users on a long-term basis to identify and encourage talent pools.

In the teaching profession too, professors are now using *Facebook* and *Twitter* as teaching tools to innovatively connect with college students through virtual lessons. Students are also using social media to reach out to experts all over the world to expand their knowledge.

The above instances exemplify the various ways that organizations are increasingly using the power of social network technologies to revolutionize their businesses and collaboratively reach out to stakeholders.

## 6.1 What is technology?

In Chapter 1, technology was depicted as one of the contextual determinants of an organization's structure. At a broad level, technology can be defined as *the combination of skills, knowledge, abilities, information, equipment (computers, machines etc.), techniques, and processes required to transform inputs into outputs in the organization*. Therefore, despite its strongly 'mechanical' connotation, this definition implies that technology as a concept is applicable to all organizations, irrespective of their field of operations. Hence, 'technology' would be as relevant to a manufacturing organization as it would be to a bank, a consumer products company, a consulting organization, an educational institution, or an NGO. Because each of them, notwithstanding the extent of usage of equipment and tools, either sophisticated or otherwise, would be using some process to convert inputs (raw materials, information, money, students, etc.) into output (products or services). Although technology is usually thought of in relation to the conversion stage, it is present in all the stages of an organization, viz. input, conversion, and output.

Technology can be defined as the combination of skills, knowledge, abilities, information, equipment (computers, machines, etc.) techniques, and processes required to transform inputs into output in the organization.

At the input stage, technology is mainly in terms of the skills, procedures, and techniques that allow each organizational function (HR, finance, materials management, etc.) to handle relationships with outside stakeholders to ensure a steady flow of resources into the organizational system. At the conversion stage, technology largely takes the form of a combination of machines, techniques, and work procedures to transform these inputs into output. Finally, at the output stage, technology (quality testing, warehousing, distribution, managing after-sales service) allows an organization to effectively dispose of finished goods and services to the external stakeholders. By using technology to deliver greater value to its external and internal stakeholders (better quality of product and service, timely delivery, and faster response time, through better and more efficient internal processes), an organization becomes more effective on all of the effectiveness parameters discussed in Chapter 2.

While this concept of technology seems elegant enough, problems arise when we attempt to drill down to more specific levels, and try to specify exactly what technology is, by means of measurable constructs. Since the concept subsumes many different ideas, it would be difficult to find a general variable describing technology. Researchers have used various conceptualizations to define and measure technology, viz. interdependence among jobs, work-flow activities, knowledge/skill level required for the job, etc. However, each of these constructs is likely to yield different values for the same organization. Hence, when attempting to understand the effect of technology on organizational structure, the major problem would be its measurement. The following sections will deal with some of the seminal contributions made by researchers in this area. At the end, these studies will be integrated to get a comprehensive idea of how technology influences an organization's design parameters. Social network technologies or Web 2.0 applications are now becoming indispensable aspects of an organization's processes and systems. Hence, the concluding section is devoted to a deliberation on the design implications of organizations and processes, in this context.

## 6.2 Technology–structure studies

### 6.2.1 Woodward's approach

One of the pioneering studies on the technology–structure relationship was undertaken by Joan Woodward, in a sample of 100 British manufacturing firms. Ironically, the initial focus of her work had nothing to do with technology: she was attempting to establish a correlation between an organization's structural configuration and its effectiveness, and identifying an optimum structure which was most effective. Her first attempts in this direction proved totally inconclusive. It was only when she grouped the organizations on the basis of the technology followed by them, that she was able to identify the relationship between structure and technology. Since all the firms were involved in manufacturing, Woodward categorized them on the basis of three types of production process: unit, mass, or process production, depending on the technical complexity of these processes. Figure 6.1 below provides a pictorial depiction of this three-stage categorization.

| Group | Type of production | Technical complexity |
|---|---|---|
| **Group I** Small-batch, unit production | 1. Production of single pieces to customer orders | **Low** |
| | 2. Production of technically complex units, one by one | ↑ |
| | 3. Fabrication of large equipment in stages | |
| | 4. Production of pieces in small batches | |
| **Group II** Large-batch, mass production | 5. Production of components in large batches subsequently assembled diversely | |
| | 6. Production of large batches, assembly line type | **Technical complexity** |
| | 7. Mass production | |
| **Group III** Continuous process production | 8. Continuous process production combined with preparation of a product for sale by large-batch or mass production methods | |
| | 9. Continuous process production of chemicals in batches | ↓ |
| | 10. Continuous flow production of liquids, gases and solid shapes | **High** |

**Figure 6.1** *Woodward's classification of manufacturing technologies*

In **unit** or **small batch technologies**, the product is manufactured in small batches, according to the customer's specifications (e.g. small machine parts, fashion-clothing, boutiques, aircraft manufacturing units). Products are highly diverse and heterogeneous. This technology is characterized by a relative lack of standardization of products, lot size, order time, delivery requirements, etc. Thus, it is difficult to strictly plan, schedule, and monitor the production operations.

At the **mass production level**, products of relatively uniform specifications are manufactured in large quantities (e.g. automobile assembly lines, bottling plants, white goods and appliances, etc.). This technology allows a high degree of routinization of operational activities, and therefore can be standardized, scheduled, and monitored.

**Continuous process technologies** are extremely complex production systems, involving highly automated and programmed activities (e.g. steel making, cement production, petroleum and chemical processing, etc.). While this process also involves outputs in large standardized quantities, the transformation happens through a series of interlinked activities through machines rather than human intervention.

Woodward concluded that there was a distinct relationship between these technology categorizations and the structural configuration of these forms, and effectiveness depended on the 'fit' between technology and structure, that is, **organizations that developed structures conforming to their technologies were more successful than those who did not**. Hence, for example, it was found that vertical differentiation increased with an increase in technological complexity. And as technological complexity increased, the proportion of administrative and support staff personnel also increased, possibly as a response to the increased need for coordination between so many differentiated units. Table 6.1 summarises Woodward's findings:

> Woodward maintained that organizations whose structures conformed to their technologies were more effective than those whose technologies did not.

Woodward's study, which was confined only to British manufacturing firms, was considered to have limited generalizability. Her methodology (subjective observations and interviews) has also been subjected to criticism. However, her greatest contribution lies in having highlighted the technology imperative, and establishing technology as a critical determinant of structure.

### 6.2.2 Perrow's approach

One of the main criticisms of Woodward's study, namely, its manufacturing bias, was addressed by Perrow's study. Perrow looked at knowledge technology rather than manufacturing technology, and defined technology as: '*...the action that an individual performs upon an object, with or without the aid of tools or mechanical devices, in order to make some change in that object.*' This definition is broad enough to subsume the concepts of both manufacturing and service operations of organizations. **Perrow's framework** described how technological uncertainty or the lack of it

> Perrow's concept of knowledge technology encompasses two dimensions of task variability and problem analyzability, which determine the extent of technological uncertainty and its effect on structure.

**Table 6.1** *Woodward's relationship between technological complexity and structure*

| *STRUCTURAL CHARACTERISTICS* | *Low* ← *Technology* → *High* | | |
|---|---|---|---|
| | *Unit production* | *Mass production* | *Process production* |
| No. of vertical levels | 3 | 4 | 6 |
| Supervisor's span of control | 24 | 48 | 14 |
| Manager/total employee ratio | 1:23 | 1:16 | 1:8 |
| Proportion of skilled workers | High | Low | High |
| Overall complexity | Low | High | Low |
| Formalization | Low | High | Low |
| Centralization | Low | High | Low |
| Approximate shape of Organization | 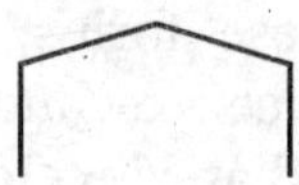 | 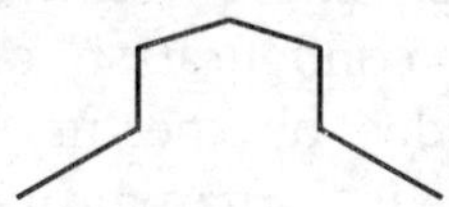 | 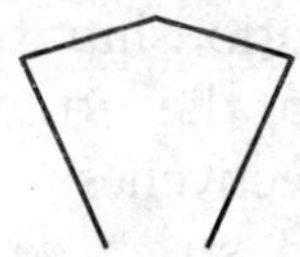 |
| | Relatively flat, with narrow span of control | Relatively tall with wide span of control | Very tall with very narrow span of control |

determined an organization's structure, and suggested that (1) task variability and (2) problem analyzability were the two dimensions of technology which affected the extent of this uncertainty.

**Task variability** refers to the number of exceptions an individual is likely to encounter in his work. A highly routine job would have fewer exceptions, whereas a job with a great deal of variety would have many exceptions. Hence, task variability is evaluated along a *variety–routineness* continuum. Some commonly asked questions to measure this dimension (on a seven-point scale) include items such as:

- ❒ *How many of these tasks are the same from day to day?*
- ❒ *To what extent would you say your work is routine?*
- ❒ *People in this unit do about the same job in the same way most of the time.*
- ❒ *Basically, unit members perform repetitive activities in doing their jobs.*
- ❒ *How repetitious are your duties?*

**Problem analyzability**, on the other hand, refers to the degree to which search activities are needed to solve a problem. At one extreme, the search can be very well defined, by using logic and analytical reasoning; on the other, the problem can be ill-defined, without any formal or preexisting search technique or archive to use. Some of the following items measure the degree of analyzability of the problem:

- ❒ *To what extent is there a clearly known way to do the major types of work you normally encounter?*
- ❒ *To what extent is there a clearly defined body of knowledge of subject matter which can guide you in doing your work?*
- ❒ *To what extent is there an understandable sequence of steps that can be followed in doing your work?*
- ❒ *To what extent can you actually rely on established procedures and practices to do your work?*

A two-by-two matrix of these two dimensions (Figure 6.2) identifies four different types of technology: routine, engineering, craft, and non-routine, and the structural configurations they are likely to follow:

**Routine technology**, with few exceptions and easy-to-analyze problems, appears similar to Woodward's mass production technology. These call for formal, centralized, and mechanistic structures, where control and coordination are through rigid rules and strict planning. **Engineering technology** would have many exceptions, but is also facilitated by the existence of huge databases and case studies, which make the solution easy to search for and analyze in a systematic and logical manner. This

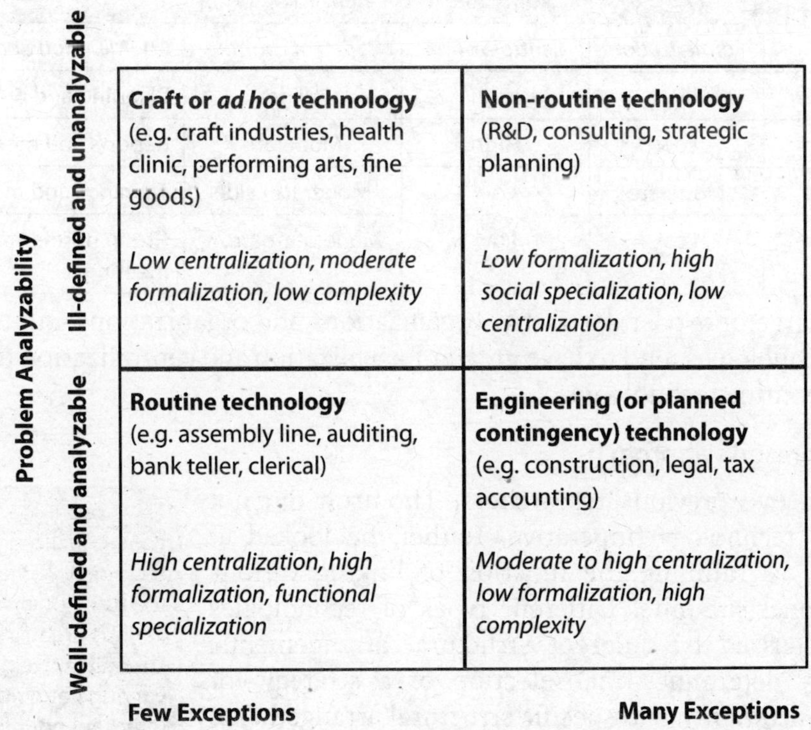


**Figure 6.2** *Perrow's classification of technologies*

requires a more flexible though centralized and formalized structure, to ensure consistency in output quality. Frequent reports and meetings of technical personnel form the integration and coordinating mechanisms. **Craft technologies** deal with relatively difficult problems but with a limited set of options compared to engineering. These are characterized by decentralized decision-making among the specialists lower down the ranks; meetings and training are the coordinating mechanisms. Finally, **non-routine technologies** have many exceptions, and very often, problems which are difficult to search for or analyze. They are similar to Woodward's unit production technology. Structurally, these organizations would require a high degree of flexibility and team work, with decentralization, and coordination achieved through informal interactions and adjustments.

At a more simplistic level, routine and engineering can be subsumed under 'routine', while non-routine and craft can be subsumed under 'non-routine', on a routine–non-routine continuum. Perrow's technology–structure predictions have been summarised in Table 6.2.

**Table 6.2** *Perrow's technology–structure predictions*

| *Structural Characteristics* | | | | |
|---|---|---|---|---|
| *Technology* | *Formalization* | *Centralization* | *Span of control* | *Coordination and control* |
| Routine | High | High | Wide | Planning and rigid rules |
| Engineering | Low | High | Moderate | Reports and meetings |
| Craft | Moderate | Low | Moderate-wide | Trainings and meetings |
| Non-routine | Low | Low | Moderate-narrow | Group norms and group meetings |

By and large, it is postulated that organizations and organizational subunits with routine technologies tend to have greater formalization and centralization than those with non-routine technologies.

### 6.2.3 Thomson's approach

> Thompson conceptualized technology as fulfilling the function of linking various organizational subunits through the varying nature of task interdependence.

Unlike the two previous researchers, Thomson did not go by the technology imperative. Rather, he looked at technology as fulfilling the function of linking various organizational subunits. Different types of technologies are characterized by different structural arrangements. Technology determines the selection of a strategy for reducing uncertainty, and specific structural arrangements can facilitate uncertainty reduction. The type of technology would be influenced by the nature of task interdependence existing between organizational subunits. Interdependence can be of three types:

(1) long-linked or sequential interdependence
(2) mediating or pooled interdependence
(3) intensive or reciprocal interdependence

**Long-linked technology** (Figure 6.3) is characterized by a fixed sequence of repetitive steps, as exemplified by organizations involved in mass production goods, cafeterias, restaurants, etc. Here, the output of the preceding subunit becomes the input of the succeeding subunit.

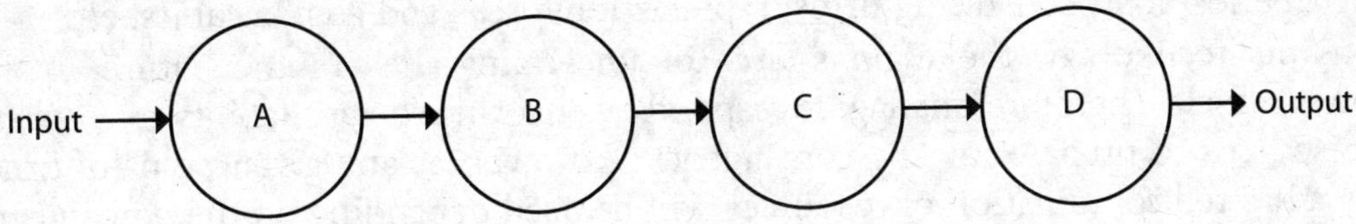


**Figure 6.3** *Sequential interdependence*

Thus, the arrangement of activities in each subunit is linked to the activities of the subunits which precede or follow in the chain. Hence, the main sources of uncertainties for the management lie in the input and output sides of the organization's chain. Acquiring raw materials and inputs, and disposing of finished goods become major areas of concern. As a result, management would try and control the input and output. A common strategy by managers in this case is maintaining slack resources or extra inventory of raw material and finished goods to offset uncertainties due to sudden emergencies. However, this has implications in terms of higher inventory carrying costs, wastage, etc. Vertical integration (both forward and backward) is one of the most popular strategies adopted by organizations to try and encompass the input and output sides of the chain within its boundaries.

**Mediating technology** (Figure 6.4) is one which attempts to link the input and output sides of an organization. Some common examples would include banks, post offices, recruitment agencies, retail stores, marriage bureaus, online auction sites, etc. The mediator performs an interchange function, linking units that are otherwise independent. The clients on either side do not know each other, but the mediator's success depends on attracting both. In this case, the organization's main source of uncertainty lies in its potential dependency on its clients on both sides.

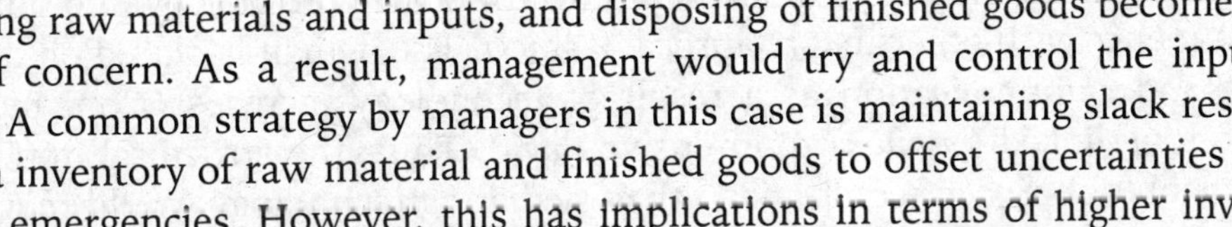


**Figure 6.4** *Pooled interdependence*

A common strategy to deal with this uncertainty would be to increase the population of clients served, to reduce dependence on one or a handful of clients and client transactions.

**Intensive technology** (Figure 6.5) is designed to meet the requirements of complex tasks, in which the variety of problems that might be encountered cannot be accurately predicted beforehand. In other words, this represents a customized response to a diverse set of contingencies. The exact response depends on the nature of the problem and the variety of problems. Common examples would include specialty hospitals, consulting firms, rapid action forces and combat units, etc.

In this technology, the main source of uncertainty lies in the nature of the problem itself. Therefore, managers respond by ensuring the availability of a variety of resources to prepare for any contingency. However, at any given point of time, only a limited combination of resources will be used depending on the demands of the situation. Coordination is achieved through mutual adjustment among these multiple resources. The selection, combination, and ordering of these resources would depend on reciprocal feedback from the output.

In long-linked technology, procedures are highly standardized and must be performed in a specified serial order. In mediating technology, two or more units each contribute separately to a larger unit. In intensive technology, the outputs of units influence each other in a reciprocal fashion. The demands placed on decision-making and communication as a result of technology increases from mediating (*low*) to long-linked (*medium*) to intensive (*high*). Thus, the structural implications of Thomson's approach would mean that mediating technology would require low complexity and high formalization; long-linked technology would call for moderate complexity and formalization, while the huge amount of flexibility required in intensive technology would imply high complexity, low formalization, and moderate to high decentralization, at least for the specialized activities.

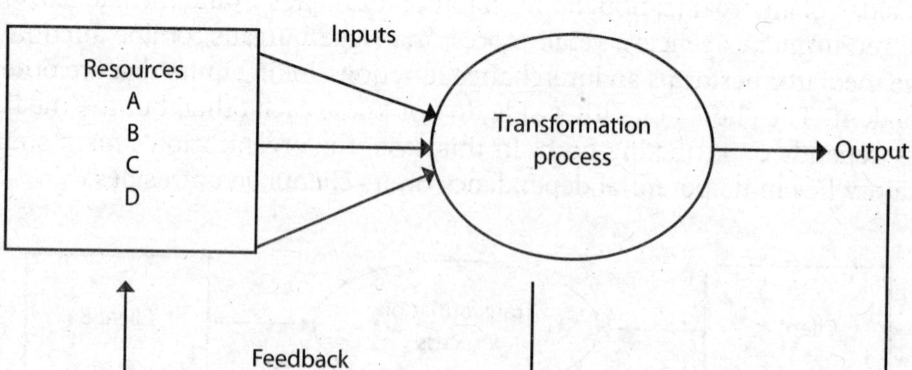


**Figure 6.5** *Reciprocal interdependence*

Table 6.3 summarises Thomson's categorizations described above.

**Table 6.3** *Technology and task interdependence: Thomson's typologies*

| *Type of technology* | *Form of task interdependence* | *Main type of coordination* | *Strategy for reducing uncertainty* | *Cost of coordination* |
|---|---|---|---|---|
| Mediating | Pooled | Standardization | Increase in number of customers served | Low |
| Long-linked | Sequential | Planning and scheduling | 1. Slack resources<br>2. Vertical integration | Medium |
| Intensive | Reciprocal | Mutual adjustment | Specialism and diversity of task activities | High |

### 6.2.4 Common theme

A comparison of the above three approaches indicates that whatever might be the terminology adopted, all three have addressed some common themes. Table 6.4 summarises the commonality among the three approaches.

**Table 6.4** *Common themes*

| *Contributor* | *Technology* | |
|---|---|---|
| | *Routine* | *Non-routine* |
| Woodward | Mass, process | Unit |
| Perrow | Routine, Engineering | Craft, Non-routine |
| Thompson | Long-linked, mediating | Intensive |

It is clear that the approaches to technology taken by the researchers would be relevant to both manufacturing and service organizations. However, there are certain inherent differences between manufacturing (product) and service technologies (Table 6.5), which would have serious structural implications.

**Table 6.5** *Manufacturing and service technologies*

| *Service technology* | *Manufacturing technology* |
|---|---|
| 1. Intangible product<br>2. Production and consumption take place simultaneously<br>3. Labor and knowledge intensive<br>4. Customer interaction generally high<br>5. Human element is very important<br>6. Quality is perceived and difficult to measure<br>7. Rapid response time usually necessary<br>8. Site of facility is extremely important | 1. Tangible product<br>2. Production can be inventoried for later consumption<br>3. Capital asset intensive<br>4. Little direct customer interaction<br>5. Human element may be less important<br>6. Quality is directly measured<br>7. Longer response time is acceptable<br>8. Site of facility is moderately important |

A representative structural dimension for each of these technology types might be as shown in Table 6.6 below:

**Table 6.6** *Structural dimensions: Service vs product technologies*

| *Structure* | *Service* | *Product* |
|---|---|---|
| 1. Separate boundary roles | Few | Many |
| 2. Geographical dispersion | Much | Little |
| 3. Decision making | Decentralized | Centralized |
| 4. Formalization | Lower | Higher |
| | *Human Resources* | |
| 1. Employee skill level | Higher | Lower |
| 2. Skill emphasis | Interpersonal | Technical |

## 6.3 Technology–structure relationship

A summary of the above discussions appears to indicate the following relationships between technology (on a routine–non-routine continuum) and various structural dimensions:

6.3.1 *Technology and complexity:* Routine technology is positively associated with low complexity. While functional specialization might be comparatively higher to handle repetitive tasks, it would not need too many different units or high level of skills. The span of control is also likely to be higher, requiring lower vertical differentiation. On the other hand, non-routine technology would require highly complex structures, both in terms of skill levels required, as well as different units to handle specialized functions, narrow spans of control, and hence, high vertical differentiation. Customized responses require greater use of specialists, and the problems confronted by managers are unique and non-programmable.

6.3.2 *Technology and formalization:* Routine technology appears to be positively correlated to high formalization. It is associated with standardization and consistency in output quality, both of which require formal procedures and rules to be followed, and the presence of detailed job descriptions. The cost for developing such detailed set of rules and procedures is offset by the economies that result from the volumes associated with mass production. Non-routine technology on the other hand, calling for unique, customized responses which are likely to differ on a case-by-case basis, requires a great degree of flexibility and autonomy, implying low formalization, and coordination achieved through meetings and interactions, rather than formalized procedures.

6.3.3 *Technology and centralization:* Unlike the above two dimensions, this relationship is not immediately apparent or direct in nature. While intuitively it might appear as if routine technology is positively associated with high centralization, it might also be argued that in routine technology, decision-making can be delegated to lower levels since tasks are repetitive, require far lower levels of skills, and hence are more amenable to decentralization. As opposed to this, in non-routine technology, requiring very specialized skill levels, decision-making can only be concentrated in the hands of a few top specialists. Hence, the technology–centralization relationship appears to be ambiguous. However, when this relationship is moderated by the extent of formalization, a clearer explanation appears possible. Hence, routine technologies can have decentralization provided a high degree of formalization exists, since the existence of well-defined sets of rules implies that even lower-level employees will know what to do. In cases where the extent of formalization is low, however, decision-making will have to be more centralized. For non-routine technologies calling for customized responses, decision-making will have to be decentralized among specialists lower down in the ranks, to allow greater flexibility and autonomy for faster speed of response.

## 6.4 Social network technology, knowledge management, and organizational design

With the proliferation of the Internet and the worldwide web, people and organizations are now living increasingly hybrid lives, where the physical and the digital, the real and the virtual, interact. This technology-enabled *'blurring'* of real and virtual boundaries has affected the flow of knowledge and information in both industrial and social situations (Jordan, 2009). As technological advancements enable increased communication and faster information-flow among different groups of stakeholders, organizational boundaries are becoming more permeable to community and social influences, with an informed public demanding that organizations become socially, financially, and environmentally accountable in their business dealings.

Online social networks are webs of relationships that grow from computer-mediated discussions. The webs grow from conversations among people who share a common affinity (e.g., they work for the same company, department, or in the same discipline) and who differ in other ways (e.g., they are in different locations, keep different hours, specialize in different disciplines, work for different companies). When the people are distributed across time and space, these conversations need to take place online, over an intranet or private internet forum. Within a company, a well-tuned online social network can enhance the company's collective knowledge and sharpen its ability to act on what people know in time to be effective. Social networks grow from the personal interactions of human beings over time, as well as from the technological infrastructure that connects those humans. This means that growing a successful online social network requires social know-how as well as technical expertise.

The term Web 2.0 or 'social software' covers a range of software tools which allow users to interact and share data with other users, primarily via the web. Blogs, wikis, social networking websites, such as *Facebook* and *Twitter*, are examples of some of the tools that are used to share and collaborate in educational, social, and business contexts. The key aspect of a social software tool is that it involves wider participation in the creation of information, which is shared (Minocha, 2009). The rationale underpinning social networking is the virtuous circle of:

- generating something of personal use
- which benefits the larger network as a whole
- which in turn creates additional value for the original user

Clearly, the potential for its contribution to overall organizational learning is immense (Bartlett-Bragg, 2009). The interactivity of Web 2.0 or social software provides two-way communication and so lends itself to collaboration, co-operation and the development of a learning community. This is in contrast with the more traditional approach of individuals working in isolation and often in competition with each other. By integrating social software, organizations can generate powerful learning networks which create a platform that extends from simple individual actions, to links that connect people for a common learning goal, to connecting learners with others beyond the boundaries of their current learning contexts. From a knowledge management perspective, enterprise social networks benefit organizations by helping to connect employees, promote information discovery and spark knowledge sharing (Kleinschmidt, 2009).

Social software tools fit into social network theory, harnessing the 'strength of weak ties': if we want novelty and innovation, our weak ties, or our more distant colleagues and acquaintances, are actually the place to go first, because they have less overlap with our knowledge base and our social network (Mangelsdorf, 2010). Another body of social network literature talks about the tragedy of not having a tie at all. This happens when social networks are isolated from each other and there is a structural hole between them; there may be great work going on in both networks, but they are not aware of each other, and hence, no cross-pollination can occur. This is a place where a weak tie could be a bridge between the two networks. Social software tools like *Facebook* provide just such a bridge. The same thing is true at the level of potential ties. A blogosphere where everybody is narrating their work is a great way to find people whose work one should know and to convert potential ties into actual ones.

Social software tools have transformed the online landscape to the extent that information sharing is now the norm for multitudes of people. Many companies, however, remain pretty skeptical about the implications of welcoming social networking tools into the workplace. The openness that characterizes this development goes against established principles, especially those founded on command and control. To be fair, these apprehensions are perfectly understandable, given potential issues that include:

- Security concerns such as the fear of confidential systems or information being accidentally or deliberately leaked to external sources.
- Trust and privacy: For instance, contacts made through social networking may potentially be unknown or unverified.
- Knowing what, how much, when and how to share.

There is no getting away from the fact that the trend is here to stay. According to *Facebook* records, many employees of leading organizations are already subscribers, including 33,000 from *IBM*, 30,000 from *Microsoft* and 20,000 who work at *Accenture* (Lavenda, 2008), and the numbers are growing exponentially. Companies that refuse to acknowledge the significance of such evidence clearly do so at their peril. All this does not stop some organizational leaders from clinging on to the perception that social networking sites are a waste of time. At the end of the day, business is all about building and sustaining relationships, be it with employees, customers, or stakeholders.

The openness that characterizes this development goes against established principles, especially those founded on command and control. With increased usage, it is hoped that company leaders may start to appreciate that social networking tools and technologies can be utilized to:

- Enable speedier location, access, and sharing of information
- Enable more efficient leverage of contacts and knowledge
- Help retain key employees by improving satisfaction in the workplace
- Break down time and geographical boundaries to improve communication between widely dispersed personnel
- Reduce expenses
- Improve productivity and competitiveness

Thoughtfully planned and knowledgeably implemented, online social networks can enable an organization to:

- Create an early warning system.
- Make sure knowledge gets to people who can act on it in time.
- Connect people and build relationships across boundaries of geography or disciplines.
- Provide an ongoing context for knowledge exchange that can be far more effective than memoranda.
- Attune everyone in the organization to each other's needs – more people will know who knows what, and will know it faster.
- Multiply intellectual capital by the power of social capital, reducing social friction and encouraging social cohesion.

- Create an ongoing, shared social space for people who are geographically dispersed.
- Amplify innovation – when groups get excited by what they can do online, they go beyond problem-solving and start inventing together.
- Create a community memory for group deliberation and brainstorming that stimulates the capture of ideas and facilitates finding information when it is needed.
- Improve the way individuals think collectively – moving from knowledge-sharing to collective knowing.
- Turn training into a continuous process, not divorced from normal business processes.
- Attract and retain the best employees by providing access to social capital that is only available within the organization.

Some organizations are recognizing the potential for Web 2.0 technologies to impact within specific business areas. Customer service is one such example. Times change and trends come and go, but there is no escaping the fact that interaction with one's clients remains crucial. That it also functions as a key source of market intelligence should likewise not be ignored. The concept of 'extra-preneurship' (Snyder, 2005) is gaining recognition. Social software facilitates online collaborations between employees of a company and the employees of their outsourced suppliers and service providers to create virtually integrated networks of efficient, high-quality specialists from independent firms, and enhances the ability to leverage customers as a key input to production.

However, notwithstanding the benefits of such network usages (attracting and retaining talent, encouraging creative work environments, enabling work–life balance, improving managerial decision-making, greater transparency of processes, greater involvement of customers and employees in improving business performance), challenges to their successful implementation are immense. Not the least among them is the culture and mindset change required, moving away from a change in perspective, from turfs to teams, from hoarding knowledge to sharing knowledge, from ownership (of knowledge) to access (to knowledge), and from competition to collaboration. While digital technology enables organizations to respond faster to stakeholder concerns, it also throws up attendant challenges in the form of new business configurations, new circles of power, new connections, new networks, issues pertaining to data security, greater possibilities for attrition of talent, increased dependence on trust and the need for strict regulatory mechanisms to discourage wrongful exploitation of its potential.

These are merely an indication of the dichotomous nature of the issue under discussion, namely, the potential of IT usage for greater business effectiveness and economic growth, and the attendant challenges for exploitation of the same. It remains to be seen how, through a process of effective structuration and design, organizations are proposing to address these issues and contribute more meaningfully for more ethical and socially relevant economic growth.

### 6.4.1 Organizational design implications

The transition from an economy based on materials to an economy based on flows of information has created considerable challenges for organization design by unfettering many organizational aspects from physical constraints. From a structural perspective, organizations are realizing that the traditional organizational chart is no longer an accurate depiction of how and by whom work gets done in modern organizations (McCluskey and Korobow, 2009). In today's increasingly dynamic and unpredictable environment, centralized and/or hierarchical organizational forms can no longer be pursued: some key questions that the organizational chart fails to answer are 'who knows what' and 'where do I go for information?' In the new digital economy, where intra- and inter-organizational collaborations are becoming more central to organizational effectiveness, attention must be paid to the relationships that people weave and draw upon while accomplishing their work. One of the starkest contrasts between conventional thinking about organizations and the newer models is that change is taken for granted in the new forms. Rather than view organizations as stable structures designed to absorb uncertainty, many thinkers today suggest that new organizations must build in flexibility and the capacity to handle constant change. Thus, we expect both efficiency and innovation, both global control and local responsiveness, both centralized vision and decentralized autonomy, and so on.

### 6.4.2 Organization design challenges

In order to address these apparent contradictions, the resulting new organizational forms will have to cope with four core issues or challenges: *interdependence*, *disembodiment*, *velocity*, and *power* (Child and McGrath, 2001).

- *Interdependence*: Traditionally, the extent to which an organization could operate interdependently with other organizations was constrained by limits imposed by information-processing capacity and physical distance. As information and communications technologies have advanced, interdependent operations are a much more cost-effective possibility than they were formerly. This development, combined with changes in regulatory regimes and capital flows, has made interdependent operations desirable. Although any social system exhibits interdependence, the level of interdependence that is possible today is unprecedented. A key aspect of interdependent systems is that the outcome for any party to a transaction is fundamentally entwined with the actions of and outcomes for other players. Further, actions taken by one player in an interdependent system can have unforeseen and far-reaching consequences for other actors. This meshing makes the management of interdependent systems particularly complex, because although authority is dispersed, the actions taken by any member of an interdependent network influence others. A change in one component of an interdependent system produces unpredictable changes in others, thus leading to coordination problems.

- *Disembodiment*: Traditional organizations presumed tight links between the outputs, ownership and control of assets. Performance had to do with how efficiently assets were deployed, relative to those of other firms. The major shift that has taken place in the information economy is to disembody performance from asset ownership. In information-intensive businesses, it is not necessary to physically own an asset to utilize it. For instance, to the extent that general purpose assets can be used to create an offering, a firm can elect not to own the asset.
- *Velocity*: Greater velocity has come to characterize virtually all aspects of organizational functioning, from internal communications to product development to competitive interchange. Apart from the enabling effects of new communication technologies, increased velocity can also be attributed to the liberalization of trade and of capital movements and to decreases in the cost of travel and transportation. One effect of this is to increase the speed at which organizations are expected to respond. When capital can swiftly and inexpensively move across borders and into and out of securities portfolios, the result is greater volatility.
- *Power*: One of the most profound shifts in the economy is the shift from power derived from the possession of tangible assets and inputs to power derived from the possession of knowledge and information. A longstanding practical concern with concentration of power at the top of bureaucracies is now exacerbated by the increasing scope of these organizations. For example, the number of banking institutions in the United States has declined by 36% since 1984, at the same time that financial activity has enjoyed significant growth. Although mega global firms often compete fiercely among themselves, there is nonetheless a growing asymmetry of power between the managerial agents in charge of them and most other groups in society, including consumers, employees and members of the local communities in which the firms' operations are located. Addressing new power asymmetries is thus a key challenge for new organizational forms. At the individual level too, this entails a shift in power center concentration, from hierarchically designated positions of authority to individuals who possess knowledge and information, irrespective of their formal designations in the organizational hierarchy.

### 6.4.3 Networked organizations

Organizations are facing design and performance issues as their environments, markets, products and service offerings, and stakeholder relationships have become more complex. The adoption of social software in organizations is fundamentally altering the way information is shared and knowledge is created and used, for enhanced organizational performance. The open nature of social networking, the flexibility of the Internet, the cultural diversity and enhanced interactivity, and the fact that they can simultaneously serve several different audiences turns them into an environment that businesses can no longer ignore. As a result, networked forms of organizations are increasingly becoming the norm. However, they also bring with them attendant challenges which need to be addressed.

### 6.4.4 Converting social networks in organizations into internal value-creating networks

Organizational networks can be considered value conversion networks, or value networks (Allee, 2009). A value network can be defined as 'any purposeful group of people or organizations creating social and economic good through complex dynamic exchanges of tangible and intangible value' (Allee, 2009). Tangible exchanges are formally structured or contractual interactions directly generating revenue or funding. Intangible exchanges consist of all the informal, often *ad hoc*, yet critical supporting exchanges of information, support, and benefits. Participants in a value network, either individually or collectively, utilize their tangible and intangible asset base by assuming or creating roles that convert those assets into more negotiable forms of value that can be delivered to other roles through the execution of a transaction. In turn, the true value of deliverables received is realized by participants when they convert them into gains or improvements in tangible or intangible assets. The basic challenge of the network orientation is the same challenge we have been dealing with in organizations for two decades with the focus on business processes: the world of human interactions and the world of business transactions are treated as two completely different worlds. Human interactions are dealt with in organizational charts, team charters, performance reviews, organizational culture, change management, and training. Business transactions are managed in the world of process maps, workflow systems, applications, and technology. Supporting network patterns of organization requires addressing several key issues:

*Supporting 'roles'*: Most staffing and resource efforts focus on filling seats or 'jobs' on the formal organization chart. Common HR practice is not to seek people who can fill multiple roles, but to create a job description of specific credentials and skills and then seek candidates who have done exactly that same work for many years. Reorienting toward networks means supporting people in wearing different 'hats' and filling roles in multiple value creating networks. Their formal position then just becomes a 'home base' while they are more flexibly deployed where needed in different roles. The role does not care who plays it. In companies where value networks have been implemented, a daily duty roster first lists the role, then the individual who is assigned to the role and then what organization or 'box' they come from.

*Supporting the learning curve*: In the past, when companies were moving into process tools and learning to work as teams there was a huge amount of training support. Today, we tend to throw people into new technologies or toss a few buzz words at them like 'collaboration' or 'networks' and expect them to suddenly begin behaving differently. The shift into the process orientation and team structures required significant investments in training and education. However, comparable support appears to be seriously lacking as we move into the world of networked organizations. There are new skills sets, mindsets, toolsets, and behaviors that must be mastered. Otherwise 'networks' comes out our lips but 'processes' and 'organization charts' run our lives.

## CHAPTER SUMMARY

Technology can be defined as *'the combination of skills, knowledge, abilities, information, equipment (computers, machines, etc.) techniques, and processes required to transform inputs into outputs in the organization.'* Therefore, technology as a concept is applicable to all organizations, irrespective of their field of operations, be it a bank, a consumer products company, a consulting organization, an educational institution, or an NGO. Although technology is usually thought of in relation to the conversion stage, it is present in all the stages of an organization, namely, input, conversion, and output.

Various researchers have attempted to understand the relationship between an organization's technology and its structure. Woodward categorized manufacturing firms on the basis of three types of production process: unit, mass, or process production, depending on the technical complexity of these processes. She concluded that there was a distinct relationship between these technology categorizations and the structural configuration of these firms, and that effectiveness depended on the 'fit' between technology and structure, that is, organizations that developed structures conforming to their technologies were more successful than those who did not. Perrow introduced the concept of knowledge technology, defining it as *'...the action that an individual performs upon an object, with or without the aid of tools or mechanical devices, in order to make some change in that object.'* Perrow's framework described how technological uncertainty or the lack of it determined an organization's structure, and suggested that (1) task variability and (2) problem analyzability were the two dimensions of technology which affected the extent of this uncertainty. Based on these two dimensions, Perrow identified four categories of technologies employed by organizations – craft technology, engineering technology, routine technology, and non-routine technology, and predicted the type of structural configurations required in each type.

Thomson looked at technology as fulfilling the function of linking various organizational subunits. Different types of technologies are characterized by different structural arrangements. Technology determines the selection of a strategy for reducing uncertainty and specific structural arrangements can facilitate uncertainty reduction. The type of technology would be influenced by the nature of task interdependence existing between organizational subunits. Interdependence can be of three types: (1) long-linked, or sequential interdependence, (2) mediating, or pooled interdependence, and (3) intensive, or reciprocal interdependence. Routine technology is positively associated with low complexity. Non-routine technology requires highly complex structures, both in terms of skill levels required, as well as different units to handle specialized functions, narrow spans of control, and hence, high vertical differentiation. Routine technology is associated with standardization and consistency in output quality, both of which require formal procedures and rules to be followed, and the presence of detailed job descriptions. Non-routine technology requires a great degree of flexibility and autonomy, implying low formalization, and coordination achieved through meetings and interactions, rather than formalized procedures. Finally, while usage of social network technologies are becoming a common feature among organizations, networked forms of organization are recommended in order to exploit the potential of these technologies to deliver maximum value to all stakeholders.

## Review Questions

(1) How does the concept of 'knowledge technology' vary from the traditional meaning of technology?

(2) Explain the statement: 'Technology is present at all stages of an organization's processes'.

(3) Compare and contrast Woodward's, Perrow's, and Thomson's conceptualizations of technology.

(4) Discuss various categories of technology that organizations normally employ, and the structural configurations suitable for each category. Give examples to support your answer.

(5) What are the design challenges that networked organizations of the future are likely to face?

## Project Assignment

Undertake a comparative study between two organizations, one in the manufacturing sector and the other in the service sector. In light of the concepts discussed in the chapter, analyze the type of technology followed by both organizations. Compare the extent of fit between the technology and structure in both organizations, and the extent to which this fit is helping the organization to be effective.

## CASE ILLUSTRATION: BHARTI-AIRTEL

*Bharti Airtel Limited*, formerly known as *Bharti Tele-Ventures LTD* (BTVL), is the largest cellular service provider in India, with a customer base of more than 135 million as of May 2010. It is now the world's third-largest, single-country mobile operator and the sixth-largest integrated telecom operator. It offers its telecom services under the *Airtel* brand, and provides telephone services and broadband

Internet access (DSL) in 95 cities in India. It also acts as a carrier for national and international long distance communication services. The company has a submarine cable landing station at Chennai, which connects the submarine cable linking Chennai and Singapore.

Globally, *Bharti Airtel* is the third largest in-country mobile operator by subscriber base, behind *China Mobile* and *China Unicom*. In India, the company has a 24.6% share of the wireless services market, followed by 17.7% for *Reliance Communications* and 17.4% for *Vodafone Essar*. It is the first mobile phone company in the world to outsource everything except marketing and sales. Its network (base stations, microwave links, etc.) is maintained by *Ericsson* and *Nokia Siemens Network*, with business support from *IBM*, using the transmission towers of another company.

The businesses at *Bharti Airtel* are structured into four individual strategic business units (SBUs) - Mobile Services, Airtel Telemedia Services, Enterprise Services and Digital TV services. The mobile business provides mobile and fixed wireless services using GSM technology across 23 telecom circles, while the *Airtel Telemedia Services* business offers broadband and telephone services in 95 cities and has recently launched a Direct-to-Home (DTH) service, *Airtel Digital TV*. The company provides end-to-end data and enterprise services to corporate customers through its nationwide fiberoptic backbone, last mile connectivity in fixed-line and mobile circles, VSATs, ISP and international bandwidth access through the gateways and landing station. The main brands offered by *Bharti* include *Airtel*, a brand of telecommunication services in India, Bangladesh and Sri Lanka; *BlackBerry*, a result of a tie-up between *Bharti Tele-Ventures Limited* and *Research In Motion* (RIM); digital TV; a Direct-to-Home Television service; iPhone 3G and iPhone 3GS.

Traditionally, *Airtel* has always been at the cutting edge of technology. Given the fact that it functions in an environment in which seamless information flow is critical for its progress, the technology implementation at *Airtel* in the form of Web 2.0 services is highly advanced and aids in quick decision-making. The company's use of technology is reflected in four prominent information technology systems that are used on a diurnal basis:

*Intranet*: With multiple internal messengers and Web 2.0 tools, the company ensures rapid flow of information. *Airtel* is also looking to implement some aspects of Web 3.0 such as social networks within its network so that it becomes easy for employees to collaborate.

*CRM*: *Airtel*'s focus on customers is reflected in its extensive use of customer relationship management systems. *Airtel*'s CRM includes employee training and special purpose software. There is an emphasis on handling incoming customer phone calls and email, although the information collected by CRM software is used for promotion, and surveys such as those polling customer satisfaction. The CRM system includes various aspects which relate directly to one another:

- Front office operations: Direct interaction with customers, e.g. face-to-face meetings, phone calls, e-mail, online services, etc.
- Back office operations: Operations that ultimately affect the activities of the front office (e.g. billing, maintenance, planning, marketing, advertising, finance, manufacturing, etc.)
- Business relationships: Interaction with other companies and partners, such as suppliers/vendors and retail outlets/distributors, industry networks (lobbying groups, trade associations). This external network supports front and back office activities.

*ERP*: *Airtel*'s ERP system is highly complex and collates and distributes information about the company's order processing, services design, purchases, payments, inventory, distribution, HR, etc.

Although *Airtel* is largely a service industry wherein its products are its mobile service packages, its ERP system is very robust given the high volume of transactions. This has greatly enabled the organization to take a holistic view of its activities.

*MIS*: To ensure that management decision-making is rapid, the information systems are highly evolved with multiple marketing plans over each week being planned with the help of the MIS. The company also uses the EIS (Executive Information System) to map customer needs in different geographical regions.

In addition to these, *Airtel* also accords high importance to Knowledge Management (KM). KM strategies followed at *Airtel* include rewards, knowledge mapping, expert directories, competency management, training, knowledge repositories, and knowledge brokers. Accordingly, the company has in place a web-forum: 'E-learning portal' which intends to integrate existing explicit and tacit know-how from all units. The web forum acts as a single point for requesting training, posting feedback, referring process documents, and tracking performance records. The e-portal gives employees a 'one-stop-shop' to effectively store, contribute, and access knowledge.

### Critical enquiry

*How relevant do you think are the categories discussed in the chapter in terms of understanding the technology followed by Bharti-Airtel? What other ways would you suggest to describe the technology followed at Bharti-Airtel?*

***Key words and phrases***: routine technology; non-routine technology; task inter-dependence; knowledge technology; social network technology

# CHAPTER 7

# Organizational Culture

**CHAPTER OUTLINE**

- Defining organizational culture
- Functions of organizational culture
- Types of organizational culture
- Strength of organizational culture
- Creating, transmitting, and sustaining organizational culture
- Situational factors affecting management of organizational culture
- Culture's effect on structure

## ORGANIZATIONAL INSIGHT

A diversified business conglomerate with varied business interests in finance, infrastructure and housing, tourism and hospitality, media and entertainment, consumer products, manufacturing, services and trading, the Rs 50,000-crore *Sahara India Pariwar* represents an emotionally integrated family with over 9 million employees on its rolls. Subrata Roy Sahara, the Managing Worker and Chairman of the *Sahara group*, takes pride in being the guardian of the 'world's largest family' as he refers to the group. The organization's espoused values include emotion, discipline, duty, no discrimination, quality, self-respect, giving respect, honesty, and collective materialism as their core commitments. In fact, it is this last value of 'collective materialism' which is expressly stated as their organization's philosophy and which differentiates them from many other business conglomerates. The philosophy is described thus:

*In any human relationship, it becomes imperative to take into consideration the materialistic aspect of life – we do so but by giving it second priority. The first priority is given to (the) emotional aspect and with perfect blending of materialism with emotionalism, results in continuous collective growth for collective sharing and caring, that gives an impetus to our philosophy – COLLECTIVE MATERIALISM.*

Another espoused value of the organization is termed *BHARTIYATA* ('Indianness' or Indian Nationality): the group believes that *Bhartiyata* is a religion higher than religion itself. And this belief and the value of 'Indianness' is reinforced repeatedly in multiple ways, not the least among them being the group name itself. Internally, in *Sahara India* offices, employees not only greet each other using the *Sahara Pranam*, they also mention *Sahara Pranam* at the end of their emails. *Bharat Parva* is celebrated every year on 26th January and 15th of August with a great deal of enthusiasm. The *Kartavya council* with its tagline *Response Will Never Be Delayed and Justice Will Never Be Denied* safeguards the rights (no discrimination, quality, justice) of its stakeholders. Externally, the same value becomes more visible in the group's endorsements and sponsorships of various sports – including cricket, hockey, boxing, wrestling, and archery – that Indian sportsmen and sportswomen participate in, both nationally and internationally.

These behaviors and values represent the essence of organizational culture at *Sahara India Parivar*.

## 7.1 Defining organizational culture

Organizational culture is represented by a pattern of basic assumptions that has worked well enough to be taught to new members as the correct way to perceive, think and feel in relation to those problems

Organizational culture has been one of the most widely studied and researched constructs in management literature, and continues to be so, given the current focus on globalization and the need for firms to be effective in a multicultural context. Business successes and failures have often been attributed to corporate culture. Managements of organizations are increasingly recognizing the importance of an effective corporate culture, taking proactive steps to define and protect cultural identity and orchestrating cultural changes as part of their reorganization (Carrillo and Gromb, 2007). Barnard (1968) looked at culture from the perspective of 'informal structure', and posited that one of the main functions of top leaders in an organization was to 'set the tone' for the entire organization, a euphemism for organizational culture. Peters and Waterman's (1982) 'culture of excellence' motivated a resurgence of interest in the topic of culture.

Researchers have repeatedly stressed the importance of organizational culture in impacting organizational outcomes such as productivity, employee commitment and motivation, financial performance, and ultimately, business success (e.g. Holmes and Marsden, 1996; Ritchie, 2000). Burton and Beckman (2007) have shown that the culture established by top executives can indeed be a strong legacy which can impact the functioning of an organization, through the formal structures that it shapes. Expectedly enough, various meanings and definitions have been ascribed to this variable, some of the most popular ones being:

1. Fairly stable set of taken-for-granted assumptions, shared meanings and values that form a kind of backdrop for action (Smircich, 1985)
2. Shared values and beliefs, assumptions, perceptions, norms, artefacts, and patterns of behavior (Ott, 1989)
3. Observed behavioral regularities in the interactions, language, and rituals of organizational members (Schein, 1992)

4. The norms which evolve over a period of time in working groups, the dominant values which are espoused by the organization or its dominant members, the philosophy which guides the decisions and policies of an organization (Schein, 1992)
5. The rules of the game ('the ropes') one must learn in order to survive and be accepted in the organization (Schein, 1992)
6. The feeling and climate that pervades and gets conveyed in the day-to-day functioning of the organization (Schein, 1992)
7. Shared jargon, slang, humor, and jokes (Trice and Bayer, 1993)
8. An organization's values, beliefs, practices, rituals, and customs (Marguardt, 2002)
9. The psychological assets of an organization, which can be used to predict what will happen to its financial assets in five years' time (Hofstede, 2003)
10. The collective programming of the mind which distinguishes the members of one organization from another (Hofstede, 2003)

From the above definitions, it can be inferred that organizational culture refers to the underlying set of beliefs, assumptions, values, shared feelings and perceptions, which influence the actions and decisions taken by the organizational members. It also affects the way people perceive various organizational situations and react to them. Hence, organizational culture is defined as:

*'A pattern of basic assumptions – invented, discovered, or developed by a given group as it learns to cope with the problems of external adaptation and internal integration – that has worked well enough to be considered valid and therefore, to be taught to new members as the correct way to perceive, think, and feel in relation to those problems.'* (Schein, 1985)

Culture is a multi-level construct comprising three concepts: the *organizational ethos*, consisting of the values which give a distinct identity to a group, the *organizational climate*, defined as the perceived attributes of an organization and its subsystems, reflected in the way it deals with its members, associated groups and issues, and finally, *organizational culture*, comprising the cumulative beliefs, values and assumptions underlying interpersonal transactions, and depicted through rituals, artefacts, etc. Pareek (2007) has identified a set of eight core values (OCTAPACE – an acronym) which make up the ethos of an organization, viz.

- Openness: *receiving and giving spontaneously*
- Confrontation: *facing, rather than shying away from, problems*
- Trust: *maintaining confidentiality of information, integrity in dealings*
- Authenticity: *congruence between claims and actions*
- Proactivity: *taking initiative, pre-planning, taking preventive action*
- Autonomy: *using and giving the freedom to plan and act in one's sphere*
- Collaboration: *giving and asking for help*
- Experimentation: *using and encouraging innovative approaches to solve problems*

Organizational climate is identified through an organization's motivation focus. Thus, while industrial organizations might be motivated by an *achievement* focus, educational institutions and research organizations might be motivated by an *influence* or expert focus. Similarly, typical bureaucracies would be expected to have a *control* focus, while traditional one-man organizations would have a *dependency* focus. On the other hand, community or social organizations would have an *extension* focus, while clubs would have an *affiliation* focus. And each of these dimensions would affect various processes in the organization such as orientation, interpersonal relationships, supervision, problem management, management of mistakes, conflict management, communication, decision-making, trust, management of rewards, risk-taking, innovation, and change.

## 7.2 Functions of organizational culture

Organizational climate indicates the motivation orientation of the organization.

Apart from influencing an organization's structural configurations, culture performs various other functions. Organizational culture

- provides shared patterns of perceptions, communicating to organizational members about how they are expected to think and behave.
- provides shared patterns of feelings, i.e. an emotional sense of involvement and commitment to organizational values and moral codes – of things worth working for or believing in – so organizational members know what they are expected to value.
- defines and maintains boundaries, allowing identification of members and non-members.
- functions as an implicit organizational control system, prescribing and prohibiting certain behaviors.

Cultural influences on organizational behavior operate more implicitly than explicitly. This invisibility adds to its power.

## 7.3 Types of organizational cultures

Broadly, various organizations differ in culture along various structural and behavioral dimensions, as shown below:

- *Individual initiative*: Degree of responsibility, freedom, and independence that employees have.
- *Risk tolerance*: Degree to which employees are encouraged to be aggressive, innovative, risk-seeking.
- *Direction*: Degree to which an organization creates clear objectives and performance expectations.

- *Integration*: Degree to which units of the organization are encouraged to operate in a cooperative manner.
- *Management support*: Degree to which managers provide clear communication, assistance, and support to subordinates.
- *Control*: Number of rules and regulations, amount of direct supervision used to control employee behavior.
- *Identity*: Degree to which members identify with the organization as a whole rather than with their particular work group.
- *Reward system*: Degree to which reward allocations are based on employee performance criteria in contrast to seniority, favoritism, etc.
- *Conflict tolerance*: Degree to which employees are encouraged to air conflicts and criticism openly.
- *Communication patterns*: Degree to which organizational communications are restricted to formal hierarchy of authority.

On the basis of the above dimensions, a typical organizational culture profile would differentiate organizations based on innovation, stability, respect for people, outcome orientation, attention to detail, team orientation, aggressiveness, customer focus, collaboration, quality consciousness, transparency, and integrity, among others. Hofstede's (2003) recent study has identified six dimensions along which cultural differences among organizations may be understood, through their common practices, symbols, heroes, and rituals. These dimensions can be described as:

1. **Process oriented *vs* result oriented**: In *process-oriented cultures*, signifying a concern with means, people perceive themselves as avoiding risks and making only a limited effort in their jobs, while each day is pretty much the same. In *result-oriented cultures*, signifying a concern with end-goals, people are relatively more comfortable in unfamiliar situations and put in maximal effort, as each day is felt to bring in new challenges.
2. **Employee-oriented *vs* job oriented:** In *employee-oriented cultures*, employees feel that their personal problems are taken into account by the organization, which takes responsibility for employee welfare; important decisions tend to be made by groups or committees. In *job-oriented cultures*, people might experience strong pressures to complete their jobs, decision making is highly centralized, and the organization is perceived to be only interested in the work that employees do and not about their personal and family welfare.
3. **Parochial *vs* professional:** In *parochial cultures*, organizational members derive their identity mainly from the organization they belong to, while in *professional cultures*, organizational members' identities stem more from the job or profession they are engaged in rather than the organization they work for.
4. **Open system *vs* closed system:** In *open system cultures*, as the name suggests, both the organization and its people are open to newcomers and outsiders;

almost anyone would fit into the organization and new employees would need only a few days to feel at home in the organization. Conversely, in *closed system cultures*, the organization and its people are felt to be closed and secretive, even among insiders; only 'very special' people fit into the organization and new employees need a long time to feel comfortable and at home.

5. **Loose control *vs* tight control:** In cultures with *loose control*, the general perception is that no one thinks of costs, meeting times are only kept approximately, and jokes about the company and the job are frequent. Conversely, in those with *tight control*, the overall perceptions are that the work environment is cost-conscious, meeting times are strictly adhered to, and loose comments and jokes are avoided or discouraged.
6. **Normative *vs* pragmatic:** *Pragmatic cultures* are market driven, with major emphasis on meeting customer's needs, results are more important than correct procedures, and in matters of business ethics, a pragmatic rather than dogmatic attitude prevails. *Normative cultures*, on the other hand, perceive their task toward the outside world as the implementation of inviolable rules; the main emphasis is on correctly following organizational procedures, which are perceived to be more important than results, and in matters of business ethics, the organization's standards are perceived to be high.

While the above dimensions relate to the type of work an organization does, they also partly reflect the business or industry culture in which the organization operates. Moreover, while at an overall level, these dimensions reflect the organization's culture, they could also be a reflection of subcultures existing in an organization's various units. Hence, in a manufacturing organization, the production department might have a largely process-oriented culture, while the marketing or finance departments in the same organization might be characterized by strong results-orientation.

Organizational members differ in terms of their perception of the extent of certainty or uncertainty in the environment and the nature of actions necessitated by the perceived reality. Based on these two dimensions, organizational culture can be of four types:

1. **Rational culture (or task culture)** is characterized by task-oriented environments, emphasizing performance, productivity and efficiency, and a high achievement focus. There is a high degree of certainty perceived in the environment. These cultures are likely to be found in competitive environments such as consumer products, banking and financial services, etc.
2. **Ideological/developmental culture (or person culture):** These are future-oriented, innovative environments, focusing on employee development and growth, and encouraging creativity. Creative advertising firms and R&D departments, for example, might be expected to have this type of culture.

3. **Consensual culture**: These are team-oriented, affiliative cultures whose main focus is to build and maintain relationships, allowing for open and spontaneous interactions. The overall environment is informal, and personal issues are considered to be more important than procedures and rules. Small project teams, educational institutions, etc. might signify this culture.
4. **Hierarchical cultures (or role cultures):** Strongly bureaucratic organizations are likely to have such cultures, characterized by a focus on continuity, security, and predictability in a stable environment. High-power distances and reliance on rules and procedures as instruments of control, and cautious, low-risk responses are other characteristics of such cultures.

Scholars like Denison and Mishra (1995), Quinn (1988), and Hooijberg and Petrock (1993) have characterized organizational or corporate cultures through other terminologies, though most of them are conceptually similar to the ones described above. Thus for example, an **adaptability/entrepreneurial culture** is characterized by strategic focus on the external environment through flexibility and change, in order to meet the constantly changing needs of the customer, by constantly promoting individual initiative and encouraging entrepreneurial behavior among employees. A learning culture has as its main focus a trend toward change, knowledge expansion, organizational commitment, sensitivity and responsiveness to environmental cues, and encouragement of creativity and learning. A **competitive culture** is characterized by high flexibility, low integration, focus on quantitative outcomes, low loyalty and cultural identity, and contractual relations between the employee and the organization.

A **mission culture** is somewhat similar in concept to a rational and competitive culture, characterized by emphasis on a clear vision, profit-orientation and goal achievement. The **clan culture** or **participative culture** which is characterized by focus on employee participation and development, is low on complexity and formalization, with coordination among members facilitating decentralization, and concentrates on employee needs as the route to high performance, as denoted in ideological and, to some extent, consensual cultures. Finally, a **bureaucratic culture** is very similar to the hierarchical culture described above, with its internal focus, consistency and stability orientation, relative inflexibility, affirmative leadership styles, and methodical, formalized approach to doing business.

**Table 7.1** Summarises the relationship between different types of cultures with other variables such as strategy, technology, and structure.

**Table 7.1** *Relationship between organizational culture, strategy, technology, and structure*

| *Organizational cultures* | *Organizational structure* | *Strategy type* | *Technology* |
|---|---|---|---|
| Rational | Divisional | Analyser | Engineering |
| Ideological | Adhocracy | Prospector | Non-routine |
| Consensual | Simple | Implementer | Craft |
| Hierarchical | Bureaucracy | Defender | Routine |

## 7.4 Strength of organizational culture

> The strength of an organization's culture indicates the extent of commonality of understanding and shared perceptions among organizational members.

Culture affects not only the extent to which formal structures are needed to accomplish coordination and control, but the degree to which certain formal structures are acceptable.

While culture implies commonality of understanding and shared perceptions among organizational members, any large organization is likely to have a dominant culture and multiple subcultures in different functional units. *Dominant culture* expresses the core values that are shared by a majority of the organization's members. *Subcultures* on the other hand tend to develop in large organizations to reflect common problems, situations, or experiences that members face. These can form vertically or horizontally. It would include the core values of the dominant culture plus additional values unique to members of the particular department. Subcultures are mostly defined by departmental specificities and designations, or geographic separations.

A culture is considered to be 'strong' when the organization's core values are intensely held by employees, clearly ordered, enjoys widespread acceptance among all members, with all members strongly committed to them. A strong culture increases behavioral consistency by conveying to members what behaviors they should engage in. A strong culture can also be a powerful means of implicit control and can act as a substitute for formalization. High formalization creates predictability, orderliness and consistency. A strong culture achieves the same end without any need for written documentation. Finally, a strong culture can be more potent than formal controls since it controls the mind and soul as well as the body.

However, a strong culture also has its disadvantages. The same cultural values which might be advantageous to an organization under one set of circumstances might be irrelevant or dysfunctional under another set of circumstances. Strong cultures being tenacious tend to slow down an organization's ability to respond quickly to environmental changes. Hence, for an organization's culture to contribute to its effectiveness, it should ideally be a combination of many subcultures that can deal with and integrate apparently contradictory values and needs of different organizational subunits. In the same organization therefore, while the marketing and production units might have a rational culture, the accounts and administration departments might have hierarchical cultures, the HRD division might have a developmental or ideological culture, and so on. That is, successful organizations are likely to be those whose internal cultures have a good fit with the external environment they operate in and serve.

Some scholars have also differentiated between overt ('preferred') and covert ('culture-in-use') cultures. This covert culture, or culture-behind-the-culture symbolizes the actual beliefs, values, and norms that drive patterns of behavior within the company.

## 7.5 Creating, transmitting, and sustaining organizational culture

The ultimate source of an organization's culture lies in its founders, or more specifically, the founders' vision, mission, attitudes, and values. This, in turn, forms the basis for recruitment of the initial group of employees. Organizational culture is the result of the interaction between the founders' biases and assumptions, and what the initial employees employed by the founders learn through their experiences. Some other key influences in the development of an organization's culture include the firm's history (reason and manner in which the organization was originally formed), primary function and technology, geographic location, etc. This culture is then sustained and kept alive through various organizational activities, often termed the 'culture web' (Figure 7.1), which includes:

1. The organization's selection practices to ensure proper 'person–organization fit'
2. Actions of top management, which sends out 'signals' to the employees regarding what is acceptable behavior and what is not
3. Organization's socialization methods, including orientation, mentoring, in-the-trenches training, and consistent role models, by which employees learn and internalize the values and norms of the organization
4. Control systems, power structures and reward systems

Organizational employees 'learn' this culture mostly through common expression of culture such as:

1. *Physical artefacts*: Layout, décor, availability of facilities, office stationary, 'symbols', logo
2. *Language, jargon and metaphor*: Unique jargon, terminology, phrases, acronyms
3. *Stories, myths and legends*: Narratives based on true organizational events that are then narrated and frequently shared among employees
4. *Ceremonies and celebrations*
5. *Routines, rites and rituals*: Staff meetings, training programs, appraisal forms, superiors' annual visits, picnics
6. *Behavioral norms* toward seniors, colleagues, in meetings, during breaks. These norms are transmitted to new members through socialization
7. *Shared beliefs and values*: In terms of ethical/moral codes or ideologies, which are consciously held, mental pictures of the nature of organizational reality, and what is considered right or wrong
8. *Basic assumptions*: Unconscious values, beliefs held by the organization's members.

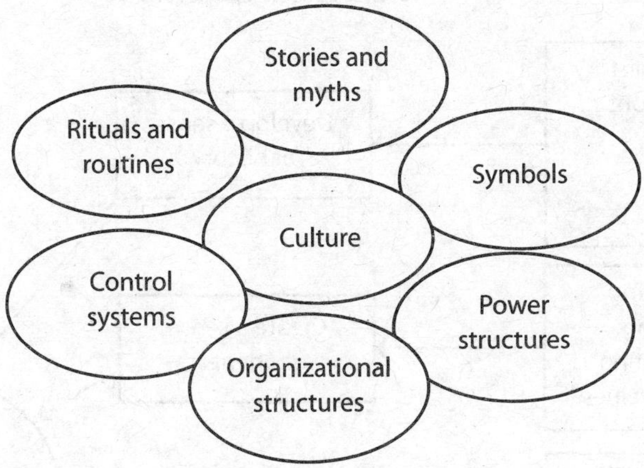


**Figure 7.1** *The cultural web of an organization*

Gross and Shichman (1987) have proposed an integrative framework which brings out this evolution of a cohesive workplace culture (Figure 7.2).

## 7.6 Situational factors affecting the management of organizational culture

While some scholars have argued in favor of the need to manage and change an organization's culture, advocating the need to constantly change and adapt to environmental changes, others have held that it would be difficult for employees to unlearn years of shared values and beliefs. However, most have agreed that various situational factors would influence the ease or difficulty in managing or changing an organization's culture. The important ones are outlined below:

- **A driving force**: Since any cultural change is difficult to sustain, there has to be an absolutely compelling reason to attempt it. Cultural change efforts are more successful when there is a clear link with business strategy.
- **A dramatic crisis** or shock that undermines the status quo (e.g sudden hostile takeover, sudden loss of market share, financial loss, dramatic technological breakthrough, and unforeseen political upheavals) can call into question current practices and values and facilitate acceptance of a different set of values and practices.
- **Leadership turnover:** Since the values of top management are a representation of an organization's value system, change in leadership can facilitate change of culture, provided the new leader has a clear set of alternative values and vision which he is willing to enact.
- **Life-cycle stage:** In the growth and maturity stages, an organization's culture is well set and entrenched; however, at startup, or in the transition periods

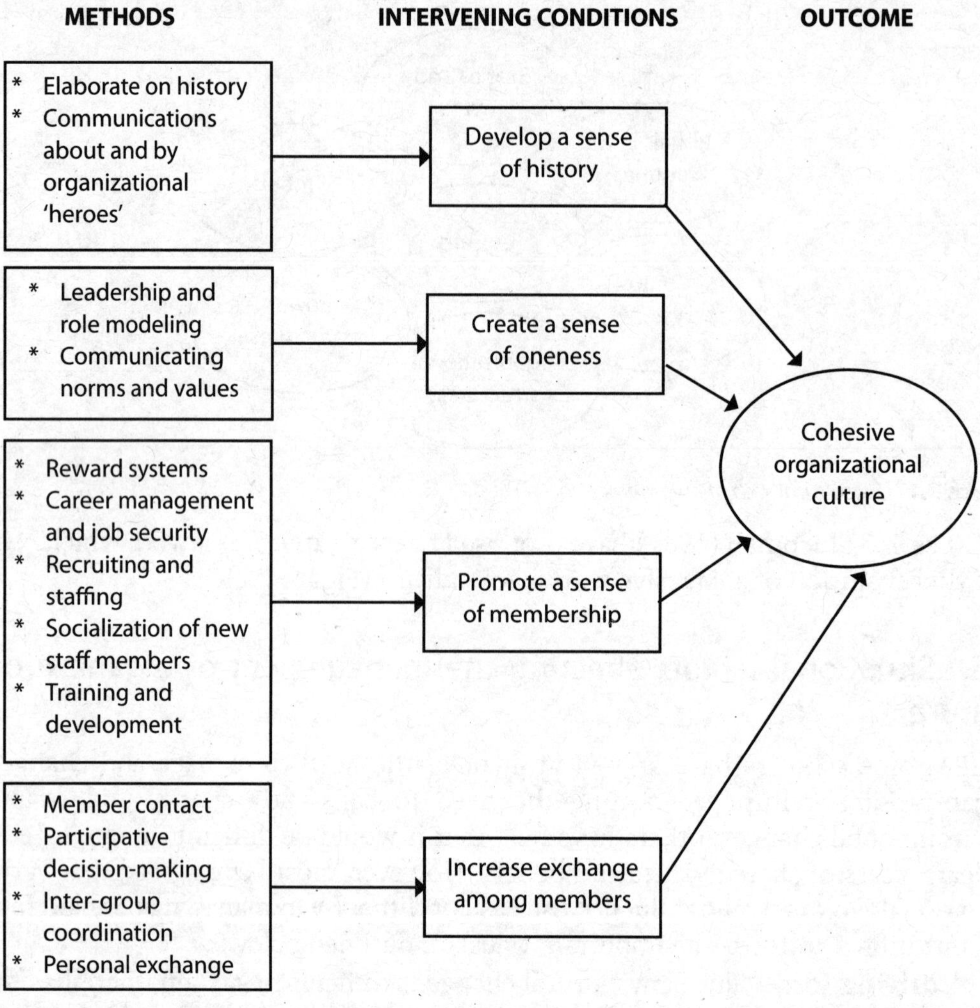


**Figure 7.2** *Evolution of a positive culture*

from startup to growth or from maturity to decline, when things are in a flux or uncertainty, cultural change becomes easier. Employees are expected to be more receptive to cultural changes if (a) the organization's past success record has been at best modest, (b) employees are generally dissatisfied, and (c) the founder's image and reputation are in question.

- **Age of organization:** Irrespective of the life-cycle stage, a younger organization will have lesser entrenched cultural values, and hence, will find it easier to change, compared to an older organization.
- **Size of organization:** Managing cultural change becomes easier in a smaller organization, since communicating to employees is easier and role models to disseminate new values are more visible in a smaller set up.

- **Strength of current culture:** Expectedly, the stronger and more widely held the current culture, the more difficult it will be for employees to unlearn them. Cultural change is facilitated in weak cultures.
- **Absence of subcultures:** Greater number of subcultures, and hence, greater heterogeneity makes it more difficult for cultural change, since each subgroup of employees will try to resist their self-interest. A uniform culture and lesser subcultures will, on the other hand, facilitate cultural change.
- **Strong organizational systems and procedures:** Effective systems and procedures can not only help to precipitate changes, but also to sustain it. For example, new methods of appraisal and metrics to measure and encourage new behaviors, revised operating procedures, communication system to promote new behaviors, different working environments and reward systems can all help to institutionalize the changed practices.

Although culture is perceived to be a 'soft' characteristic, changing it calls for some 'hard' measures (Hofstede, 2003). *Structural* changes may mean closing departments, opening other departments, merging or splitting activities, or moving people and/or groups geographically. Generally, it is found that when people are moved individually, they will adapt to the culture of their new environment; however, when they are moved as groups, they might bring their group culture along, which is quite stable and difficult to change. However, demands of new tasks or a new environment might force a renegotiation of existing patterns of interactions in the group and help to change its culture. *Process* changes mean new procedures, eliminating controls or establishing new controls, automation, new communication linkages, etc. *Personnel* changes would mean new hiring and promotion policies, with greater sensitivity toward social heterogeneity, training programs to sensitize employees to the need for a new culture, and new reward policies to cement the changes.

**Managers can facilitate cultural changes by:**

- Acting as positive role models for the new cultural values.
- Allowing 'rehearsal' of new behavior and allowing for initial failures without recriminations.
- Providing organizational support through training, coaching, and mentoring to encourage and sustain new behaviors.
- Putting in place suitable reward systems to encourage and cement the new behaviors.
- Redesigning selection and recruitment and socialization practices to reinforce the new values.
- Diluting or integrating subcultures into the mainstream organizational culture.
- Sharing the new cultural values by soliciting employee acceptance through participation.

## 7.7 Culture's effect on structure

Organizational culture shapes formal structures by influencing the need for and acceptability of different arrangements for control and supervision (Tolbert and Hall, 2010). Different characteristics of an organization's climate, which help shape its culture, are expected to have an influence on the type of structural configurations. For example, an organizational culture characterized by a climate of high trust, low conflict, high or medium morale, equitable reward, low change resistance, high leader credibility and low level of 'scape-goating' is likely to have a matrix structure or adhocracy, low to medium complexity, low levels of centralization and formalization, wide span of control, coordination and control through meetings and liaison roles, and results based on group incentives.

On the other hand, organizational cultures with a climate of low trust, high conflict, medium to low morale, inequitable rewards, high change resistance, low leader credibility and high level of 'scape-goating' would most likely result in a bureaucracy or functional structure, high complexity, high to medium centralization, high formalization, wide span of control, coordination and control through rules and procedures, planning, and individual and procedure-based incentives.

Studies have also identified relationships between organization culture and strategy. Hence, prospectors would be likely to have a culture of innovation characterized by action orientation, willingness to experiment and risk taking. Conversely, defenders would more likely have a culture characterized by focus on stability, efficiency, attention to details and internal controls. Reactors would expectedly enough have weaker cultures which are low on outcome orientations (Baird, Harrison and Reeve, 2007). Finally, value dimensions of culture, as hypothesized by Hofstede and other scholars are expected to have an influence on various organizational choices, as summarised in Table 7.2.

**Table 7.2** *Effect of culture on organizational choices*

| *Cultural dimension* | *Valence* | *Structures* | *Processes* |
|---|---|---|---|
| Power distance | High | Hierarchy:<br>*Differentiation: high*<br>Centralization: *high* | Decision-making: *authoritative*<br>Communication: *vertical*<br>Control: *tight*<br>Coordination: *vertical* |
| | Low | Hierarchy:<br>*Differentiation: low*<br>Centralization: *low* | Decision-making: *participative*<br>Communication: *lateral*<br>Control: *loose*<br>Coordination: *horizontal* |

*(Contd ...*

*... Contd)*

| | | | |
|---|---|---|---|
| Individualism | High | Horizontal differentiation:<br>*Specialization: high*<br>Rewards differential: *high* | Rewards and incentives: *individual*<br>Communication: *specific*<br>Decision-making : *contentious* |
| | Low (collectivism) | Horizontal differentiation:<br>*Specialization: low*<br>Rewards differential: *low* | Rewards and incentives: *group emphasis*<br>Communication: *diffuse*<br>Decision-making : *consensus* |
| Uncertainty avoidance | High | Formalization: *high*<br>Centralization: *high* | Locus of decisions: *hierarchical* |
| | Low | Formalization:*low*<br>Centralization: *low* | Locus of decisions: *diffuse* |

## CHAPTER SUMMARY

Organizational culture is defined as a pattern of basic assumptions and mental models that has worked well enough to be considered valid and therefore, to be taught to new members as the correct way to perceive, think, and feel in relation to those problems. Culture is a multi-level construct measured through multiple structural and behavioral dimensions such as openness, communication, experimentation and initiative, risk-taking, management support, reward systems, integrity, etc. Depending on a combination of these dimensions and the different ways in which organizations perceive uncertainty in their environment and react to it, organization cultures can be classified under various categories, namely rational culture, ideological culture, consensual culture, hierarchical culture, entrepreneurial culture, bureaucratic culture, mission culture, etc.

*Dominant culture* expresses the core values that are shared by a majority of the organization's members. *Subcultures* on the other hand tend to develop in large organizations to reflect common problems, situations, or experiences that members face. An organization's culture is often a reflection of its top management's values and attitudes and is propagated and reflected through socialization procedures, control systems and policies, management actions, physical settings, and rituals. A strong culture can be a powerful means of implicit control and can act as a substitute for formalization. Conversely, a strong culture can also build up rigidity and slow down an organization's flexibility to react to a dynamic environment. An organization's structure and processes would be significantly influenced by the type of culture characterizing it.

### Review Questions

1. Highlight the difference between an organization's ethos, climate, and culture.
2. Draw up a typology of organizational cultures based on various structural and behavioral dimensions.
3. Discuss the various situational factors that can facilitate or inhibit a change of culture.

## Project Assignment

Undertake a comparative study of four organizations in one particular sector, each in a different stage of life-cycle (start-up, growth, maturity, and decline). Using the dimensions discussed in the chapter, examine how the culture of each of these organizations varies along these dimensions.

## CASE ILLUSTRATION: CULTURAL TRANSFORMATION AT *FORTIS–MALAR HOSPITALS*

*Fortis Healthcare* is a leading hospital chain in India, with a stated vision of *'creating a world-class integrated healthcare delivery system in India, entailing the finest medical skills combined with compassionate medical care.'* The chain's national rollout plans were formulated in line with this vision. A significant milestone in their plans was reached on February 2008, when *International Hospitals Ltd*, a wholly-owned subsidiary of *Fortis Healthcare*, along with *Oscar Investments Ltd* acquired a majority stake in the Chennai-based *Malar Hospitals*, heralding the group's entry into Southern India.

*Malar Hospitals* is a multi-specialty facility offering complete medical care in various specialties, the thrust areas of which include cardiology, orthopedics, neurosciences, and women's health. However, given that the success of any acquisition depends largely on cultural compatibility between the two organizations, the culture at *Malar Hospitals* has undergone significant transformation in line with the new focus. This has been necessary in order to differentiate itself from other equally world-class healthcare facilities such as *Apollo, Lifeline*, etc. that are already successfully present in that area. The policy document of *Malar Hospitals* makes the following assertion: '*....we aspire to achieve absolute transparency, accountability and responsibility in the operations and in the interactions between shareholders, government, employees, regulatory bodies and community at large through effective corporate governance.*' Prior to the acquisition, *Malar* had been suffering from huge losses accumulated over years; planned projects could not be completed owing to lack of funds, further adding to these losses.

*Malar* finally decided to confront these issues by revamping its planning of accounts and replacing its team of accountants by a newer and more efficient team. The support of *Fortis* acted as a boon in this respect. New initiatives have now been adopted to give greater recognition and incentive to its sales and marketing teams. There is renewed clarity and focus in terms of revenue generation. Some of the stated objectives of the hospital in this regard include:

- enhancing neuro and ortho departments and commencing new medical programs to enhance the current revenue of the hospital
- improving patient-centricity and cost effectiveness of the hospital
- increasing the occupancy rate and revenues per bed
- leveraging on lower costs in India to attract patients from abroad
- using high-end technology to reduce the average length of stay in the hospital

In order to authenticate its claims about quality, *Fortis Malar* has been assessed and given the ISO 9001: 2000 certification. The hospital gives a lot of autonomy to its doctors in their daily work. For example, there is no stipulated minimum revenue from a particular department, which may force doctors to prescribe medicines and tests that the patient might not actually require. The rental arrangement model followed earlier for doctors has also been changed to a remuneration-sharing model, further enhancing this autonomy. At the same time, the hospital is very strict about upholding principles of integrity in all its processes, as is reflected in its code of ethics and procedures, the breaching of which (e.g. false certification, drinking on the job, disobeying instructions, giving away confidential information, non-performance of duties, etc.) results in instant dismissal of an employee. For offences other than critical breach of policies, the hospital is forgiving and supportive of its employees to a large extent. The usual course of action against such offenders involves a sequential pattern of (1) counseling, (2) verbal warning, (3) written warning, (4) final warning, (5) suspension, and finally (6) dismissal.

The hospital has a human resources department that is responsible for addressing employee grievances and complaints. Employees are encouraged to talk openly about their concerns with the HR department, which also solicits employee suggestions periodically during annual appraisal meetings. A very fair, merit-based reward system and participative appraisal processes are followed for employees. In order to recognize high performance, the compensation practices include performance-related extra pay for employees. There is also a substantial amount of reserve funds set aside for retention and performance incentive initiatives for talented, high-performing employees. In order to ensure that the hospital operates as a well-coordinated unit, a number of initiatives have been undertaken to ensure that all departments coordinate with each other in order to generate the requisite synergies in operations.

The hospital at its inception was positioned as an elite hospital catering to the upper middle class. Realizing the acute need for quality healthcare in the poorer sections of society, it changed its positioning to include the opening of non-air-conditioned wards, cheaper rates, subsidies for the poor, etc. Earlier, *Malar* was concentrating on a few narrow areas of specialization; following the acquisition, it is now venturing into new niches and hitherto unexplored areas such as neonatal units, plastic and reconstructive surgery, otolaryngology, etc. Recognizing its social, economical and environmental responsibilities, *Malar* has undertaken various initiatives such as subsidized healthcare for underprivileged patients, free checkups for senior citizens, hygienic disposal of wastes, and free health check-ups for kids and teenagers.

Earlier, the founding family took all major decisions, whereas in the current setup, the board of directors has been entrusted with that responsibility. The cultural change has also resulted in a more patient-centric approach overall. However, this transition of ownerships and subsequent cultural change has witnessed its share of turbulence. The beginning of the transformation has been promising; it now remains to be seen whether the two entities are able to integrate and build a strong culture, which will deliver on promises and stand the test of time.

## Critical enquiry

Identify the various dimensions of culture as are evident from the facts related above, giving examples to support your answers.

***Key words and phrases***: organizational culture, ethos, climate, dominant culture, subculture, strength of culture, cultural artefacts, propagation of culture, positive culture

# CHAPTER 8

# Organizational Failure

**CHAPTER OUTLINE**

- What is organizational failure or decline?
- Organizational ecology
- Why do organizations fail?
- Patterns of organizational failures
- Implications for managers

## ORGANIZATIONAL INSIGHT

In 1933, *Metal Box India Ltd.** (a subsidiary of *Metal Box plc*, UK) was incorporated at Calcutta, with the objective of manufacturing metal containers and closures, flexible packages, paper products, hardware and engineering products. For the next four decades, the company went from strength to strength, notching up impressive profits year on year. In 1974, the company decided to add ball bearings, cylindrical and taper roller bearings to its product range. The land for this plant was acquired in Kharagpur Industrial area. Know-how arrangements were made with a French manufacturer. In 1977, *Chrysal* kitchen canisters were added to the range of domestic containers. Soon after, however, in 1977, the bearings factory had to face several unforeseen problems relating to infrastructural facilities, industrial relations, and supplies from indigenous sources. As a result, this line of business became a heavy drain on profits.

From 1980 onwards, operations in the metals packaging business began to be affected by a shortage of imported tinplate. In an attempt to diversify further, the company introduced beer cans in the market. In the paper packaging business, profit margins were eroded by substantial increases in costs. The bearings factory continued to face a variety of problems (erratic power supply, workers' seven-month strike at Cochin and go-slow at the Mumbai and Chennai units), which resulted in substantial losses. The company embarked upon a program of modernisation of the packaging factories. This program envisaged the introduction of welded cans with wrap-around decoration, and crown corks with moulded liners. In 1982, the first part of the modernisation program was implemented with the introduction of high-speed welding technology for container manufacture. In 1983, the loss-making bearings unit was sold off to *TISCO*. Notwithstanding this sale, acute shortage of tinplate and prolonged strikes in the Calcutta units resulted in continued loss in operations.

In 1985, in an attempt to infuse fresh life into the struggling unit, a satisfactory arrangement was concluded between *Metal Box plc* in the U.K. and the *Macneill & Magor* Group, whereby *Macneill & Magor* would provide financial and other support. As financial troubles continued, in 1986, an agreement was signed with *India Foils, Ltd.* for the sale of the assets of the Company's paper and plastics unit at Calcutta. It was also proposed to sell the small installation at Kandla Free Trade Zone, which was set up to service a major customer engaged in exports, as a cost reduction measure. Continuing IR problems caused further setback affecting both production and sale. In 1987, the company came under the provision of the Sick Industrial Companies' Act. By 1989, five of its units, viz., Faridabad, Calcutta Units No. 1 and 2, Cochin, and the division at Worli remained inoperative. The Company's subsidiary *Kosmek Plastics Manufacturing Ltd.* went into liquidation. In 2000, *Metal Box India*'s prime land at Worli was put up for sale to fund the company's rehabilitation.

**Source:** *http://www.moneycontrol.com/company-facts/metalboxindialtd/history/MBI02/accessed on 1st August 2010*

## 8.1 What is organizational failure or decline?

In Chapter 1, we had discussed the life-cycle perspective of organizations and analyzed how organizations typically pass through various stages of their life-cycle, and if they are not able to manage the crises mentioned in **Greiner's model** at each stage, might even go into decline and die. Business history is replete with examples of organizations, both in India and abroad, which were phenomenally successful at some stage, gradually losing touch with reality and dying.

Organizational decline and failure happens due to failure to anticipate, recognize, avoid, neutralize, or adapt to external or internal pressures that threaten an organization's long-term survival.

Some organizations, of course, do not 'die', but might cease to continue in their present form, and be 'reborn' in another form. In fact, the previous chapters have primarily focused on how organizations strive to attain a 'fit' between their internal and external environments by aligning their strategy, environment, technology, size, and culture with their structural configurations, and hence, avoid decline or failure. Organizational decline refers to that life-cycle stage of an organization *when it fails to anticipate, recognize, avoid, neutralize, or adapt to external or internal pressures that threaten its long-term survival*. Decline is a change over time from previously efficient to inefficient organizational functioning, from previously rational to non-rational organizational and individual decision-making, from previously law-abiding to law violating organizational and individual behavior, from previously virtuous to iniquitous individual moral behavior. As important as it is for organizations to understand how to attain this fit, it is also equally important for them to appreciate the factors which can lead to decline or failure. Some of the important ones are discussed in the next section. Prior to that, however, a brief discussion if the concept of organizational ecology will help us arrive at a better appreciation of the reasons for decline.

## 8.2 Organizational ecology

Organizational ecology (also organizational demography and the population ecology of organizations) is a theoretical and empirical approach in the social sciences that is especially used in organizational studies. The concept of organizational ecology (Hannan and Freeman, 1977), which has been briefly mentioned in Chapter 1, utilizes insights from biology, economics, and sociology, and employs statistical analysis to try and understand the conditions under which organizations emerge, grow, and die. Organizational ecology examines the environment in which organizations compete and a process similar to natural selection occurs. This theory looks at the death of organizations (firm mortality), the birth of new organizations (organizational founding), as well as organizational growth and change. Organizational ecology contains a number of more specific 'theory fragments', including *inertia and change, niche width, resource partitioning, density dependence* and *age dependence*, each of which has implications in terms of an organization's survival.

### 8.2.1 Inertia and change

This theory fragment holds that organizations that are reliable and accountable are the ones that can survive (favored by selection). A negative by-product, however, of the need for reliability and accountability is a high degree of inertia and resistance to change. A key prediction of organizational ecology is that the process of change itself is so disruptive that it will result in a higher rate of mortality.

### 8.2.2 Niche width

The theory fragment on niche width distinguishes broadly between two types of organizations: 'generalists' and 'specialists'. Specialist organizations maximize their exploitation of the environment and accept the risk of experiencing a change in that environment. On the other hand, generalist organizations accept a lower level of exploitation in return for greater security. **Niche theory** shows that specialization is generally favoured in stable or certain environments. However, generalism is not always optimal in uncertain environments. The exception is produced by environments which place very different demands on the organization, and the duration of environmental states is short relative to the life of the organization.

### 8.2.3 Resource partitioning

The relationship between generalist and specialist organizations is further developed in the resource-partitioning model which includes predictions about the founding and mortality rates of both specialists and generalists as a function of market concentration. This theory maintains that more available resources should translate into better chances of success for specialists when they operate in a more concentrated market.

### 8.2.4 Density dependence

Organizational ecology also predicts that the rates of founding and mortality are dependent on the number of organizations (density) in the market. The two central mechanisms here are legitimation (the recognition or taken-for-grantedness of that group of organizations) and competition. Legitimation generally increases (at a decreasing rate) with the number of organizations, but so does competition (at an increasing rate). The result is that legitimation processes will prevail at low numbers of organizations, while competition will prevail at high numbers. The founding rate will, therefore, first increase with the number of organizations (due to an increase in legitimation), but will decrease at high numbers of organizations (due to competition). The reverse holds for mortality rates. Thus, the relationship of density to founding rates has an inverted U shape and the relationship of density to mortality rates follows a U-shaped pattern.

### 8.2.5 Age dependence

Organizational ecologists have found a number of patterns in terms of how an organization's risk of mortality relates to the age of that organization:

- *Liability of newness*: Here, the risk of failure is high initially, but declines as the organization ages.
- *Liability of adolescence*: The risk of mortality will be low at first as the organization is buffered from failure due to support by external constituents and initial endowments. But when these initial resources become depleted, the mortality hazard shoots up and then declines following the liability of the newness pattern.
- *Liabilities of aging*: Here, the risk of failure increases with organizational age. This could be due to a *liability of senescence* (internal inefficiencies arising from the aging of the organization) or a *liability of obsolescence* (a growing external mismatch with the environment).

## 8.3 Why do organizations fail?

While stories of organizational failure abound across nations, the reasons for failure could be ascribed to a variety of reasons. Some of the major factors leading to failure of organizations are explained below:

- Organizational inertia: This refers to the forces inside an organization that make it resistant to change. Factors which increase organizational inertia could be:
  - *Risk aversion:* As organizations grow and stabilize, managers might become overly concerned with protecting their positions and survival, and hence become unwilling to bear the uncertainty associated with entrepreneurial or risky activities.
  - *Desire to maximize personal rewards:* Often, managers' desire to increase their own rewards such as power, prestige, job security, etc. pushes them to increase the organizations' size to a point where it becomes ineffective, and the interests of stakeholders are adversely affected, thereby compromising the organization's long-term ability to sustain the flow of input and output resources required for its survival.
  - *Overly bureaucratic culture:* As organizations grow in size, the higher need for coordination results in bureaucratic rules and procedures which often become ends in themselves, rather than means to an end. While ensuring stability and consistency, these might result in decreased levels of flexibility in adapting to changing conditions.
- Entrepreneurial weakness: Essentially arising from the vision and actions of the founder, these might be manifested through
  - Untrained (non-professional) and inexperienced entrepreneurs in a particular trade, who are unable to read the market correctly or respond effectively to market demands.
  - Greed and profiteering: Often, entrepreneurs have limited, short-term vision, preferring to concentrate on quick profits, rather than being willing to compromise on the preset for longer-term and more sustainable gains. This is also manifested in unwillingness to buy technology and pay skilled loyal workers, fearing reduction in immediate profits.
  - Often, in their enthusiasm for success and fame, an entrepreneur might allow himself to get carried away by some immediate success experiences, and rashly launch into a too-fast growth trajectory without building systems and organization with a committed, trained, and motivated workforce (both at the worker level and at the managerial level) to sustain growth.
- Structural weakness: These are inherent in the tasks, responsibility allocations and division of decision-making, and may arise as a result of
  - Lack of robust management systems and lack of proper delegation of authority.
  - Lack of documented and well laid-out policy and procedure manuals with quality check points.
- External factors on which the organization might not have too much control, but which would nonetheless affect its survival, would include non-availability

of logistics chain and high cost of distribution, poor industrial and logistic infrastructure and lack of modern facilities for shipment and handling, global competition tending to make products obsolete and tending to push prices down, rising costs of doing business, high economic rents, political intervention, and political instability.

- The trap of success: Organizations which have been successful once, if they are not careful, might end up as victims of their own success. Strategies and subsequent processes which have been successful in one environment might not be equally effective under different environmental conditions. However, once an organization has succeeded, the tendency would be to create standardized processes and procedures in the hope of replicating that success formula. Hence, markets and customers are segmented, inventories and buffers are created, and investments made in technology to achieve economies. However, this process of decreasing dependence on the environment also makes the organization less sensitive, and hence, less responsive to its environment. Moreover, people who hold positions of power in a currently successful setup might resist any strategic reorganization and restructuring that may be required in order to respond to environmental demands, all of which decreases an organization's adaptability.
- Insensitivity to gradual changes: For many organizations, environmental changes happen not suddenly, but gradually and incrementally, over a long period of time, so much so that organizations often fail to notice such changes till it is too late to take any corrective measures. In fact, the external factors described above need not come on suddenly, but could 'creep up' gradually. More often than not, early but ambiguous signs of crisis are overlooked by organizations as exceptional or immaterial events, till they become so huge in magnitude that they overwhelm the organization. Some early but unmistakable signs of crisis which organizations need to be sensitive to would include gradual deterioration in cash flow, increasing turnover of managers, gradual growth of a competitive small-scale player, increase in overhead costs, etc.
- Bounded rationality: This refers to the inherent limitations of rational information-processing and decision-making by managers. Time constraints and information overload imply that managers cannot consider all possible alternatives and their possible consequences. Moreover, prior to taking the decision, managers can at best have a probabilistic idea of the outcome of the decision. Hence, managerial decision-making is more often a response to the *perceived* reality. Should the reality be perceived wrongly, or misinterpreted, the organizational responses would also be ineffective.
- Organizations as defenses against anxieties: The fact that all human beings die subconsciously creates a feeling of impermanence in all of us. Organizations, with their focus on rationality, reliability, control, etc. provide a feeling of predictability of continuity which acts as a psychological counter to our deep-seated anxieties.

This has implications for the perception of reality by the organizations' managers. If the decision-makers' focus is on reducing uncertainties and warding off psychologically threatening facts, they might unconsciously tend to ignore such 'unacceptable' facts and concentrate only on those aspects of 'reality' which provide some element of psychological comfort to them. In the process, it is likely that this incorrect perception would lead to ineffective responses by the organization.

## 8.4 Patterns of organizational failures

A study of organizations that have failed have yielded certain common organizational styles, which can broadly be categorized into five types of organizations as shown in Table 8.1 below. This typology includes dramatic organizations, suspicious organizations, compulsive organizations, depressive organizations and detached organizations, where the strategy, structural configurations and culture appear to predispose the organization toward failure. The *dramatic* or 'impulsive' organization is normally dominated by an over-ambitious, dominating, egoistic CEO, seeking constant excitement through bold and risky ventures and unconventional mega moves. It is when such moves or strategies represent an extension of the CEO's personality rather than a well-planned response based on intelligent market analysis that organizations start becoming ineffective. The *suspicious* organization, characterized by low trust level, has an overwhelming focus on tight controls, and distrust is institutionalized as a way of working.

**Table 8.1** *Patterns of organizational failure*

| | *Strategy* | *Structure* | *Culture* |
|---|---|---|---|
| *Dramatic organization* | Hyperactive; over-ambitious and inconsistent goals | Primitive and rudimentary; weak second-tier management, over-centralized | Dependency; passivity among subordinates |
| *Suspicious organization* | Reactive and conservative; analytical and diversified | Elaborate information-processing; centralized | Lack of trust; 'fight or flight'; power oriented |
| *Compulsive organization* | Narrow, focused, and tightly calculated | Rigid, formal, and segmented; hierarchical | Rigid, inward, and insecure; bureaucratic |
| *Depressive organization* | Lack of focus and direction; antiquated | Ritualistic and bureaucratic; poor internal communication | Inward; lack of initiative and leadership |
| *Detached organization* | Vacillating; narrow and parochial | Blocks to smooth communication; no scanning mechanisms | Lack of warmth; conflicts; inward-looking |

*Compulsive* organizations are 'stagnant bureaucracies' with enormous focus on rules and procedures, which have become ends in themselves, and where the organization, in the process, has lost touch with reality. *Depressive* organizations are another form of such bureaucracies, characterized by general apathy and listlessness, lack of sense of purpose, diffidence and pessimism, mediocrity, ineptitude and a sense of powerlessness. Finally, the *detached* organization suffers from lack of strong leadership, lack of involvement and commitment from the organization, with managers pursuing their individual goals often at the cost of organizational objectives. Managers have to be able to identify signals or patterns of failure that exist outside organizational consciousness, and might include 'scape-goating', lack of problem ownership, division of the organization into permanent, mutually exclusive informal subgroups, individual awareness of problems limited to private group discussions, no open sharing, lack of problem-solving approach, etc.

Table 8.2 illustrates some early warning signs that managers would do well to heed, and a possible explanation for the concerned problem.

**Table 8.2** *Early warning signals of organizational failure*

| *Early warning signals* | *Possible problem* |
|---|---|
| Sales are unpredictable and irregular | Customers are acquired more by luck than design or effort |
| Not many customers place a repeat order and few new customers are from 'word of mouth' recommendations | Either the product is not up to quality or the company fails to live up to its promises |
| Prices and profit margins are being squeezed down | Market is getting more competitive, and the company's product is failing to hold its value. Customers are starting to believe they can get better products elsewhere |
| Sales are falling | Firm's market is in decline. Services are either not as good as they were/or promised, or customers' needs and desires are changing so that they no longer require the firm's services (obsolescence or substitutes) |
| Constant fire-fighting | Firm is reacting to problems rather than proactively seeking to solve them. Management skills or resources need improving |
| Large cash flow fluctuations | Financial management skills or systems are not effective |
| No capital reserves | Firm is probably either under-capitalized or trading unprofitably |
| Staff retention is poor | People lack belief in the company. Firm's people management skills and recruitment practices need to be improved |

(Contd...

... Contd)

| | |
|---|---|
| Culture of 'excuses' | The firm has accepted defeat. No one is responsible, it is everybody else's fault, and nothing can be done! |
| Always focusing on the rosy future, never the problematic present | Managers cannot cope with things as they are and console themselves hoping for improvements tomorrow |

Cameron, Whetten, and Kim (1987) have identified certain dysfunctional consequences of organizational decline. Hence, it is likely that, for an organization in decline:

- Decision-making becomes centralized and downward-directed, and less participative.
- Long-term, strategic planning is replaced by short-term, crisis-management planning.
- Innovation is deemphasized, with risk-averse decision-making and discouragement of experimentation.
- Convenient scapegoats, mostly leaders, are blamed for the decline.
- Interdepartmental, interpersonal conflicts increase and become dysfunctional.
- There is high resistance to any new change initiatives, with turf protection and conservative decision-making.
- Morale and motivation is low among the workforce, with high turnover, high politicking by special interest groups, abundance of rumors, and general apathy toward work.

Managers need to ask questions periodically, however uncomfortable they might be, to ensure that warning signs are not being ignored. Some of the questions could be:

- Is the firm facing difficulty paying its bills?
- Is the firm experiencing a shrinking market for its product?
- Is the firm frequently losing customer sales?
- Is there an increase in customer complaints, revealing that the firm's business is failing to meet their needs?
- Are inventory levels climbing faster than sales, and is more inventory being built up than sales warrant?
- Is the firm highly leveraged and thinly capitalized?
- Is the firm essentially a one-person management team?
- Is the firm suffering from poor management communications?
- Are decisions not being disseminated down from the top?
- Is the firm late in producing financial statements?
- Is the firm experiencing sales growth but no growth in net income?
- Does the firm have a tight grip on expenditure, or is the firm committing to expenditure before cash is in hand?

**Weitzel and Jonsson's (1989) model** (Figure 8.1) traces the degrees through which an organization declines and finally dies. The model also suggests some actions of management at each stage that can halt the decline, except of course at the final dissolution stage.

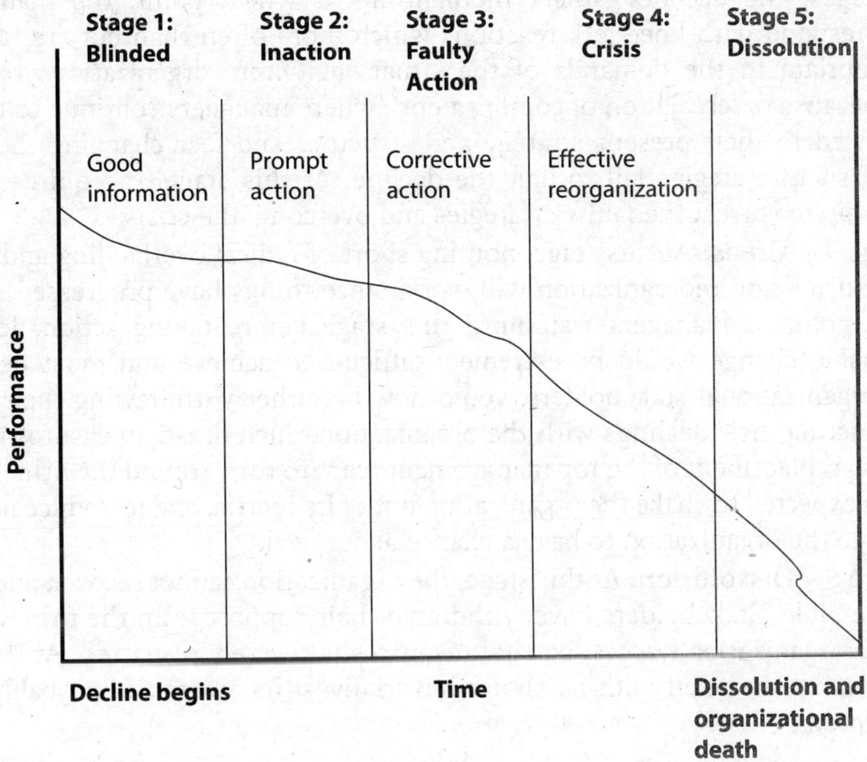


**Figure 8.1** *Organizational failure and decline*

**Stage 1 – Blinded:** At this stage, organizations are either unable or unwilling to recognize the internal or external symptoms of problems that might threaten their long-term survival. This could either be because of lack of proper monitoring or information-gathering systems in place, or because of psychological unwillingness to acknowledge unpleasant realities. At this stage, access to good information and a strong top management team can prevent decline and allow the organization to continue its growth pattern.

**Stage 2 – Inaction:** In the first stage, in spite of signals that exist of impending crisis, top management fails to take cognizance of the facts, and hence, does not take any action to stem the rot, perhaps from a mistaken hope that these are temporary phenomenon that would get rectified over time. Organizational inertia might also be another reason for this inaction. In order to prevent further decline, management might have to take some prompt action in the form of downsizing, or other cost-cutting measures, which, though short-term, would help to stabilize matters for a while.

**Stage 3 – Faulty action:** When corrective actions are not taken in the first two stages, the decline gathers momentum, at which point, the management might respond with knee-jerk reactions which more often than not are faulty and inappropriate to the demands of the situation. Often, organizations reach this stage because of 'escalation of commitment', where managers continue to be overly committed to their present strategy and structure and fear changing them, even though such strategies fail to halt the decline. At this stage, it requires a strong leadership to correct the faulty strategies and overcome the crisis.

**Stage 4 – Crisis:** At this stage, nothing short of radical overhauling and massive restructuring and reorganization will work, since things have progressed to a very critical point. If managers wait until this stage before taking action, long-term sustainable change would be extremely difficult to achieve and must be drastic, since organizational stakeholders would now be either withdrawing their support or restricting their dealings with the organization. Such drastic measures normally call for a replacement of the top management team to turn around the firm. The new team is expected to shake the organization out of its inertia, and introduce new ideas to enable the organization to have a chance at survival.

**Stage 5 – Dissolution:** At this stage, the organization cannot recover, and decline is irreversible. Stakeholders have withdrawn their support from the firm, implying that the organization's access to vital resources is severely restricted. At this stage, the organization is left with no choice but to divest its assets and probably file for bankruptcy.

## 8.5 Implications for managers

The need to manage the process of organizational decline is as great as the need to manage growth. However, organizations do not die as 'neatly' as living beings: they might make turnarounds, get merged, or are taken over, and continue to survive in some form. A manager's effectiveness lies in being able to identify signals of impending crisis and taking precautionary and/or corrective action. In the process, managers have to remember that there are no isolated or single causes for an organization's failure or decline; it is normally a combination of several factors. This would require the manager to continually analyze the organization's structure to pinpoint any sources of inertia that might have emerged, as well as continuous scanning of the environment to identify any changes that have to

> To prevent failure, managers have to continually analyze the organization's structure to pinpoint any sources of inertia that might have emerged, as well as continuously scan the environment to identify any changes that need to be responded to.

be responded to. Sometimes, by virtue of being a part of the organization, it might be difficult for the manager to identify internal or external problems. Hence, other managers, board members, and influential stakeholders may be called on to analyze and give feedback about the organization's current situation.

## CHAPTER SUMMARY

Organizational decline refers to that life-cycle stage of an organization when it fails to anticipate, recognize, avoid, neutralize, or adapt to external or internal pressures that threaten its long-term survival. Organizational failure occurs because of a number of reasons, predominant among them being: organizational inertia owing to risk aversion, desire to maximize personal rewards, overly bureaucratic culture, entrepreneurial weakness, structural weakness, external factors, the trap of success (overconfidence and complacence), insensitivity to gradual changes, and bounded rationality.

A typology of failure in organizations yields five different patterns: dramatic organizations, suspicious organizations, compulsive organizations, depressive organizations, and detached organizations. The *dramatic* or 'impulsive' organization is normally dominated by an over-ambitious, dominating, egoistic CEO, seeking constant excitement through bold and risky ventures, and unconventional mega moves. The *suspicious* organization, characterized by low trust level, has an overwhelming focus on tight controls, and distrust is institutionalized as a way of working. *Compulsive* organizations are the 'stagnant bureaucracies' with enormous focus on rules and procedures, which have become an end in themselves, and where the organization, in the process, has lost touch with reality. *Depressive* organizations are characterized by general apathy and listlessness, lack of sense of purpose, diffidence and pessimism, mediocrity, ineptitude, and a sense of powerlessness. The *detached* organization suffers from lack of strong leadership, lack of involvement and commitment from the organization, which leads to managers pursuing their individual goals often at the cost of organizational objectives.

Weitzel and Jonsson's model traces the degrees through which an organization declines and finally dies, namely, stage 1 (blinded), where organizations are either unable to or unwilling to recognize the internal or external symptoms of problems that might threaten their long-term survival; stage 2 (inaction), where top management fails to take cognizance of the facts, and hence does not take any action to stem the rot; stage 3 (faulty action), when management might respond with knee-jerk reactions which more often than not are faulty and inappropriate to the demands of the situation; stage 4 (crisis), where nothing short of radical overhauling and massive restructuring and reorganization will work, since things have progressed to a very critical point, and finally, stage 5 (dissolution), where the organization cannot recover, and decline is irreversible.

## Review Questions

1. Define organizational failure.
2. How does organizational ecology help to explain the reasons for organizational decline?

3. Discuss the main reasons why organizations fail. How can mangers prevent failure?
4. Describe the structural characteristics of various types of organizations which are more prone to failure.
5. Discuss the various stages through which organizations pass during decline and failure.

## Project Assignment

Look through old issues of business magazines and identify five large professional organizations which were once successful but which have since failed and no longer exist, or exist in a different form. Identify the main reasons – both internal and external – to understand why each of them failed. Suggest ways in which each of these organizations could have prevented failure.

## CASE ILLUSTRATION: '*PEUGEOT* LEAVES INDIA'

In October 1994, Europe's fourth largest automobile major, *Peugeot* of France, entered the Indian automobile market through a joint venture with *Premier Automobiles Ltd.* (*PAL*), christened *PAL-Peugeot Ltd.* As *Peugeot* was one of the first automobile MNCs to enter India, the early mover advantage was expected to help the company make its mark in the Indian automobile market. According to reports, *Peugeot* was set to achieve cash break-even within two years and to begin generating profits by 1998. *Peugeot* decided to enter the Indian market with its passenger car model – *Peugeot 309*, as the car was believed to be the best suited for Indian terrain. Production began at the Kalyan plant and the car was launched in 1995, positioned in the mid-size segment, against *Daewoo's Cielo* and *Maruti's Esteem*. The initial response to the car was positive, with the company selling around 10,000 units in the first year of the launch. However, *Peugeot*'s ambitious plans soon went haywire when production at the Kalyan plant was disrupted due to labor unrest in mid-1996. Production of the *Peugeot 309* had to be halted resulting in mounting losses and a severe cash crunch. Problems surfaced with *PAL* regarding certain strategic issues including infusion of fresh funds and violation of the *PAL-Peugeot* MoU. By 1997, the company's accumulated losses touched over Rs 3 billion. In November 1997, *Peugeot* announced its decision to exit from the JV and leave the Indian market, claiming that it was moving out of India because of a policy decision by its parent company to concentrate only on European markets.

*Peugeot*'s partner, *PAL*, was one of India's first automobile manufacturing companies, established in 1944 by the Walchand Hirachand family. The family owned many other businesses, including *Hindustan Shipyard, Hindustan Aeronautics, Hindustan Construction, Rayalgaon Sugar*, and *Walchandnagar Industries*. In the early 1950s, *PAL* entered into a technical agreement with the Italian automobile major *Fiat*, for manufacturing *Fiat 500* in India. Despite the impressive 10,000 unit sales in its first year, *Peugeot* recorded a loss of Rs 920 million for the year 1995-96. The company's problems could, by and large, be traced to *PAL*'s association with *Fiat*. After having partnered *Fiat* in India for a significant time, *PAL* entered into a new technical agreement to assemble the *Fiat Uno* at its Kurla plant and the technical agreement was changed into a joint venture in 1997. The June 1996 production slowdown at the Kalyan plant had its roots in the problems at *PAL*'s Kurla plant where the workers had gone on strike over issues related to wages, incentives, and VRS. *PAL* was manufacturing the *Premier Padmini* and the *Premier 118NE* at the Kurla plant (later the *Uno* and *Siena* models as well), and the *Peugeot 309* and the *118NE* at the Kalyan plant. The Kurla and Kalyan plants were dependent on each other, as the Kurla unit was the sole supplier of components such as gearboxes and rear axles to the Kalyan plant. *PAL* was reportedly unhappy with *Peugeot* over the *309* which was only 24% indigenised. This made the spare parts very expensive and the company was unable to reduce the price of the car. *PAL* claimed that *Peugeot* was just not interested in increasing the indigenization level of the vehicle. There were reports of disagreements over the high price of the CKD kits from *Peugeot* as well. Due to the 1996 labor problems, the company had to bear heavy inventory carrying costs. To compensate for this, *PAL* reportedly asked *Peugeot* to cut down the CKD prices and release funds as loan to the joint venture. *PAL* sources said that *Peugeot* could have advanced loans to the company by treating CKD and other equipment with the venture as security for the loan. *PAL* even requested *Peugeot* to use its name to raise bank loans abroad for the joint venture, where the cost of funds was much lower than in India.

*Peugeot*'s announcement in August 1999 that it had agreed to license its diesel engines to *PAL* for 5 years took observers by surprise. *Peugeot* also decided to write-off claims on *PAL* amounting to Rs 850 million on account of license and technical fees. The deal did not involve any royalty payments and *Peugeot* had agreed to transfer its stake in the joint venture to *PAL*; this added to the mystery. In January 2001, *Peugeot Citroen* and *Telco* began discussions for introducing a luxury car in India. There were also reports of *Peugeot* planning a tie-up with the Indian two-wheeler major, *Hero Honda*, to enter the motorcycle segment in India. Interestingly enough, the FIs were reported to be planning to use their clout in the Foreign Investment Promotion Board (FIPB) to protest against the re-entry of *Peugeot*. However, in July 2001, after the completion of various feasibility studies, *Telco* and *Peugeot* decided against going ahead with the project for the time being.

### Critical enquiry

What learning does this case hold for an MNC desirous of doing business in India?

***Key words and phrases***: Organizational decline, ecology, warning signals, blindness, inaction, inertia, dissolution

# CHAPTER 9

# Managing Organizational Change

**CHAPTER OUTLINE**

Why do organizations need to change?

❖

The changing paradigm of organizational design

❖

Organizational readiness for change

❖

Change leadership

❖

Approaches to change management

❖

Creating a learning organization

## ORGANIZATIONAL INSIGHT

In the middle and late 1990s, the automotive industry in India was experiencing significant turbulence and upheavals. *Maruti Udyog Limited* (*MUL*) (renamed *Maruti Suzuki India Ltd* in 2007), one of India's leading automobile manufacturers, was no exception to this. Increasing competitiveness of the external market and a lax work culture internally, coupled with increasing demands from unions without any improvement in the organization's performance forced the *MUL* management to take the unpleasant decision to downsize their workforce, through a Voluntary Retirement Scheme (VRS). This decision was further reinforced when, following a three-month strike called by the unions in 2000, the management managed to run the plant on reduced manpower, without a drop in production levels or productivity. The main criterion for reducing manpower was inefficiency and non-performance, though employees approaching retirement age were also targeted. The senior managers in charge of implementing the downsizing were unanimous about the necessity for downsizing, in terms of weeding out non-performers.

Prior to launching the VRS, a team of senior officials were sent to other automobile companies in India that had already gone through downsizing, to learn from their experiences and mistakes. Another group of managers were given training to act as VRS counselors. Around six months of planned and focused effort went into this downsizing exercise. The main aim of the VRS was to provide a financial buffer to the downsized employees to start life afresh in some alternative career. The separation package was a mix of monetary and non-monetary components: monetary in terms of a lumpsum amount of money, and non-monetary in terms of helping downsized employees to set up businesses, arranging for/sponsoring their training in alternative skills, or helping them to get placed elsewhere through managers' personal contacts. Prior to starting the downsizing exercise, job rotations and other proactive measures were introduced to increase the organization's flexibility and efficiency in working with less manpower.

Of the 1100 downsized employees, 50% took VRS voluntarily; the remaining half, comprising non-performing or medically unfit employees or those nearing retirement age were counseled and motivated into taking VRS. The main outcome from downsizing was envisaged as not merely cost-cutting through headcount reduction but a way of utilizing technology to achieve maximum value for money for its products, and pave the way for the generation of more employment opportunities for the correct skill mix of people. The envisaged outcome was successfully achieved. However, the implementation process did encounter its share of challenges. Expectedly enough, the unions were extremely hostile, right from the beginning. Notwithstanding this, the top management and managers kept up extensive communication to employees before, during, and after downsizing. Managers repeatedly communicated with employees at different forums, to keep up the morale of the surviving employees, and to overcome feelings of isolation among the downsized employees. Though the decision to downsize was taken by the top management, actual implementation was widely delegated to senior managers across various hierarchical levels in the plant. While these designated managers had been broadly briefed about their role, the finer details of how to handle the employees while counseling them were left to the individual manager.

Following the VRS exercise, a number of large-scale interventions were introduced to iron out the initial resentment among employees and power play by supervisors, etc. As expected, there was widespread resentment after the VRS, but sustained and extensive communication by the top management to the employees at various forums helped to mitigate and lessen the initial negative feelings.

## 9.1 Why do organizations need to change?

Over the last two decades, the business environment throughout the world has witnessed phenomenal upheavals in the form of technological innovations, opening up of new markets, deregulation, developments in information technology, and communication practices. Such upheavals and the challenges posed by the information revolution have led to heightened competition and greater struggle for survival among organizations, forcing them to take a fresh look at traditional ways of conducting business (Venkatraman and Henderson, 1998). Organizations have now begun to realize that in order to remain competitive in this turbulent scenario, they need to reduce costs. Further, organizations are also realizing that today, their formula for success lies not just in superior technology, efficiency, or manufacturing capacities, any or all of which can be replicated by competitors, but rather, in effective management of their human resources (Pfeffer, 1998).

Change management refers to the process of renewing the organization's direction, structure, and capabilities to serve the ever-changing needs of the marketplace, customers, and employees

The need for effectively managing the human resources of an organization is further emphasized through the concept of 'knowledge economy'. This concept underscores the importance of intellectual ability in providing the leading edge for success in an organization, by having a knowledgeable and committed workforce who can contribute to its survival and growth. The need to cut costs to remain competitive has provided organizations with the impetus to initiate a spate of organizational change programs. These change efforts have taken various forms such as restructuring, downsizing, rightsizing, mergers and acquisitions, takeovers, delayering, etc.

Change management refers to *the process of renewing the organization's direction, structure, and capabilities to serve the ever-changing needs of the marketplace, customers, and employees* (Holbeche, 2006). By definition, this implies that any change in organizations will involve some degree of re-visioning and restructuring. In fact, reorganizations are a popular move with organizational leaders, who believe that making big structural changes will lead to better performance (Blenko et al, 2010). However, whether reorganizing merely for the sake of changing benefits organizations is a subject of continuing debate among scholars and practitioners alike. We need to have a clear understanding of why organizations change or need to change, in order to resolve this dilemma.

Given the dynamic nature of the business scenario today, the environment exerts enormous pressure on organizations to continuously reinvent themselves. Some of the major environmental forces include:

- **Political pressure** in the form of changes in government legislation, international laws and wars. For example, following the recent court judgment on the Bhopal gas tragedy, there is mounting pressure on the government to bring in stricter environmental regulations for MNCs operating in India, with clear punitive measures for non-compliance spelt out. In 1991, following deregulation of the Indian markets, there was heavy pressure on Indian corporates to become globally competitive, resulting in widespread restructuring among companies.
- **Economic factors**, including actions of competitors, changes in the world economy, market decline, obsolescence of products, fluctuations in exchange

rates, etc. For example, the recent economic downturn brought about by the irresponsible actions of foreign financial institutions had a cascading effect on almost all countries worldwide, with large-scale downsizing and restructuring of organizations and economic depression. A host of strict regulations is now being brought in to prevent such meltdowns in the future, which is going to further affect how organizations function.

- **Technological factors** such as the proliferation of the Internet, new production processes, changes in transport technology, etc. have radically altered the way in which organizations are becoming more responsive to customers' demands and the market. For example, the increasing use of ERP application software has not only made end-to-end processes faster and more efficient, it has also resulted in large-scale delayering and leaner organizational hierarchy. Likewise, the advent of social networking software has at one level opened up innovative and new ways for organizations to market their products and reach out to their customers, while at the same time, by making organizational boundaries more vulnerable and permeable to social influences, increased the stakeholders' expectations that organizations become socially, financially, and environmentally accountable in their business dealings.
- **Socio-cultural factors** such as changes in customer demographics, changes in customer expectations, life-style changes, diversity in the workplace, diverse skill availability, increasing mobility of the workforce, and increasing number of women in the workforce are changing the way organizations function. For example, the increasing environmental consciousness on the part of consumers is forcing organizations to 'go green' and adopt environmentally responsible approaches to doing business. Likewise, with increasing social consciousness, corporations are now adopting various CSR (Corporate Social Responsibility) initiatives to project a 'humane' image to society.
- **Fashion fads,** which lead organizations to mimic or copy their more successful competitors. For example, many downsizing and restructuring initiatives taken up by organizations are a mimetic response to benchmark with the best in class, and are not dictated by the actual needs of the organization.
- **Internal environment,** including organizational structures, processes, routines, and practices, which, if not changed periodically, might result in 'silos' and build-up of 'corporate cholesterol' (Vermeulen et al, 2010), affecting an organization's health and adaptability. While most managers would be averse to rocking an apparently well-functioning boat, periodic restructuring helps to shake up organizational inertia, forces people to start forming new networks, disrupts all innovation-stifling routines in an organization, and most importantly, breaks up outdated power structures and entrenched interests that may be quietly misdirecting a company's allocation of resources.

## 9.2 The changing paradigm of organizational design

While the basic dimensions of organization design remain unchanged, approaches to designing organizations are undergoing rapid changes. Considerations of efficiency are rapidly being replaced by a focus on organizational learning. While issues such as the size and scope of operations, how to break down tasks and create lines of authority, how to improve communication and clearly defined duties and responsibilities, and issues of centralization and decentralization are still relevant and important, they have been superseded by other contextual considerations, namely,:

- Flexibility, to support organizational learning and innovation, and to adapt to environmental changes
- The challenge of globalization, to manage diversity and multicultural markets
- Facilitation of knowledge creation by exploiting individuals' skills and capabilities, as well as the transfer and sharing of this knowledge throughout the organization
- The enhancement of relationships with external partners beyond normal organizational boundaries, through strategic alliances and networks

Clearly, the new norm today is constant change (Vermeulen et al, 2010) and organizations have to constantly reinvent themselves in order to survive. As a result, some significant changes have resulted in organizational design paradigms:

a) *From vertical to horizontal structures*: The traditional focus on hierarchy, control through differences in formal designations and reporting relationships are now giving way to leaner and flatter structures, where vertical layers are being reduced. Organizational learning is facilitated by creating structures around horizontal workflows and processes rather than departmental functions. However, a flat structure might give rise to problems of self-identity, self-esteem, and growth needs, as well as have negative implications in terms of perceived lack of career growth.

b) *From routine tasks to empowered roles*: A task is a narrowly defined piece of work assigned to a person. A role carries with it discretion and responsibility, shaped by one's own and others' expectations from that role. With increase in knowledge levels and awareness of the average worker, organizations are now able to empower their employees with greater responsibilities and autonomy, rather than merely giving them precise and detailed instructions about how to carry out a particular task.

c) *From formal control systems to shared information*: In traditional organizations, formal systems are required to manage large amounts of complex information flow and to control possible deviations. In learning organizations, however, widespread sharing of information keeps the organization functioning at an optimum level. Hence, formal systems are geared more for information sharing purposes than controlling the behavior of members.

d) *From competitive to collaborative strategy*: Advances in knowledge management concepts have reinforced the fact that sharing information and knowledge among various hierarchical levels facilitates organizational learning. Collaboration has long been accepted as a win-win strategy in various organizational processes. The increasing numbers of strategic alliances among organizations serve to reinforce this paradigm shift toward collaboration.

e) *From rigid to adaptive culture:* For an organization to survive and grow, its culture should encourage adaptation to the external environment. Organizations that are highly successful in a static environment might become victims of their own success when the environment changes. In a learning organization, the culture would encourage openness, continuous improvement and change, experimentation, and respect for others' ideas and opinions. While a perfect learning organization might be a difficult concept to implement, organizations today are increasingly striving to move toward that objective.

## 9.3 Creating organizational readiness for change: role of power, politics, and conflict management

Different organizations respond differently to pressures for change, due to a variety of reasons. For example, market decline causes some organizations to respond positively by learning from the problems and adopting innovative approaches to close the gap between performance and aspirations, and in the process, change into a learning organization. In others, environmental pressures might inhibit innovative change as managers' cognitive and decision-making processes become restricted when faced with threatening problems (Mone et al, 1998). The 'trap of success' is another issue. Some companies which have had a winning business formula become overconfident and arrogant about their success formula and market dominance. This is reinforced by an inherent belief in the correctness of their approach, routines, and practices that become embedded in the organization as the 'correct way' and by self-seeking shareholders who inhibit exploration of other areas and approaches. Gradually, it results in a 'learning-disabled organization' which is unwilling and unable to change.

Finally, any organization has to maintain an optimum balance between stability and change. Depending on the extent to which an organization's mission is institutionalized in stakeholders, the extent of diffusion of power and resources throughout the organization, and the rationale managers employ to explain decline, the organization will respond positively to change or to stability. The less institutionalized the mission, the more concentrated the power in the organization, which makes decisions and allocates resources for change; and the more the causes of decline are perceived to be permanent, the more an organization is likely to introduce innovative change (Palmer et al, 2006).

In the present business environment, a company ought to be willing to accept chaos in its industry, the global economy, and its own market place as part of the reality of doing business. The present global economy is in flux with a constant state of growth and expansion, which is characterized by both incremental change and long-term systematic transformations. It has been accepted that in the long run, linear thinking will kill an organization. The traditional importance accorded to organizational hierarchies is declining, with increasing focus on creating organizations that are built for speed and for customers. In the process, organizations need to develop 'organizational intelligence' about the constantly shifting business environments in which they operate. There is a shift in business from being about 'transactions' to being about 'value-added' interactions with customers, and in the present scenario, customer care becomes the only true and lasting differentiator.

While most organizations, as part of their everyday activities, undergo incremental changes in processes and approaches, what is of importance here is long-term, sustainable changes with organization-wide impact. Before attempting to undertake any long-term change, it is vital to adopt the right attitude toward sustainable change. Organizations have to appreciate that change involves not only learning something new, but unlearning something that is integrated into an individual's self/social system. Moreover, no organizational change can be brought about unless there is motivation to change. Ways to create this motivation could include instilling some fear or discomfort in the minds of individuals regarding the present state or shaking them out of their complacency; it would also mean addressing the question in people's minds about 'what is in it for them'. Most adult changes involve changes in attitudes/values/self-concept and can be painful and threatening, implying that management of change is not necessarily only rational management, but also emotional management of people, where change leaders would have to lend their supportive shoulders and handhold affected employees through the period of transition.

Organizational changes are effected through individual changes in key members; hence, it is crucial to appoint change leaders/change agents from within the organization who enjoy the rapport and confidence of their colleagues and subordinates and who can therefore act as role models during and after the change process. Finally, change is a multistage cycle and all stages must be planned for and negotiated. Some scholars are of the opinion that since most changes can be painful, a surgical approach ('clean cut') is preferable to prolonging the pain through multiple rounds of change. However, there is no ideal solution, and each organization needs to decide on the phasing of the change process based on the realities of its own situation, rather than going by pre-established templates of action. A readiness-focused change builds awareness of the need for change and communicates a vision for change, creates a climate that is supportive of the desired change by realigning organizational culture, rewards, policies, procedures, and systems, and builds up a participative culture by equipping people throughout the organization with the skills needed to participate meaningfully in planning and implementing strategic change. Planning for change has to be an open process, with an emphasis on establishing general goals and direction, using pilot programs to build commitment within the organization.

An organization's propensity to change can be influenced by freeing the system from redundant structures, processes or functions, generating new patterns of systems in keeping with envisaged/desired future state, reflecting the desired future state or pattern around which the organization is to be reformed, and building individual and organizational cohesiveness to move the organization toward the envisioned state.

While restructuring and change have been ongoing activities for organizations for decades, it is true that nearly two-thirds of change efforts fail to achieve their intended objectives, for various reasons:

- Managers often fail to establish a sense of urgency among their employees regarding the need to change, especially when things appear to be going well. This also calls for clearly articulating a powerful vision of the future to energize the employees and shake them up from their complacency.
- Pressure to act quickly often undermines values and culture. Hence, leaders often tend to take drastic steps without due consideration of other alternatives. In the process, values such as participation, buy-in, and commitment are often compromised. Managers should avoid the temptation to announce instant decisions, and instead find issues that can benefit from employee inputs (Kanter, 2010).
- Sometimes, management exercises too much control. In crises, decision-making tends to get pushed to the top, while people below tend to be passive and wait to be told what to do. Initiative declines and innovation is put on hold. It is necessary to establish short-term tasks that empower employees to seek quick wins, giving them a sense of control over results.
- Urgent tasks divert the attention of leaders from the mood of the organization. Managers get so carried away with the burdens of meetings and decisions that they fail to monitor the culture and note the pulse of employees or assess the impact on employee motivation and performance.
- Communication is often haphazard and erratic. As a result, rumors abound and can destroy the organization's morale.
- Cutting, either people or budgets, seems easier than redeploying – either reallocating resources or reassigning people. Often, strong performers are lost when they could have served elsewhere. Managers often restructure by removing the weakest or newest people, without regard to business needs. It is advisable to establish a pool of strong performers from areas with cutbacks who might be able to help the business in other ways or be called back for special assignments.

- Sometimes, leaders, in their desire to appear 'humane', spend so much on the 'casualties' or victims that they tend to neglect the survivors on whom the future of the organization depends. In the process, these employees might feel ignored and unvalued, and decide to leave.
- Managers fail to form a powerful guiding coalition of influential role models to steer the change in a participative manner, involving all affected parties.
- Managers often fail to effectively manage individual resistance to change.

Knowing what to change is important, but it is equally important to conduct a pre-change audit of the organization's readiness for change to help identify key areas where further action could significantly enhance the prospects of success.

### 9.3.1 Resistance to change

#### *9.3.1.1 Individual and organizational sources of resistance*

Any change process, irrespective of the intended benefits, will encounter resistance; but what has to be put into perspective is the fact that people do not necessarily resist the change *per se*, but the individual transition that a change entails. Change, typically operationalised through different policies, processes and structures, is perceived to be external, situational, event-based, fast, objective and is the same for all. Transition on the other hand is internal, a psychological reorientation that people have to go through before the change can work. It is perceived to be subjective, unpredictable, involving emotions and feelings, and different for different people. More often than not, it is this transition, and not the change *per se*, that employees resist.

> Any change effort, irrespective of the expected benefits that might accrue, will encounter resistance, at both the individual and the organizational levels.

Resistance to change could be manifested at both individual and organizational levels. At the *individual level*, force of habit and discomfort with uncertainty could be powerful inhibitors to acceptance of change. In fact, research has shown that individuals have difficulty in giving up established patterns of behavior and embracing new behavior, however beneficial the new behavior might be. Moreover, because of uncertainty regarding the future, some employees might be perceived as standing to benefit more at the cost of others, because of the proposed change. Often, managers fail to communicate clearly the expected benefits and rationale for the change, resulting in uncertainty and cynicism regarding whether the change is required by the organization as a whole or is intended to benefit a few. Sometimes, the amount of change proposed could be perceived to be excessive and hence, threatening; in case of earlier negative experiences with change efforts, this could serve to reinforce the resistance.

At the organizational level, structural inertia brought on by established patterns of routines and practices and group inertia could account for resistance. Moreover, an inability to see the larger picture and overall benefits of the change, along with perceived threat to individual expertise, established power relationships and preferential resource allocations might further accentuate this resistance. It is often observed that resistance to change tends to move through a life cycle comprising five phases. In *phase 1*, there are only a few people who see the need for change and take reform seriously. As a fringe element of the organization, they might face open criticism, ridicule and persecution, along with massive resistance. The larger the organization, the higher is the resistance at this stage. In *phase 2*, as the movement for change begins to grow (assuming it has not died out in the first phase itself), the forces for and against it become identifiable. The change is discussed, and is more thoroughly understood and appreciated by more of the organization's members. Greater understanding may lessen the perceived threat of the change. In *phase 3*, there is a direct conflict and showdown between the forces for and against the change, and unless handled properly, might result in the death of the change efforts. In *phase 4*, the supporters of the change see any residual resistance as a nuisance, since the detractors, though not too many in numbers, might still try to derail the change efforts. In the final phase, *phase 5*, the resistors to the change are as few in number and alienated as were the supporters in phase 1.

#### *9.3.1.2 Utilizing the power of resistance*

While it is an accepted fact that any proposed organizational change will meet with some degree of resistance, managers have to be sensitive to the fact that this resistance could be either covert or overt. While active resistance is often overt and therefore, easier to understand and tackle, covert or passive resistance, which is more difficult to detect, and therefore handle, could be equally problematic. Common signs of active resistance to change from employees could include being critical and finding fault continuously, openly ridiculing and undermining others' efforts, appealing to others' fear of the unknown to garner more support for resistance, using facts selectively to project only the negative aspects of the change, while remaining silent regarding potential benefits, and therefore manipulating and distorting facts, blaming or accusing the change leaders, intimidating or threatening, sabotaging change efforts by word and action, starting unfounded rumors, blocking information and arguing. On the other hand, passive resistance is harder to detect and could include signals such as agreeing verbally but not following through, procrastinating, withholding information, standing by and allowing change to fail and feigning ignorance.

#### *9.3.1.3 Overcoming resistance to change*

It is true that for a change leader, resistance can be a source of frustration and acute despair. However, for any change effort to be successful, the first requirement for implementation would be to identify the sources of resistance and overcome the same. In fact, addressed positively, resistance can actually become a source of strength in a change initiative rather than a hindrance. But for this to happen, it is essential that managers in a way embrace resistance by actively looking for and identifying the real reason for resistance. Rather than getting diverted and discouraged by initial resistance, one has to persevere and maintain focus, attempt to join the resistance and look for commonalities, and avoid 'pushing back' when attacked by resistance.

The 'resistor' is to be respected and listened to with an open mind; he/she might have important insights to offer regarding genuine problems, which will have to be addressed as part of the change plans. Appearing to be sympathetic to the resistors is likely to facilitate managing and overcoming resistance rather than being perceived to be opposing and ignoring it. Change leaders would have to be trained or sensitized to the power of persuasion in overcoming resistance to change. Table 9.1 below tabulates the principles of persuasion (Cialdini, 2001) and the change management tactic that can be used to overcome resistance and to persuade detractors.

**Table 9.1** *Using principles of persuasion in change management*

| *Principle* | *Change management tactic* |
|---|---|
| **Liking**: Individuals like people who are similar to them, who like them, who praise them. | Use first level supervisors and employees to communicate change to other employees; be appreciative of employees and their past efforts |
| **Reciprocity**: Individuals feel obligated to repay in kind, when they receive help, gifts or praise without asking. | Practice generosity and benevolence; offer help to peers and staff who need it |
| **Social proof**: People are influenced by others who are similar to them | Arrange visits to other organizations that have implemented similar change efforts; build a critical mass of change supporters and influence others through this critical mass |
| **Consistency**: People feel compelled to fulfil voluntary, public and written commitments | Enlist employee support in a public forum by asking people to indicate their commitment openly (do not coerce or pressurize them to commit) |
| **Authority**: Individuals are influenced by others who are perceived as experts | Develop professional and technical competence in your job so that others around you see you as being competent |
| **Scarcity**: People tend to value things that are relatively in short supply | Share strategic information with employees; identify the opportunities they are likely to miss if the organization does not undergo change |

As in any management approach, the change leader has available to him/her a range of approaches to overcome resistance. Based on an analysis of the specifics of the situation, and the perceived life-stage of the resistance, the change leader has to decide which approach is likely to be the most effective in the given context. Often, a combination of approaches is likely to be required, for different profiles of employees. A few approaches are discussed here:

**Education and communication:** This involves informing people about the rationale for the proposed change, providing information regarding the expected benefits of change, the desired future envisioned, and broad details pertaining to the change process. For example, when *Tata Steel* decided to take up its manpower rationalization exercise in 1996, in a bid to reduce by half its huge manpower over the next ten years, the then MD, Mr J. J. Irani took it on himself to talk about and communicate the necessity for change at every press conference, newsletter, and public meeting from six months before the actual downsizing exercise started. This is effective where resistance to change is due to lack of information or misinformation. However, this approach is time-consuming and might be a problem in situations which demand a quick response.

**Participation and involvement:** This implies involving people in the change process as active participants. It can be a powerful means of persuasion, in situations where resistance is a reaction to a sense of exclusion from the change process. However, managers have to remember that the act of getting employees to participate actively may slow down the process and introduce an element of compromise in decisions that could reduce the optimality of the change. Moreover, participation implies knowledgeable and intelligent inputs from participants. However, if employees affected by the change are unaware of the specifics or unable to contribute meaningfully to the discussion process, or when the change process involves decisions that are bound to be adverse to the participants, this approach might not be effective. For instance, in the case of *Tata Steel*, at the beginning of the exercise, meetings were held with union leaders in an effort to convince the workforce about the need to retrench and cut down. However, given the family-friendly image enjoyed by the *Tata* group and its long history of job security for its employees, this was neither effective nor convincing.

**Facilitation and support:** Where resistance is due to anxiety and uncertainty, managers may use this approach by providing resources – both technical and emotional, to address the anxieties. Hence, when *Philips India Ltd.* decided to shut down its Kolkata factory, its top management sponsored training programs and counseling sessions for the downsized employees to enable them to take up alternative careers. However, this requires financial resources, time, and interpersonal support that the already overburdened and stressed out managers may not feel able or prepared to give.

**Negotiation and agreement:** This involves offering incentives to actual or potential resistors, especially when the resistors are in a strong position to undermine the change if their concerns are not addressed. For example, during the restructuring exercise taken up by a leading hotel chain in India, the head chef was proving to be the main resistor, threatening to quit and take the entire kitchen staff with him to set up a competitor establishment next door. One-on-one discussions with him revealed that he had grave monetary liabilities which would get aggravated if the restructuring went through. Almost overnight, 'unofficial' arrangements were made to provide him with the necessary funds to address his monetary needs, with the sole mandate of withdrawing his resistance and getting his kitchen staff to support the process. While special circumstances may necessitate such an approach, it might lead to a 'watering down' of key elements of the change, if not handled well.

**Manipulation and cooptation:** This approach works where participation, facilitation, or negotiation is too time-consuming or resource-demanding, and involves selective use of information, and 'buying' the support of certain individuals by giving them key roles in the change process. However, it runs the risk of creating a backlash if it is seen as a crude and unethical attempt to trick or bribe them into compliance.

**Coercion:** When all other conciliatory approaches and tactics fail, this approach would involve punitive measures of threatening people with undesirable consequences (e.g. firing) if they resist. For example, in the late 1990s, a number of nationalized Indian banks had undertaken restructuring exercises to rationalize their inflated manpower and retrench non-performing and poorly-performing employees. As per Indian law, the only way to rationalize workers was through a VRS (Voluntary Retirement Scheme). In the first few rounds of VRS, it was found that the majority of those applying for VRS were the star performers, who, well aware of their worth, took the attractive separation package offered by the bank and joined private sector organizations at very attractive remuneration packages. Those who steadfastly refused to sign the VRS forms were the poor performers who were apprehensive and felt that it would be difficult for them to get jobs in the private sector. Finally, the bank managers had to 'coerce' them and threaten them with dire consequences if they did not resign. Here, the change recipients have little capacity to effectively resist, as the survival of the organization is at risk if change does not occur quickly. The desired change may occur; however, 'support' achieved in this manner is likely to be superficial and a threat to the enduring nature of the change, since underlying resentment from 'colleagues' who remain could come back later to 'haunt' managers.

#### 9.3.1.4 *Managing conflict during organizational change*

While discussing the life-stages of resistance to change, it was seen that phases 3 and 4 are characterized by direct conflict and confrontation. Though the description seems to imply that a battle is being waged between the supporters and resistors of change, the actual conflict is usually more subtle and may surface in small verbal disagreements, questions, reluctance, etc. Even in normal times, organizational stakeholders are in a state of competition over their share of rewards and resources. Each group of stakeholders has its own goals and vested interest, which might clash with those of other groups. Notwithstanding this, all stakeholders have a common interest in the survival of the organization, and therefore in their own survival. Since any organizational change is likely to threaten the survival of some stakeholders, it is likely that intergroup clashes will occur where the goal-directed behavior of one group of stakeholders is likely to jeopardize or thwart the goals of another. Such clashes, termed **organizational conflicts**, are almost inevitable in any organizational change; the more transformational the change, the more pronounced is the conflict.

Attitudes toward organizational conflict have traversed a spectrum of transformation, from the classical approach, which viewed any conflict as bad for the organization and hence, to be avoided at all cost, to passive acceptance of conflict as a way of organizational life. The contemporary approach is far more interactive in nature and views conflict as something which, managed wisely and in optimum amounts, is actually good for the organization and can result in organizational creativity, innovation, and heightened performance. However, the key word is 'optimum'; while the right amount of conflict can benefit an organization, too much conflict can be harmful and counterproductive to an organization's health. In times of trouble, different groups might perceive the organization's problems in different ways and be willing to act based on their different beliefs. This would definitely help to jolt the organization out of its inertia, improve decision-making, and allow the organization to adapt itself to the changing environment. However, beyond a point, such task-based conflicts might soon take on interpersonal implications where managers cannot even agree on strategic decisions such as resource allocation and organizational priorities. Managers spend so much time arguing and fighting over petty decisions that the process of change can get stalled, letting the organization decline further. Hence, while organizations have to be open to the value of conflict, they should be able to manage conflict in such a way that it does not go beyond an optimum range.

**Pondy's** (1967) **model** describes five stages through which the process of organizational conflict plays out. The same concept would be relevant in the context of conflict during organizational change as well and is discussed later. In stage 1 – **latent conflict** – there is no outright conflict, but several factors create an atmosphere of conflict-producing situations. These factors could include interdependence of tasks, differences in goals and priorities, bureaucratic controls, incompatible or inequitable performance and evaluation criteria, competition for resources, etc. An example of this is the fact that managers must frequently compete for scarce resources. Although there is potential for conflict in the situation, conflict itself will not arise until a demand for limited resources is actually made. In stage 2 – **perceived conflict** – different stakeholder groups become aware of conflict and begin to analyze it. In stage 3 – **felt conflict** – different stakeholder groups may start responding to each other emotionally, with 'us versus them' attitudes polarizing them. The conflict becomes personalized. Hostile feelings may accumulate. Stage 4 represents what is known as **manifest conflict** where intergroup fighting and aggression are common and organizational productivity is likely to suffer. Demonstrated behaviors can include arguments, lack of contact, or even overt contact with covert intentions. The last stage is the **conflict aftermath** where the conflict is resolved or managed. Pondy refers to this stage as the legacy of a conflict episode. Managers who tend to 'smooth over' or suppress conflict will find that the legacy of a conflict situation is much like 'latent' conflict; it still has the potential to explode at any time.

A case in point is that of the appointment of R.S.S.L.N. Bhaskarudu as the Managing Director of India's passenger car market leader *Maruti Udyog Ltd.* (MUL) by the Government of India in August 1997. This was strongly opposed by *Suzuki Motors Corporation (SMC)* of Japan, the GoI's 50% partner in the *MUL* joint venture, claiming that since a majority (five out of nine) of the *MUL* board had opposed the appointment, it was illegal.* According to the government, however, in the 1992 amendment in the GoI-*SMC* joint venture agreement, both the partners were entitled to nominate the MD for five years in turn, and there was no need for any consultation on it. It was alleged that *SMC* was opposing the appointment of Bhaskarudu as it wanted Jagdish Khattar, Executive Director, *MUL* (reportedly an *SMC* loyalist) to become the MD. Heated letters were exchanged between *SMC* and the Industry ministry; in the AGM held on September 22, 1997, *SMC* and GoI representatives even resorted to verbal violence. *SMC* asked for Bhaskurudu's resignation claiming that the minutes of the meeting when Bhaskurudu was appointed, did not fully record its objections to the same. However, the GoI refused to remove Bhaskurudu and reportedly even started looking for a prospective partner in the event of *SMC*'s exit. When Bhaskarudu's appointment was put to vote and met with a tie, Prabir Sengupta, the then Chairman of the *MUL* board, with the backing of the GOI, used his casting vote to ratify the appointment. Following this, *SMC* nominees passed a no-confidence motion against Sengupta and proposed the name of Yoshio Saito for the chairmanship. *SMC* also lodged an arbitration petition against Bhaskarudu's appointment in the International Court of Arbitration. In June 1998, the government intervened and negotiated an out-of-court settlement between the parties. As per the settlement deal, Bhaskarudu was to step down in December 1999, two years ahead of schedule and Khattar was to replace him in January 2000. Further, Saito was to replace Sengupta as the chairman. This dispute between GOI and the *SMC*, though unpleasant, was just one of many frequent conflicts between the partners.

The implication is that managers can predict that, in most cases, the most violent reactions to change will come from those who perceive that their areas of control are likely to be violated. Further, an individual's response to change is highly dependent on the individual's or area's predisposition to change. Managers of change must plan accordingly and formulate a strategy to best create buy-in among the workforce and

* ***Source***: *http://www.icmrindia.org/casestudies/catalogue/Businessstrategy1/TheMaruti-SuzukiConflict.htm accessed on 25th June 2010*

other key stakeholders. While incompatible personalities can be a potential source of individual conflicts in organizations, what would be more worrisome in the context of organization-wide change would be structurally derived sources of conflicts, some of which are discussed below.

**Mutual task dependence** refers to the extent to which two organizational units depend on each other to complete their respective tasks effectively. While mutual dependence by itself need not lead to conflict, any antagonistic interaction would have the potential to escalate conflict. In **one-way task dependence**, one unit is unilaterally dependent on the other, making the latter more powerful than the former. In such a case, since the more powerful unit has no incentive to cooperate with the latter, potential for conflict is high. **Horizontally differentiated organizations** have different units handling widely varying tasks and face widely varying environments and differences in subunit goals. Consequently, approaches to doing business would be very different for such units, creating potential conflict situations. Similarly, organizations with **low formalization** would have ample scope for jurisdictional ambiguity among units, and increased possibility of disputes and conflicts. **Scarcity of resources** gives rise to disputes among units, and control of resources is seen as a zero-sum game where availability for one unit is dependent on depriving another unit of the required resources. **Perceived inequity in reward and appraisal techniques** is another possible area of conflict, giving rise to political and self-seeking behaviour on the part of organizational members, especially if reward practices are felt to be subjective and lacking in transparency. **Participative decision-making**, while democratic in approach, also allows more disagreements and differences of opinions to surface, and if not managed firmly, can escalate pre-existing antagonism into full-scale conflict. **Communication approaches** which lack transparency and objectivity are likely to lead to distortion and generate ambiguity, leading to conflict among units and members.

**Conflict management** refers to a combination of conflict resolution (for high and dysfunctional levels of conflict) and conflict stimulation (in cases where there is too little conflict and high levels of complacency). Structural approaches to resolving conflicts would include a variety of measures. A *super-ordinate goal* is a common goal for multiple units, which cannot be achieved by any one unit operating singly. Hence, in their own interest, units will be forced to work cooperatively, putting aside their internal conflicts. In order to reduce interdependence between units, *buffer stock* can be created of one unit's output which will feed into the next unit as input. Further, *coordination positions* manned by individuals with experience in both the conflicting units can also be used as mediators between the units. *Increasing opportunities for interaction* between groups can facilitate cooperation and help resolve differences. When conflict arises due to scarcity of resources, the ideal way to resolve it would be to *expand available resources*. However, that might be easier said than done since the organization might not have the wherewithal and capability to generate extra resources. A widespread method of conflict resolution is the use of *formal authority* by seniors over their conflicting subordinates. *Mutual problem solving* has been described as the soundest method for resolving intergroup conflicts. Since this method entails both parties meeting face-to-face, understanding the underlying causes for the conflict and taking shared responsibility for seeing that the solution works, it implies that the focus is on actually solving the problem rather than merely accommodating different viewpoints. Sometimes, *merging conflicting units,* where one unit expands its boundaries and absorbs the source of its irritation, can be an effective method of resolving conflicts. Finally, when none of these are effective, an *appeals system* can be set up, comprising formal channels for grievance hearing and settlement.

All these structural approaches are designed to lessen conflict; however, it is possible that levels of conflict could also be too low, in which case it is necessary to 'stimulate' opposition and actively encourage functional conflict. Though a relatively recent notion, organizations have used a variety of approaches to stimulate conflict in order to maintain optimum levels of conflict. By purposely using *ambiguous communication techniques* in which the meaning is left open to multiple interpretations, managers can stimulate conflict by reducing apathy and forcing members to confront their differences. One way to 'shake up' a complacent group is to introduce some *heterogeneity* in the form of 'outsiders' to the group, who come with very different values, experiences, and approaches. The outsider can also help play the role of the 'devil's advocate', with the assigned task of questioning, attacking, inquiring, and otherwise resisting any homogeneity in views. Finally, artificial *competition* can be created by creating zero-sum reward practices, intergroup contests, etc., to generate more conflict.

## 9.4 Change leadership

> People who act as catalysts and assume the responsibility for managing the change process are called change agents or change leaders.

Interest in the theory of planned change has created a new professional role, that of the *change agent,* whose job is to develop a climate for planned change by overcoming resistance and rallying forces for positive growth. Such skills are needed in conditions of rapid change, particularly in systems that do not respond appropriately to changing environmental forces. Hence, people who act as catalysts and assume responsibility for managing the change process are called *change agents* or *change leaders*. Change leadership refers to a set of principles, techniques, or activities applied to the human aspects of executing change to influence intrinsic acceptance while reducing resistance (Griffith-Cooper and King, 2007). Intrinsic acceptance implies individual internalization of a change – a choice to move forward with a future state. Change leadership is the guided coordination of the social ecology, focusing on the intrinsic motivation of individuals (both staff members and leaders), who are subject to the change or define the change. Expertly designed change leadership involves collaboration between leaders and staff in which they construct change together. Hence, good leaders do not merely lead, but recruit collaborators to a shared purpose (Maccoby, 2010). If the design concept is shared between employees and leaders, rather than directed from the top, the acceptance and ownership of change will be embraced with less resistance. Change leadership helps promote the success of a change effort by guiding affected members through the inevitable stages of human reactions to change. According to Kotter (1998), the focus of change leadership is on crafting a vision and then aligning and motivating people affected by the change so that they are prepared to support and adopt it. In fact, for any transformational change, commitment of change leaders is one of the most crucial dimensions for success.

It has been seen that change leaders typically need to wear multiple 'hats' and play different roles. As a **cognitive tuner**, the leader has to expose himself to variety, introspect and reflect on his mental models, forego his mental models periodically, and expose himself to dissent and feedback. As a **people catalyser**, he has to prepare himself before engaging people, use all forums and media for influencing people, be bold enough to take tough decisions, and develop credibility, trust and respect. As a **systems architect**, he is required to clarify individual roles and contribution, select/recruit team leaders carefully, create mechanisms for sharing best practices, and eliminate routines that are barriers to change. Finally, as an **efficacy builder**, he has to demonstrate faith in people, select and develop individuals for leadership positions, establish processes for storing and sharing organizational knowledge, and promote resilience.

Change leaders anticipate change, which is often anticipated, gradual, incremental, paced and solves problems; it is a conscious decision and provides new opportunities. Hence, the leader is in a position to be mentally prepared for the change. On the other hand, for 'followers' and other employees, change is often unexpected, sudden, dramatic, rapid, creates problems, is seen to be imposed and disruptive. Hence, change for them is far more traumatic and threatening. Therefore, as a change agent, it is advisable not to take others' reactions personally, and accept it for what it is: an individual's instinctive reaction to perceived threat. One also has to be clear of those aspects that remain unchanged and acknowledge it. Change agents must recognize the necessity of stability as a basis for growth. Respect for structural mechanisms and roles that promote stability must be maintained, even while one is trying to radically alter the existing system. In some cases, the functions of a change agent and an agent for stability will overlap. Further, an individual may have to shift back and forth between the behaviors characteristic of these two areas of emphases. In fact, a critical variable of organizational success is a leader's ability to stabilize and maintain the setting after the initially enthusiastic phase of new creation has subsided. For example, when a major change has to be initiated, change-agent behavior is called for. If successful, it will lead to a desired change in the circumstances and thus require, in turn, different behaviors or mechanisms to stabilize that change. The environment, however, will continue to change around this newly re-stabilized organization, creating the need at some later time for yet another major change (Westover, 2010). People should also be actively encouraged to express their feelings, be sad and talk about it. The process can be facilitated by giving people some reward for dealing with the ending, while at the same time honoring the past. People need to be encouraged to seek clarification in order to understand the reason for the ending. Finally, the change leader has to remember that everyone goes through emotional ups and downs at different speeds and have different degrees of change resilience, and hence, have a need to be treated differently.

A change leader should be knowledgeable about business domains and be aware of the environment and market competition in order to envision the desired future for the organization. While empathy and a humane approach are critical, he is also required to be familiar with different strategies of implementing change, which would help to convince and take senior management along. Finally, he has to be courageous to be able to take bold, or sometimes, unpopular decisions in the larger interest of the organization's well-being, and have the conviction to stand by his beliefs.

Managing change and transition happens through three phases, with respect to its impact on individuals. **Stage 1** represents the 'ending' of the status quo. For the change leader, this implies describing the change in detail, identifying who needs to let go of what, compensating for the losses, and communicating constantly. **Stage 2** implies 'managing the neutral zone'. It is not so much that individuals are afraid of change or in love with the old ways, but it is that place in between that they fear, where there is nothing 'certain' to hold on to. The change leader has to create a transition monitoring team, create temporary support systems, use all communication channels, improve roles, structure and work flow, and encourage creativity. **Stage 3** represents the 'beginning' of the changed state. To consolidate this change, the change leader has to communicate clearly the new purpose and vision, clearly describe who fits in where, create a plan for implementation, and reinforce the desired culture.

Hence, being a change leader would in essence mean establishing relevance by empathizing with employees, asking the right questions, changing the mindset, declaring early victory, becoming one's own competitor rather than following or benchmarking other success stories, establishing coalition to garner collective support, and understanding that success can be a paradox. Some interventions that managers can utilize in being an agent for change would include (Ryan, 1996):

1. *Setting a new leadership style*: Managers should use a new leadership style, called 'participative leadership' to describe the involvement of supervisors, managers, and leaders as partners.

2. *Creating a shared vision for quality results*: Managers must recognize the importance of involving customers and representatives of the workforce in the command's strategic planning sessions.
3. *Establishing process improvement through department teams*: Managers should value teams. The establishment of teams at the department level can introduce employees to the concept of continuous process improvement and help them understand how individual units support the organization.
4. *Fostering employee buy-in through empowered work teams*: Managers must empower teams through training.
5. *Specifying measurements to observe systems in action*: Managers should provide team members with training to help them gather meaningful data about their work processes so that analysis and improvement can begin.
6. *Incorporating leadership and teamwork-skills training*: Managers should provide training on team problem-solving skills and leadership for supervisors.
7. *Continuous improvement through ongoing feedback and review*: Managers can initiate a customer satisfaction survey to serve as a report card for the teams so that they can identify opportunities for improvement.

## 9.5 Approaches to change management

It has been established that a majority of organizational change initiatives fail to achieve their desired results (Beer and Nohria, 2000) for a variety of reasons. Often, implementation takes more time than originally allocated or planned for, major problems surface during implementation, coordination of implementation activities is not effective enough, competing activities and crises might detract attention from implementation, capabilities and skills of employees involved in implementation are not sufficient, or training and instruction given to lower-level employees are not adequate. Additionally, uncontrollable factors in the environment also have an adverse impact on implementation. Notwithstanding the poor statistics, however, attempts at corporate renewal and restructuring, as well as other long-term changes continue unabated. It is widely accepted that change strategies need to encompass a mix of 'soft' (employee oriented) and 'hard' (process, task, structure oriented) approaches, and 'successful' change efforts need to look at both objective, measurable indicators as well as subjective, hard-to-measure criteria. Some indicative measurement criteria for a successful change initiative could therefore include:

- Improved business performance in chosen domain/marketplace
- Positive financial performance and sustained growth
- Customers notice no drop in service levels, but do notice improvements in service or products
- Customer 'delight' leads to their ongoing loyalty

- Organization benefits from continuous innovation and an increase in knowledge capital
- Organization has a successful image in the marketplace, a good market position

However, a lot of this would be contingent on the willingness of employees themselves to readily modify their skills, behavior, and performance to what is required, enhance their skills and experience as a result of the change, learn to become flexible and adaptable to ongoing change efforts, and remain committed to the organization.

By and large, organizational change initiatives can be classified under two broad categories: Theory E and Theory O. **Theory E** maintains that organizational change is focused on changing the economic value of the organization. **Theory O** views organizational change from a capability-enhancing, organization development perspective. Most successful change activities use a judicious mix of both perspectives, with both people- and process orientation being given equal priority. Beer and Nohria (2000) have succinctly summarised the differences in these two approaches, as given in Table 9.2.

**Table 9.2** *Comparison of theories of change*

| | *Theory E* | *Theory O* | *Theory E + O* |
|---|---|---|---|
| *Goals* | Maximize shareholder value | Develop organizational capabilities | Embrace 'paradox' between E and O |
| *Leadership* | Manage change from top down | Encourage change from bottom up | Set direction from top and engage people from below |
| *Focus* | Emphasize structure and systems | Build up corporate culture, employee behavior and attitudes | Focus simultaneously on the hard (structures and systems) and the soft (corporate culture) |
| *Process* | Plan and establish programs | Experiment and evolve | Plan for spontaneity |
| *Reward system* | Motivate through financial incentives | Motivate through commitment – use pay as fair exchange | Use incentives to reinforce change but not to drive it |
| *Use OD consultants* | Consultants analyze problems and shape solutions | Consultants support management in shaping their own solutions | Consultants are expert resources who empower employees |

Over the years, various scholars have proposed various models of change, the more popular among which are described here. **Lewin's** (1975) **model** of planned change, based on the 'force-field concept', posits that any system exists in a state of equilibrium when the 'driving forces' (forces that push an organization toward change) equal the 'restraining forces' (forces aimed at maintaining the status quo). Any change that happens will therefore have to work toward either decreasing the restraining forces (e.g. internal resistance to change, structural inertia, resource crunch), or increasing the driving forces (e.g. benchmarking against best in class, envisioning a better future, changing domain of operations), or both. Figure 9.1 below provides a pictorial depiction of his model.

According to the 'force-field concept', any system exists in a state of equilibrium when the 'driving forces' equal the 'restraining forces'.

The process is likened to that of a solid mass which unfreezes first, moves to a newer state, and refreezes again to stabilize at the new state of solidity. '*Unfreezing*' implies disturbing the status quo by creating the motivation to change in the minds of the employees, through constant messages from top management and senior officials about the changing environment and the need for the organization to change, and subsequent disconfirmation of present behavior/attitudes. Discomfort/

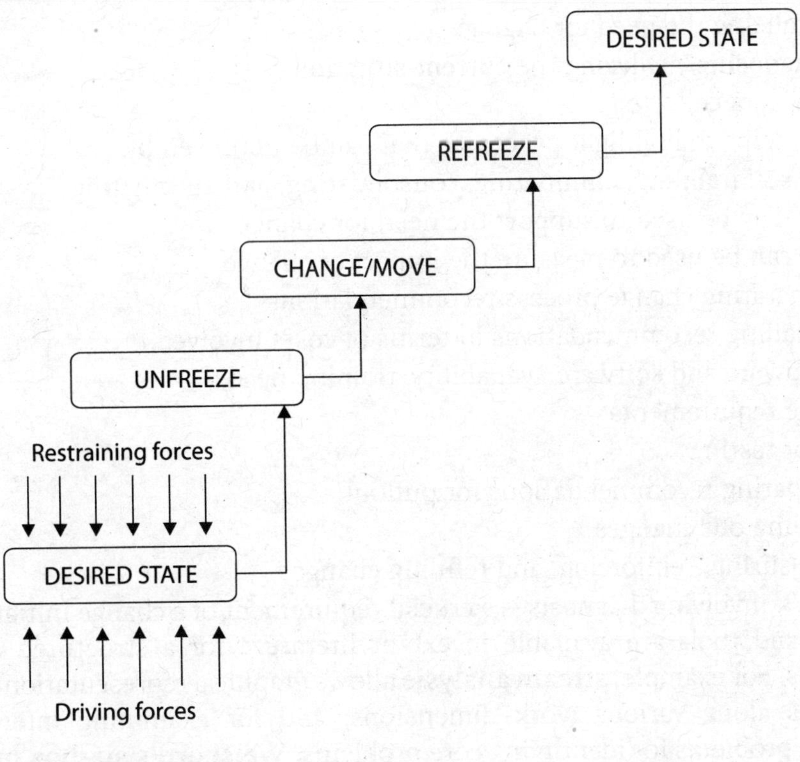


**Figure 9.1** *The force-field model of change*

disconfirmation will shake up people from their present complacency and lead to mental anxiety to motivate a change. At the same time, to counter the debilitating effects of anxiety and mental stress, managers also have to create psychological safety for the employees by holding up before them the vision of a better future if the change is successful, along with communication regarding how the organization will provide support to them to help them manage this transition. *'Moving to a new state'* implies developing new attitudes and behavior, through identification with some role model or mentor, and scanning the environment for information, especially relative to one's particular problem. *'Refreezing'* the change is the process of stabilizing the changes by allowing testing of new attitudes and behavior without being evaluative, instituting rewards to reinforce new changed behavior, and focusing on team training in addition to individual training, in order to reach the desired stage.

This model has been further refined to include nine stages, where, in addition to specifying sub-processes, a rough idea of timelines for each process is also provided, though the actual time taken would vary from organization to organization depending on the extent of their readiness, resource availability, and other contextual factors. The nine stages include:

| Stages | Timeline |
|---|---|
| 1. Establishing the need for change<br>2. Developing and disseminating a vision for change; vocalizing the need for change | 1–2 months |
| 3. Diagnosing/analyzing the current situation. The data collected<br>• helps to highlight processes that can be improved by streamlining, eliminating, consolidating, and automating<br>• may be used to support the need for change<br>• can be used to measure the impact of change.<br>4. Generating change process recommendations | 4–6 months |
| 5. Detailing recommendations in terms of costs involved, hardware and software availability, training needs, time requirements<br>6. Pilot testing | 4–6 months |
| 7. Preparing recommendations for pullout<br>8. Rolling out changes | 4–6 months |
| 9. Measuring, reinforcing, and refining changes | |

Stage 3, involving diagnosis is a crucial requirement of a change initiative. Various models and tools are available in extant literature for a structured approach to diagnosis. For example, **stream analysis** allows graphical representation of perceived problems along various work dimensions, and for examining interconnections between problems for identifying core problems. **Weisbord's six-box model** allows diagnosis of the extent of alignment between an organization's *purpose, structure, helpful mechanisms, rewards, relationships,* and *leadership.* Action research uses an iterative approach of gathering data, consultation with experts, feedback, action and further data collection to take a cyclical and ongoing approach to diagnosis. Once the diagnosis has been done, organizations can use Kilman's model or the Burke-Litwin model to plan and implement change. Irrespective of the tools used, the content of any large-scale change would cover technology, marketing, quality and cost, in different combinations. However, this will be supported by the context in the form of a fit between envisaged strategy and resultant structure, with suitable HRM practices, supportive culture, and a strong leadership providing an enabling environment. Bjelland and Wood (2008) have proposed five distinct, reproducible ways of radically altering organizations:

1. *Holism*: This is the standard type of transformational change. A crisis unfreezes the organization, then the leaders decide how it should change, plan and manage the process of change, and change systems to ensure that the new ways are supported.
2. *Ambidextrous form*: In this approach, managers recognize new opportunities and create separate business units to pursue them, while the existing business continues to exploit old opportunities. Often, the new businesses grow far larger than the old, transforming the nature of the firm.
3. *Acquisition/restructuring*: Leaders seek alterations in the firm through buying new elements from others or separating out existing elements. After purchases and other legal restructuring, leaders nurse a new and different kind of organization into existence in the often-chaotic process of integration and re-launch.
4. *Good to great*: Leaders seeking dramatically better organizations spend years developing a group of managers to work with and determining how to focus their efforts, finally focusing on doing a core group of things really well.
5. *Improvisational transformation*: In a crisis, leaders promote a strong but vague strategic intent and encourage improvisation to move the organization toward it. After initial successes, those in the organization seek to learn from them and the largely improvised innovation processes evolve into innovation routines.

To summarise, some prerequisites of successful change would include:

- Ensuring the commitment of senior management to the proposed changes; this has to be visible to all participants throughout the organization. A change initiative seen to enjoy the blessings of the top management will be perceived as credible and convincing.
- Producing a written statement about the future direction of the organization that makes clear its new objectives, values, and policies. A written statement not only makes the initiative appear more credible (willingness of the organization to commit to it in writing), but also acts as a documented source of plans for the successor.

- ❐ Creating a shared awareness of conditions to produce a common perception that change must be implemented.
- ❐ Assembling a body of key managers and other important opinion-formers to gain their commitment to the change process so that this may be disseminated more widely. While the change may be the brainchild of one manager, implementing it successfully would require a team of 'implementers' who enjoy the rapport and confidence of their colleagues, and who can therefore be used as role models to spread the message of change and convince others.
- ❐ Generating an acceptance that this type of change will require a long time to implement fully even though there may be short-term, dramatic changes as part of the overall process of transformation. This is important since managers sometimes might tend to get carried away by the initial successes, and set expectations unrealistically high regarding the ultimate outcome of the change, often resulting in a perceived violation of the psychological contract by employees from the organization.
- ❐ Recognizing that resistance to change is part of the normal process of adaptation so that managers can be educated to be aware of this and equipped to manage this reaction.
- ❐ Educating participants about the need for change and training them with the necessary competence to be effective, to overcome resistance and gain commitment.
- ❐ Persevering with the change process and avoiding blame where an attempt to implement a facet of this process fails. Such negative action will generate resistance and reduce necessary risk-taking behavior.
- ❐ Facilitating the change process with necessary resources.
- ❐ Maintaining open communication about progress, mistakes and subsequent learning.

### 9.5.1 Managing cultural change

While the above discussions on models have been predominantly process-oriented, it has to be firmly borne in mind that no change is going to be sustainable in the long run without a radical change in the organization's culture. Hence, implementation plans for any change initiative would have to factor in processes geared toward cultural transformation. For example, the unfreezing stage in Lewin's model also implies that the embedded culture has to be unfrozen and made more receptive/susceptible to change. The refreezing stage also includes stabilizing and institutionalizing the new culture. Thornhill et al (2000) have consolidated some general principles for successful cultural change:

- Accepted and appropriate patterns of behavior within organizations are defined by values and basic underlying assumptions.

- Successful organizations tend to be those where the values and basic underlying assumptions encourage practices and behaviors which match the organizations' strategies.
- If an organization is contemplating change, it first has to establish whether the strategy necessitates a shift in values and basic underlying assumptions or if change can be achieved some other way.
- Prior to any culture change, senior management must understand the implications of the new culture for their own practices, artefacts, and espoused values and be involved in all the main change phases.
- Adequate resources have to be allocated to support culture change and maintain it once it has been achieved.
- Culture-change programmes must pay attention to the organization's power-bases and opinion leaders, such as trade unions and employees' associations.
- Culture-change programmes must take into account an organization's existing practices or artefacts such as approaches to recruitment, selection and retention, training, performance management, and employee relations.
- Every opportunity should be taken to reinforce the practices or artefacts and restate the espoused values and basic underlying assumptions of the new culture.

Strategies for managing cultural change include both top–down (top management driven) and bottom–up (collective participation) approaches. Both these approaches have inherent strengths and limitations across various parameters; hence, depending on the specific situation, managers have to decide on which approach to use. For example, top–down approaches are high in expressiveness, dealing as they do in simple messages and specializing in communicating these effectively and reasonably quickly at the practice/artifact level. Highly structured top–down programs are also likely to reach a larger cross-section of employees. On the other hand, bottom–up approaches are high in commonality since they operate through shared understanding and create a culture of trust and understanding. Moreover, adaptability is higher in the bottom–up approach, since it works on willingness to accommodate others' views and opinions. Durability of the change is also higher here, since there is a collective sense of ownership and employees are keen to preserve what they have created.

## 9.6 Creating a learning organization

For many change initiatives, the long-term outcome envisioned is to evolve into a learning organization. Many consultants and organizations have recognized the commercial significance of organizational learning and the notion of the 'learning organization' has been a central orienting point in this.

The learning organization is an ideal, toward which organizations have to evolve in order to be able to respond to the various pressures they face. It is characterized by the recognition that individual and collective learning are central to it. The concept of a learning organization has been popularized by several recent authors, most notably Senge (1990). According to Garvin (1993), a learning organization is one that is 'skilled at creating, acquiring, and transferring knowledge, and at modifying its behavior to reflect new knowledge and insights.' Similarly, Easterby-Smith (1997) describes the learning organization as an ideal type of action- and change-oriented enterprise in which learning is maximized. Most organizations engage in single-loop learning; where errors are corrected based on past routines and present policies. In contrast, learning organizations use double-loop learning; where error corrections involve the modification of an organization's objectives, policies, and standard routines. Double-loop learning challenges the assumptions and norms of an organization; and therefore, it can provide possibilities for dramatic jumps in improvement.

A learning organization is one that is skilled at creating, acquiring, and transferring knowledge, and at modifying its behavior to reflect new knowledge and insights.

One reason for the growing interest in the learning organization is its suitability for today's fast-paced, global business environment. From a strategic perspective, the learning organization is especially important in highly competitive situations because it builds the capacity to change strategies, to be creative, and to avoid a narrow and rigid dependence on the status quo. Baldwin et al. (1997) claim that 'the dynamics of rapid change, heightened global competition and advancing technology mean that organizational success will be increasingly dependent on learning'. The capacity to innovate is sustained by organizational learning. The main characteristics of a learning organization include:

- *Existence of a shared vision which everyone agrees on*
- *People discard their old ways of thinking and the standard routines they use to solve problems*
- There is an *open systems approach* among all members
- People *openly communicate* with each other horizontally and vertically without fear of criticism and punishment
- People *sublimate their personal self-interest* to work together to achieve the organization's shared vision
- *Employee development and continuous learning*: Organizational learning depends on employees who are growing and developing on the job.
- *Information-sharing and collaboration*: Organizational change is a shared responsibility and innovation and change require employee participation and involvement. Innovation is much more likely to occur when people participate in the solution rather than having it handed to them. This inclusive approach

to planning brings new voices, new perspectives and new energy to the process. It allows the organization to tap into the knowledge of its people, a key to competitive advantage (Bartlett and Ghoshal, 1995).

- *Team building and shared purpose*: Creating a sense of shared purpose, an *esprit de corps*, is a view aptly stated by Senge et al (1994): 'Thus, at the heart of building shared vision is the task of designing and evolving ongoing processes in which people at every level of the organization, in every role, can speak from the heart about what really matters to them and be heard by senior management and by each other. The quality of this process, especially the amount of openness and genuine caring, determines the quality and the power of the results. A true shared vision cannot be dictated; it can only emerge from a coherent process of reflection and conversation.'

Change agents can often help their firms by adopting notions of the learning organization within a framework of 'change proofing' (Drew and Smith, 1995). This means preparing an organization for necessary transformation by developing the ability to recognize and respond to early signals of change or unanticipated opportunities. Change proofing is not a means of resisting or avoiding change, but a process for becoming more flexible and responsive in order to cope with it. To help identify and assess the critical factors for change proofing, a 'change audit' is recommended. This includes an audit of organizational learning processes and their impact on strategic focus, motivation, and core capabilities.

The underlying assumptions of a learning organization are (Senge, 1990):

- When motivation is present, employees will respond
- Employees can continuously learn and expand given the correct motivation
- The motivation must be linked to results that employees desire
- Collective learning does not contradict individual learning
- Facilitation of employee learning will lead to successful business transformation

Thus, there is an overarching learning organization paradigm that views employee participation in the form of learning as consistent with successful organization change and growth. The *learning organization* is a model of the organizational type that allows the human spirit to flourish so that creativity and innovation are possible (Porth et al, 1999). However, it is also true that the concept of 'learning organization' is not without inherent limitations (Finger and Brand, 1999), predominant among them being that the concept:

**Focuses mainly on the cultural dimension** and does not adequately take into account the other dimensions of an organization. To transform an organization, it is necessary to attend to structures and the organization of work as well as the culture and processes.

**Favours individual and collective learning processes** at all levels of the organization, but does not connect them properly to the organization's strategic objectives. Popular models of organizational learning assume such a link. It is, therefore, imperative, that the link between individual and collective learning and the organization's strategic objectives is made. This shortcoming makes a case for some form of measurement of organizational learning – so that it is possible to assess the extent to which such learning contributes or not toward strategic objectives.

**Remains rather vague.** The exact functions of organizational learning need to be more clearly defined. Organizational learning is just a means to achieve strategic objectives. But creating a learning organization is also a goal, since the ability permanently and collectively to learn is a necessary precondition for thriving in the new context. Therefore, the capacity of an organization to learn, that is, to function like a learning organization, has to be made more concrete and institutionalized, so that the management of such learning is more effective.

There is a need to develop a true management system of an organization's evolving learning capacity. This can be achieved through defining indicators of learning (individual and collective) and by connecting them to other indicators.

Finally, it is important to understand that becoming a learning organization is not a goal to reach and to pass. It is an ongoing process, of a lifetime. Just as people have to learn all the time, so do organizations in order to survive and grow.

## CHAPTER SUMMARY

The business environment throughout the world has witnessed phenomenal upheavals in the form of technological innovation, opening up of new markets, deregulation, developments in information technology and communication practices. The need to cut costs in order to remain competitive has provided organizations with the impetus to initiate a spate of organizational change programs. These change efforts have taken various forms such as restructuring, downsizing, rightsizing, mergers and acquisitions, takeovers, delayering, etc. Change management refers to the process of renewing the organization's direction, structure, and capabilities to serve the ever-changing needs of the market place, customers, and employees.

Environmental pressures which might force organizations to change would include political pressures, economic factors, technological factors, socio-cultural factors, fashion fads, and the internal environment. Different organizations respond differently to pressures for change, depending on the difference in their extent of readiness to change. A readiness-focused change builds awareness of the need for change and communicates a vision for change, creates a climate that is supportive of the desired change by realigning organizational culture, rewards, policies, procedures and systems, and builds up a participative culture by equipping people throughout the organization with the skills needed to participate meaningfully in planning and implementing strategic change. Planning for change has to be an open process, with an emphasis on establishing general goals and direction, using pilot programs to build commitment within the organization.

Before attempting to undertake any long-term change, it is vital to adopt the right attitude toward sustainable change. Any change process, irrespective of the intended benefits, will encounter resistance. Resistance to change could be manifested at both individual and organizational levels and tends to move through a life-cycle comprising five phases. Change leaders have to be trained or sensitized to the power of persuasion in overcoming resistance to change. Since any organizational change is likely to threaten the survival of some stakeholders, it is likely that intergroup clashes will occur where the goal-directed behavior of one group of stakeholders is likely to jeopardize or thwart the goals of another. Such clashes, or organizational conflicts, are almost inevitable in any organizational change; the more transformational the change, the more pronounced is the conflict.

Managing conflict during organizational change would include a mix of conflict resolution and conflict stimulation tactics. Those who act as catalysts and assume the responsibility for managing the change process are called *change agents* or *change leaders*. Change leadership refers to a set of principles, techniques or activities applied to the human aspects of executing change to influence intrinsic acceptance while reducing resistance. Change leaders typically wear multiple 'hats' and play different roles, namely, as a cognitive tuner, a people catalyser, a systems architect, and an efficacy builder. Change strategies should encompass a mix of 'soft' (employee oriented) and 'hard' (process, task, structure oriented) approaches, and 'successful' change efforts have to look at both objective, measurable indicators as well as subjective, hard-to-measure criteria. A Theory E approach to organizational change is focused on changing the economic value of the organization, while Theory O views organizational change from a capability-enhancing, organization development perspective. Most successful change activities use a judicious mix of both perspectives, with both people and process-orientation being given equal priority.

Various models of change management, both process and content-oriented, are available in extant literature to help managers manage the transition between the current and desired state. No change is going to be sustainable in the long run without a radical change in the organization's culture. Hence, implementation plans for any change initiative should factor in processes geared toward cultural transformation. Finally, for many change initiatives, the long-term outcome is evolving into a learning organization. A learning organization is one that is skilled at creating, acquiring, and transferring knowledge, and at modifying its behavior to reflect new knowledge and insights. Change agents can often help their firms by adopting notions of the learning organization within a framework of 'change proofing' – preparing an organization for necessary transformation by developing the ability to recognize and respond to early signals of change or unanticipated opportunities. It is important to understand that becoming a learning organization is not a goal to reach and pass. It is an ongoing process of a lifetime.

## Review Questions

1. How are the following terms relevant in change management? (a) *Long-term attitude toward change*, (b) *Theory E + O*, (c) *Resistance to change*

2. Assume that you are planning to implement a change initiative in your organization, for which you have to appoint a change agent (either internal or external). What are the roles that you will require him/her to play as a change leader? What type of capabilities would he/she need to possess for this responsibility, and why?
3. Briefly explain the steps needed to bring about successful cultural change in organizations.
4. What are the various approaches to change management described in the chapter?
5. What do you think could be the possible challenges that organizations are likely to face during each stage of the nine-stage approach?
6. What are the characteristics of a learning organization?

## Project Assignment

Assume that you are a professional consultant retained by a small organization to guide them in their transition from an entrepreneur-driven start-up to a more professionally managed entity. Prepare a report detailing how you would help the organization in this restructuring exercise. Your answer should comprise two parts:

(a) the diagnostic process, including understanding the organization's current situation – its structure and design, in relation to its strategy, technology, effectiveness parameters currently used, the environment that it currently faces, its culture, size, its evolution to its current life-cycle stage, and the crises points that it has faced till date. In this portion, list the key questions for every dimension that you will need answers for, to help you in your diagnosis and the expected benefits the organization might be looking for, from this restructuring exercise.

(b) your suggested roadmap for the organization's transition based on the above diagnosis. This portion should cover suggestions for changes in the organization's design and structure based on your suggested changes in its contextual parameters, and the resultant cultural changes that this would require. Try and identify the possible problems that the organization might face in this journey of transition, and your suggestions to overcome these roadblocks. Justify all your suggestions, and explain how these actions would help the organization to achieve competitive advantage and increased effectiveness, and the effectiveness parameters along which it might evaluate itself.

## CASE ILLUSTRATION: 'DOWNSIZING IN A MANUFACTURING ORGANIZATION'

The Indian subsidiary of a globally reputed MNC, engaged in the manufacture of electrical and electronic appliances, with its worldwide headquarters in the Netherlands, had two factories, one located in Kolkata (West Bengal) and the other in Pune (Maharashtra). Special attention was paid to the Kolkata unit, with considerable investments made to build it up as a world class manufacturing unit, with highly skilled and trained staff, and state-of-art equipment and technology. Fresh talent was recruited, with promises of a bright future and enviable career growth opportunities in the new set-up. However, barely two years into the new revamped operations at Kolkata, it was decided that in line with the parent company's global business model, each country would have only one manufacturing facility. For India, Pune was chosen as the location. The Kolkata operations were downsized through a Voluntary Retirement Scheme (VRS) for employees; some employees were redeployed to other units, and all its operational activities were shifted to Pune. While employees by and large accepted the decision to downsize, they questioned the rationale to shut down Kolkata and retain Pune. With no clarifications forthcoming from the top management in India, there was widespread skepticism regarding the motivation behind the downsizing decision. Employees felt that instead of taking into account the improved performance of the Kolkata unit following its modernization, the top management had allowed itself to be swayed by 'extraneous' and 'softer' issues such as negative perceptions regarding the work culture in the state, the political situation, etc. It was also felt that Pune had greater negotiating power on account of its proximity to Mumbai, the India headquarters.

During the time the top management at Mumbai negotiated with prospective buyers for the sale of the Kolkata unit on an as-is-where-is basis (without any consultation with or communication to the Kolkata employees), the workforce there (around 350 in number post-downsizing) was retained at the factory with full pay and benefits and trained in alternative skills by outside agencies; this, coupled with absence of any production during this period, resulted in monthly losses of Rs 50 lakhs for the company.

At Kolkata, three senior managers were entrusted with the responsibility of overseeing the downsizing process. The downsizing process itself was characterized by a number of noteworthy approaches on the part of the implementers (change agents) and management:

- The implementers enjoyed excellent rapport and high credibility with the workforce at Kolkata, owing to their professional yet humane handling of their jobs and their interpersonal relations with the employees.
- The organization provided the implementers with substantial autonomy and financial resources to implement the procedure according to their discretion. Hence, the empowered implementers could take a number of positive initiatives in managing the implementation process.
- The implementers organized counseling sessions and training programs, often at the factory premises, and at company's expense, to enable downsized employees to make a fresh start in life. This served to reinforce the credibility of the management in the eyes of the employees, despite the adverse nature of the downsizing decision.
- Efforts were initiated to try and fit employees into other sister units of the company. For those with mobility problems, the organization made special efforts to find suitable positions in units situated in and around Kolkata, while the rest were transferred to Pune.

- In order to help employees make a smooth relocation to Pune, the personnel department of the company provided support by arranging for accommodation, schools, and other facilities for the families at Pune.

The process itself was psychologically stressful and traumatic for the implementers. The dilemma of their personal dissatisfaction with the rationale given by the top management and their organizational role as official 'defenders' of the downsizing decision created tremendous internal stress, affecting their ability to convince and persuade others about the legitimacy of the decision. Not only did they have to deal with their personal feelings of betrayal, anger, frustration, and uncertainty, they also had to put their own emotions on the backburner in order to act as counselors and guides to their colleagues and subordinates. To make matters worse, they had to contend with severe feelings of guilt, since they had been involved in recruiting a large number of fresh professionals into the Kolkata unit barely two years prior to this, and had convinced them regarding the bright future that awaited them in the organization. They now had to counsel those same people to start looking for alternative career options. Finally, despite the high regard and respect that they enjoyed among fellow workers, direct and indirect accusations from workers and unions for not preventing the closure and a suspicion that they had been fall guys in the situation, added to their feelings of personal helplessness and incompetence.

Coping with this experience was difficult and traumatic for the implementers. One took out his anger and resentment by blaming the workers, while the other two relied on expert counseling and personal willpower to overcome their initial frustration. What did assuage the guilt to some extent was the knowledge that they had done their utmost to provide support and assistance to the affected employees.

## Critical enquiry

*How important or relevant do you think is the role of an individual implementer or change agent in today's context where change is inevitable in organizations? Given the above scenario, what could have been the probable reactions of the survivors and victims of the downsizing process? What learning can be gleaned from the facts given in the case regarding effective change implementation?*

***Key words and phrases:*** resistance to change, change strategies, change leaders, cultural change, learning organization

# References


1. Adizes, I (1988). *Corporate Life-Cycles: How and Why Corporations Grow and Die and What to do about it*. Englewood Cliff, New Jersey: Prentice Hall.
2. Allee, V (2009). "Value-creating networks: organizational issues and challenges". *The Learning Organization*. 16 (6), 427–442.
3. Baird, K.,Harrison, G and Reeve, R (2007). "The Culture of Australian Organizations and its Relation with Strategy". *International Journal of Business Studies*. 15 (1), 15–41
4. Baldwin, T.T., Danielson, C. and Wiggenhorn, W (1997). The evolution of learning strategies in organizations: From employee development to business redefinition. *Academy of Management Executive*, 11(4). 47–57.
5. Barnard, C I (1938). *The Function of the Executive*. Cambridge, MA: Harvard University Press; pg 73
6. Bartlett-Bragg, A (2009). "Reframing practice: creating social learning networks". *Development and Learning in Organizations*. 23 (4), 16–20
7. Bartlett, C A and Ghoshal, S (1995). "Changing the role of top management: beyond systems to people". *Harvard Business Review*, May-June, pp. 132-42.
8. Beer, M and Nohria, N (2000). "Cracking the code of change". *Harvard Business Review*. May-June. 133–141.
9. Bjelland, O M and Wood, R C (2008). "Five ways to transform a business". *Strategy & Leadership*. Vol. 36 (3) 4–14.
10. Blenko, MW, Mankins, M C and Rogers, P (2010). "The Decision-Driven Organization". *Harvard Business Review*. June, 42–48.
11. Bhargava, S., and Sinha, B (1992). "Predictions of Organizational Effectiveness as a Function of Type of Organizational Structure." *Journal of Social Psychology*, 132, 223–232.
12. Burger-Helmchen, T and Llerna, P (2008). "A case study of a creative start-up: governance, communities and knowledge management". *Journal of Innovation Economics*. 2(2). 125–146
13. *Burton, M D and Beckman, C M (2007)*. "Leaving a Legacy: Position Imprints and Successor Turnover in Young Firms". *American Sociological Review*. 72 (2), 239–266
14. Burton, R M, Eriksen, B, Hakonsson, D D and Snow, C C (2006). *Organization Design: The Evolving State-of-the-Art*. New York: Springer
15. Cameron, K, Whetten, D A and Kim, M U (1987). "Organizational Dysfunctions of Decline". *Academy of Management Journal*, 30, 126–138.

16. Carrillo, J D and Gromb, D (2007). "Cultural Inertia and Uniformity in Organizations". *Journal of Law, Economics and Organizations*. 23 (3), 743–771
17. Child, J (1972). "Organizational Structure, Environment and Performance: The Role of Strategic Choice". *Sociology*, 6(1), 1–22
18. Child, J and McGrath, R G (2001). "Organizations Unfettered: Organizational Form in an information-intensive economy". *Academy of Management Journal*, 44 (6), 1135–1148
19. Cialdini, R. B. (2001). "Harnessing the science of persuasion." *Harvard Business Review*, 7915, 71–80.
20. Daft, Richard L (2004). *Organization Theory and Design*; 7th ed; Singapore: Thompson South-Western
21. Dawar, N and Frost, T (1999). "Competing with Giants: Survival Strategies for Local Companies in Emerging Markets". *Harvard Business Review*. Mar-April.
22. Denison, D R and Mishra, A K (1995). "Toward a theory of organizational culture and Effectiveness". *Organization Science*, 6 (2), 204–223
23. DiMaggio, P J and Powell, W W (1983). "The Iron Cage Revisited: Institutional Isomorphism and Collective Rationality in Organizational Fields". *American Sociological Review*; 48 (2), 147–160
24. Drew, S A W and Smith, P A C (1995). "The learning organization: change proofing and strategy". *The Learning Organization*. 2(1), 4–10.
25. Drucker, P F (1954). *The Practice of Management*. New York: Harper & Row
26. Drucker, P F (1974). *Management: Tasks, Responsibilities, Practices*. London: Heinemannn
27. Easterby-Smith, M. (1997). Disciplines of organizational learning: contributions and critiques. *Human Relations*, 50 (9), 1085–106.
28. Evans, P, Pucik, V and Barsoux, J L (2002). *The Global Challenge*. NY:McGraw-Hill Irwin
29. Finger, M. and Brand, S B (1999) 'The concept of the "learning organization" applied to the transformation of the public sector' in M. Easterby-Smith, L. Araujo and J. Burgoyne (eds.) *Organizational Learning and the Learning Organization*, London: Sage.
30. Garvin, D.A. (1993). "Building a learning organization", *Harvard Business Review*. July-August, 78–91.
31. Geiger, S W, Ritichie, W, Marlin, D (2006). "Strategy/structure fit and firm performance". *Organization Development Journal*, 24 (2), 10–22
32. Gibson,J L, Ivancevich, J M, Donnelly, J H and Konopaske, R (2003). *Organizations*; 11th ed; New York: Mc-Graw Hill
33. Glueck, W F (1976).*Business Policy: Strategy Formulation and Management Action*, 2nd ed; New York: McGraw Hill.
34. Greiner, L.E. (1972), "Evolution and revolution as organizations grow". *Harvard Business Review*, 50, 37–46
35. Griffith-Cooper, B and King, K (2007). The Partnership Between Project Management and Organizational Change: Integrating Change Management with Change Leadership. *Performance Improvement*. 46 (1). 14–20.

36. Gross, W and Shichman, S (1987). "How to grow an organizational Culture". *Personnel*. 52–56.
37. Hannan, M and Freeman, J (1977). "The Population Ecology of Organizations". *American Journal of Sociology*; 82 (5), 929–964
38. Hofstede, G (2003). "*Cultures and Organizations*". In *The Successful Strategist Series* ed. Bob Garett, London, Profile Books Ltd.
39. Holbeche, L (2006). *Understanding Change: Theory, Implementation and Success*. New Delhi: Elsevier
40. Holmes, S and Marsden, S (1996). "An Exploration of the Espoused Organizational Cultures of Public Accounting Firms". *Accounting Horizons*. 10 (3), 26–53
41. Hooijberg, R and Petrock, F (1993). "On Cultural Change: Using the Competing Values Framework to Help Leaders Execute a Transformational Strategy". *Human Resource Management*, 32 (1), 29–50
42. Hrebiniak L (2008). "Making Strategy work: Overcoming the obstacles to effective execution". *Ivey Business Journal Online*. 72 (2), 1
43. Jackson, B (1999). "*Perceptions of Organizational Effectiveness in Community and Member Based Nonprofit Organizations*." Doctoral dissertation, University of La Verne. ProQuest Digital Dissertations, AAT9918843.
44. Jordan, B (2009). "Blurring Boundaries: The "Real" and the "Virtual" in Hybrid Spaces". *Human Organization*. 68 (2), 181–193.
45. Kanter, R M (2010). "Thirteen unlucky mistakes in managing traumatic change – How to avoid them". *Harvard Business Review*. March 2010.
46. Kleinschmidt, J (2009). "Cross-Company Knowledge Sharing: How enterprise social networking transforms the workplace". *Information Management*. 19 (8), 56–60
47. Kotter, J P (1998). Wining at Change. *Leader to Leader*, 10, 27–33.
48. Lewin, K (1975). *Field Theory in Social Science*. Greenwood, West Port, CT
49. Maccoby, M (2010). "Learn Change Leadership from Two Great Teachers". *Research Technology Management*. 53 (2). 68–69.
50. Mangelsdorf, M E (2010). "Connecting the Dots in the Enterprise". *MIT Sloan Management Review*. 51 (2), 9–12
51. Marguardt, M J (2002). *Building the learning organization*. New York: McGraw Hill
52. McCluskey, T and Korobow, A (2009). "Leveraging Networks and Social Software for Mission Success". *The Public Manager*. 66–70
53. Minocha, S (2009). "Role of social software tools in education: A literature review". *Education & Training*. 51 (5/6), 353–369
54. Mintzberg, H (1980). "Structures in 5's: A Synthesis of the research on organization design". *Management Science*. 26 (3), 322–341
55. Mintzberg, H (1981). Organization Design: Fashion or fit? *Harvard Business Review*. 59 (1), 103–116
56. Mintzberg, H (1983). *Structures in Five: Designing Effective Organizations*. Engelwood Cliffs (NJ): Prentice Hall.

57. Mone, M A, McKinley, W and Barker, V L (1998). "Organizational decline and innovation: A contingency framework". *Academy of Management Review*. 23 (1), 115–132
58. Mullins, L J (2005). *Management and Organizational Behavior*; 7th ed; UK: Pearson Education.
59. Ott, J S (1989). *The Organization Culture Perspective*. Chicago: Dorsey Press.
60. Palmer, I, Dunford, R and Akin, G (2006). *Managing Organizational Change: A Multiple perspectives approach*. New Delhi: Tata McGraw Hill.
62. Pareek, U (2007). *Understanding Organizational Behavior* (2nd ed). New Delhi: Oxford University Press.
63. Pennings, J M (1992). "Structural Contingency Theory: A Reappraisal". *Research in Organizational Behavior*. 14, 267–309.
64. Peters, W and Waterman, R (1982). *In Search of Excellence*. New York: Harper and Row.
65. Pfeffer, J (1998). *The Human Equation*. Massachusetts: Harvard Business School Press.
66. Pfeffer, J and Salancik, G (1978). *The External Control of Organizations: A Resource Dependent Perspective*. New York: Harper & Row
67. Pondy. L R (1967). Organizational Conflict: Concepts and Models. *Administrative Science Quarterly*. 12 (2), 296–320.
68. Porth, *S J, McCall*, J and Bausch, T A (1999). "Spiritual themes of the learning organization". *Journal of Organizational Change Management*. 12 (3). 211
69. Quinn, R E (1988). *Beyond Rational Management: Mastering the Paradoxes and Competing Demands of High Performance*. San Francisco: Josey-Bass.
70. Ridley, C R and Mendoza, D W (1993). "Putting Organizational Effectiveness into Practice: The Preeminent Consultation Task". *Journal of Counseling and Development*. 72 (2), 168–177.
71. Ritchie, M (2000). "Organization Culture: An examination of its effect on Internalization processes and Member Performance". *Southern Business Review*. 25 (2), 1–13
72. Robbins, S P (2000). *Organization Theory*. 3rd Ed. New Delhi: Prentice Hall of India
73. Rojas R (2000). "A Review of Models for Measuring Organizational Effectiveness Among For-profit and Non-Profit Organizations". *Non-Profit Management and Leadership*. 11(1), 97–104
74. Ridley, C. R., and Mendoza, D. W (1993). "Putting Organizational Effectiveness into Practice: The Preeminent Consultation Task." *Journal of Counseling and Development*, 72, 168–178.
75. Ryan, B. (1996). "Managing Change in the Public Sector". *Journal for Quality and Participation*, 19 (4). 42–50.
76. Schein, E H (1985). *Organizational Culture and Leadership* (1st ed). San Francisco: Jossey-Bass.
77. Schein, E H (1992). *Organizational Culture and Leadership* (2nd ed). San Francisco: Jossey-Bass.
78. Senge, P M (1990). *The Fifth Discipline*. London: Century Business.

79. Senge, P.M., Roberts, C., Ross, R., Smith, B. and Kleiner, A. (1994). *The Fifth Discipline Fieldbook: Strategies and Tools for Building a Learning Organization*, Doubleday/Currency: New York, NY.

80. Smircich, L (1985). "Is the concept of culture a paradigm for understanding organizations and ourselves?" in P Frost, L Moore, M Louis, C Lundberg and J Martin (eds.) *Organizational culture*. 55–72, Newbury Park, CA: Sage

81. Snyder, D P (2005). "Extra-Preneurship: Reinventing Enterprise for the Information Age". *The Futurist*. 39 (4), 47–53.

82. Stern, R N and Barley, S R (1996). "Organizations and Social Systems: Organization Theory's Neglected Mandate"; *Administrative Science Quarterly*; 41 (1), 146–162

83. Schein, E H (1992). *Organizational Culture and Leadership* (2nd ed). San Francisco: Jossey-Bass

84. Shukla, M (1999). *Understanding Organizations: Organizational Theory and Practice in India.* New Delhi:Prentice Hall of India

85. Thornhill, A, Lewis, P, Millmore, M and Saunders, M (2000). *Managing Change: A Human Resource Strategy Approach*. Pearson Education: New Delhi.

86. Tolbert, P S and Hall, R H (2010). *Organizations: Structures, Processes and Outcomes* (10th ed). New Delhi, PHI Learning Pvt Ltd.

87. Trice, H and Bayer, J (1993). *The Cultures of Work Organizations*, Englewood Cliff, N.J.: Prenticc Hall.

88. Vermeulen, F, Puranam, P and Gulati, R (2010). "Change for change's sake". *Harvard Business Review*. June, 57–62.

89. Van de Ven, A H (1979). Review of Aldrich's (1979) book----Organization and Environments. *Administrative Science Quarterly*. 24. 320–326

90. Venkatraman, N (1989). "The Concept of Fit in Strategy Research: Towards Verbal and Statistical Correspondence". *Academy of Management Review*. 14 (3). 429–444

91. Venkatraman, N and Prescott, J E (1990). "Environment-Strategy coalignment: An empirical test of its performance indicators". *Strategic Management Journal*. 11 (1). 1–23.

92. Venkatraman, N and Henderson, J C (1998). Real strategies for virtual organizing. *Sloan Management Review*. 40 (1). 33–48

93. Weitzel, W and Jonsson, E (1989). "Decline in Organizations: A Literature integration and Extension". *Administrative Science Quarterly*, 34 (1)

94. Westover, J H (2010). "Managing Organizational Change: Change Agent Strategies and Techniques to Successfully Managing the Dynamics of Stability and Change in Organizations". *International Journal of Management and Innovation*. 2 (1). 45–51

95. Wolin, S (1960). *Politics and Vision*. Princeton: Princeton University Press.

96. http://www.socialmediatoday.com/ClientFiles/2b461d74-0b05-4149-a6fd-33257181a2c7/sapnetworks.pdf/ (accessed 6th June 2010)

97. http://en.wikipedia.org/wiki/Social_media_marketing/ accessed 6th June 2010)

98. http://www.cio.com/article/592271/Social_Networks_in_the_Enterprise_3M_x2019_s_Innovation_Process/(accessed 6th June 2010)

99. http://www.articlesbase.com/human-resources-articles/facebook-as-an-online-recruitment-tool-for-masses-877697.html#ixzz0q2YqiwgP (accessed 6th June 2010)
100. http://wbztv.com/local/college.twitter.facebook.2.1581001.html/accessed 6th June 2010)
101. http://en.wikipedia.org/wiki/Bharti_Airtel/accessed 7th June 2010

# Index